W9-AEK-352

WITHDRAWN
NDSU

The Jossey-Bass Nonprofit Sector Series also includes:

MANAGING CHANGE
IN THE NONPROFIT SECTOR

MANAGING CHANGE IN THE NONPROFIT SECTOR

Lessons from the Evolution of Five Independent Research Libraries

Jed I. Bergman
in collaboration with William G. Bowen
and Thomas I. Nygren

Foreword by William G. Bowen

Jossey-Bass Publishers
San Francisco

Copyright © 1996 by The Andrew W. Mellon Foundation, 140 East 62nd Street, New York, New York 10021. Copyright under International, Pan American, and Universal Copyright Conventions. All rights reserved. No part of this book may be reproduced in any form—except for brief quotation (not to exceed 1,000 words) in a review or professional work—without permission in writing from Jossey-Bass Inc., Publishers, 350 Sansome Street, San Francisco, California, 94104.

Substantial discounts on bulk quantities of Jossey-Bass books are available to corporations, professional associations, and other organizations. For details and discount information, contact the special sales department at Jossey-Bass Inc., Publishers (415) 433-1740; Fax (800) 605-2665.

For sales outside the United States, please contact your local Simon & Schuster International Office.

Manufactured in the United States of America.

Library of Congress Cataloging-in-Publication Data

Bergman, Jed I., 1970–
    Managing change in the nonprofit sector: lessons from the
evolution of five independent research libraries/Jed I. Bergman.—
1st ed.
    p. cm.—(Jossey-Bass nonprofit sector series)
    Includes bibliographical references and index.
    ISBN 0-7879-0138-5
    1. Research libraries—United States—Administration.
    2. Nonprofit organizations—United States—Management.
    3. Organizational change—United States. I. Title. II. Series.
Z675.R45B47 1996
026'.00973—dc20
                                            95-4705
                                          CIP

HB Printing 10 9 8 7 6 5 4 3 2 1

FIRST EDITION

The Jossey-Bass Nonprofit Sector Series

CONTENTS

APPENDIXES

TABLES AND FIGURES

Tables

Figures

FOREWORD

Even those of us who are familiar with public libraries or with college and university libraries are unlikely to have had firsthand experience with independent research libraries—although we have probably heard of them. We may know, to cite one example, that the Folger Shakespeare Library possesses the greatest collection in the world of first folio editions of Shakespeare's plays. As unnoticed as they may sometimes seem, these institutions—numbering fewer than two dozen—have unparalleled collections of rare books and manuscripts and are among the oldest research libraries in America.

Scholars have always prized the opportunity to work at one of these libraries because of the depth and focused nature of their holdings, their unusually well-informed and helpful staffs, and the ease with which the distinctive materials on their shelves can be used. Many of the most important books in the humanities include enthusiastic testimonials by the authors to the ways in which one or more of these libraries facilitated their research. One cannot imagine, for example, a major book on American Indian history that is not based in part on research conducted at the Newberry or a work on many aspects of early American history for which the author did not consult the American Antiquarian Society.

One reason for the continuing importance of these great libraries is precisely their independence. They are called "independent research libraries" because they are not affiliated with, or part of, larger scholarly institutions such as universities. While campus libraries understandably build their collections in response to changing instructional needs or other interests of current (and therefore changing) generations of faculty and students, the independent research libraries have been able to focus over very long periods of time on their defined areas of strength—areas often specified by their founders. Such single-mindedness has enabled these libraries to become—and remain—essential institutions for scholarship and research in the humanities.

This book focuses on five leading members of this set of institutions:

- The American Antiquarian Society in Worcester, Massachusetts
- The Folger Shakespeare Library in Washington, D.C.
- The Huntington Library, Art Collections, and Botanical Gardens in San Marino, California
- The Pierpont Morgan Library in New York City
- The Newberry Library in Chicago

In his preface, Jed Bergman explains the reasons for selecting these particular libraries for intensive study. In this foreword, I have two other objectives. First, I would like to explain why we believe that a careful examination of the histories of these libraries is not only intriguing in and of itself but also instructive to people interested in other parts of the nonprofit sector. Second, I would like to locate this study within the context of the Mellon Foundation's broader research interests in the health and welfare of a wide range of nonprofit institutions.

Why Study the Independent Research Libraries?

We selected the independent research libraries as subjects for this study primarily because of their relevance for broader segments of the nonprofit world. The basic premise of a case-study approach is that the lessons learned from particular institutions will be of interest to a wider audience. This is most certainly the case with the leading independent research libraries. From a theoretical perspective, research libraries serve as useful exemplars of the much larger class of nonprofit organizations, which, for reasons explained later in the foreword, depends heavily on endowments and contributed income rather than on earned income.

In addition to exemplifying one type of nonprofit, the leading independent research libraries are useful objects of study for two quite practical reasons. First, the individual libraries are themselves compact enough, and clear enough in their structure and organization, to be understandable. The main issues can be identified fairly readily, and their financial statements can be untangled (albeit with some effort). Second, these libraries have a history that is long enough and rich enough to permit examination of trends; their histories illustrate the ways in which quite profound transformations can occur incrementally over decades.

Pervasive Trends Within the Nonprofit Sector

Case studies of these five libraries are of relevance to a broad segment of the nonprofit world because their histories, which can be told in some detail, illuminate trends that have affected many institutions. The effects of the social and economic upheavals that have taken place in the United States since the 1960s have been felt throughout the nonprofit sector. In particular, during the late 1960s and the 1970s, there were intense pressures for democratization and increased openness on the part of educational and cultural institutions of every type. At the same time, financial pressures were mounting, in the form of high inflation, low economic growth, and poor returns in financial markets. These pressures created crises for many nonprofit institutions—not least the independent research libraries. Part of the story of this book is how these five libraries responded to those crises and were transformed in the process.

All five libraries started out with much in common, despite the unique circumstances surrounding the birth of each. They began in the nineteenth and twentieth centuries as privately supported institutions with the mission of collecting and preserving historical documents. They existed as quiet, scholarly oases serving small, exclusive clienteles. Until the 1950s, they were able to continue from year to year in a fairly stable fashion, having no reason to depart from well-established routines.

During the 1960s, however, the equilibrium of all five libraries, and of many similar nonprofit institutions, began to be threatened. By the 1970s, economic difficulties and external pressures to broaden their missions created a series of crises, typically manifested in recurring deficits as revenue growth stagnated and expenditures increased rapidly and seemingly inexorably. No longer were these institutions able to survive on their investment income alone (as "income spenders," in the language of Chapter Seven), sheltered from the world around them. Now they had to become "fund seekers," with new revenue profiles and, in many ways, fundamentally altered missions. This evolution, which has taken a variety of forms in these five research libraries, contains profound lessons concerning the consequences of rapid growth, the wise and unwise management of endowments, and the critical importance of forward planning and strategic decision making.

All of the libraries represented in this study were compelled to respond to a markedly different climate in which both the scholarly community and governmental and foundation donors expected more "openness" and less "elitism." New opportunities were exhilarating, and an unprecedented aggressiveness was manifested by many of their directors. Unfortunately, however, the economics of the 1970s made it difficult to achieve new programmatic goals while maintaining financial stability. Operating deficits and the need for capital funds to address space problems created severe budgetary strains.

Eventually a new, and significantly different, equilibrium began to emerge for most of these libraries. Funding profiles had come to include significant amounts of contributed income that had to be raised annually and even some earned income. Governance had become more "professional," and new groups of trustees saw their responsibilities quite differently from their predecessors. Financial planning had become more important—and more realistic.

This book chronicles the ways in which five similar institutions, all starting from much the same circumstances, facing common pressures, and experiencing similar crises, responded in distinctive ways. The story includes both triumphs and failures, as well as many instances of simply "muddling through" while hoping for the best. For some, the outcome is not yet clear. Many other nonprofit institutions have faced, or are facing, similar challenges. They may be able to benefit from the experiences of these five libraries.

Independent Research Libraries as Providers of Public Goods

The independent research libraries are also of general interest because they serve as useful exemplars of that large class of nonprofits that cannot sustain themselves simply by selling services—as examples of organizations that must depend heavily on contributed income. To appreciate the significance of this categorization, it is useful to take a step back and consider how the independent research libraries fit into the nonprofit sector as a whole. The nonprofit sector includes a vast array of different types of organizations, operating in fields of activity as diverse as higher education and civil rights, performing arts and wildlife preservation, health and international affairs. When faced with such diversity, the task of deriving general lessons from any particular set of case studies, regardless of the field selected, seems daunting indeed. This lesson has been driven home to us many times during the course of other research the Foundation has carried out: generalizations about "*the* nonprofit sector" often conceal more than they reveal.

Nonetheless, when one examines the nature of the "output" produced by different types of nonprofits, clearer patterns emerge. The output of every organization (by which we mean the goods or services it produces) can be thought about in terms of what economists call private and public goods. Stated simply, the distinction between the two is based on who benefits from the production of a good or service: an identifiable, private individual, who can then be charged an appropriate fee, or a more amorphous constituency such as the public at large (or some part of it). At one end of the continuum based on this distinction are organizations that produce relatively pure private goods; at the other are those that produce goods that are primarily public in nature. Many nonprofits, of course, fall somewhere along the continuum, with outputs that are a mix of private and public goods.

The private/public distinction is reflected directly in the way in which an organization finances its activities. Entities at the private end of the spectrum earn most of their income by charging fees, whereas those at the public end must tap quite different sources of revenue. Examples of organizations with a large private-good component are hospitals, day-care centers, and schools. Many of the benefits they confer accrue directly to the purchaser of the service, and these organizations almost always rely heavily on fee income. Since it is possible to charge for services provided, at least in some measure, similar organizations exist in the for-profit sector.

How are the independent research libraries to be classified? They are charter members of the set of entities whose output contains a large public-good component. The benefits they provide through their collections of scholarly materials accrue mainly to the society at large, over long periods of time, through what they tell us about our history and our cultural heritage. These libraries are responsible for the preservation of their valuable collections for the benefit of future generations and for providing access for scholars who will in turn write books and articles that are potentially of interest to a broad public. More recently, these libraries have also undertaken extensive programs of education and "outreach."

There is no way that the costs of establishing and maintaining such research libraries can ever be met by imposing user charges and then seeking to exclude from the benefits individuals who would not or could not pay. Acts of philanthropy were required for the founding of these institutions and continue to be necessary for their maintenance; libraries such as these will always be dependent, in significant measure, on contributed income from donors past and present. Indeed, to our knowledge, no independent research library has been able to exist by relying primarily on revenues obtained by charging end users for services provided.

In emphasizing the centrality of "contributed income," as contrasted with earned income, it is important to avoid any implication that only private patrons make such contributions to these types of organizations. Contributions to non-profit purveyors of public goods also come from governmental entities, which use tax revenues to subsidize activities regarded as worthy. The likelihood of governmental support, relative to private donations, depends on (among other things) the breadth of the constituency served and how essential the good or service is perceived to be. Thought about from this perspective, it is not surprising that private philanthropy has been the main (but not only) source of contributed income for independent research libraries. In contrast, governmental bodies are more likely to subsidize activities such as elementary and secondary education—activities that are often carried out, as well as funded, by entities that are themselves governmentally organized and supervised.[1] More generally, the overall balance between private and governmental support for entities whose outputs have a large public-good component, as well as between private and public provision of the services in question, varies dramatically across countries and cultures, in large part as a consequence of different histories of philanthropic support and of different attitudes toward the role of government.

Whatever the particular sources of contributed income, the central point remains: independent research libraries are examples of "pure" nonprofits in that they face the challenge of funding ongoing activities that cannot be paid for by user charges. In this key respect, the independent research libraries represent a large class of entities, including historical societies, museums, organizations that promote the humanities, those concerned with environmental protection and civil rights, many types of institutions serving advocacy functions, and organizations that conduct basic research. To be sure, these entities face market tests of their own. If they fail to convince enough people with control over resources (in the private and public sectors) that they are worth supporting, they will contract or fail altogether. But this kind of market test, focused on the ability to persuade donors of the worthiness of the organization, is different from selling goods or services to individual consumers of what are essentially private goods.

Many other sets of organizations have some public-good component to their output, even though they also produce goods that can be, and are, sold to individual purchasers. Higher education and the performing arts are good examples of fields in which outputs are of a mixed nature—and, as a consequence, revenues consist of substantial amounts of both earned and contributed income. Many of the issues discussed in this study of independent research libraries are also directly relevant to the problems faced by these hybrid institutions. At the same time, we recognize that the research reported here will have less relevance for organizations clearly sited at the opposite end of the private-good–public-good continuum, especially those that are paid directly, from private or public funds, for most of the services they provide.[2]

The Mellon Foundation's General Interest in the Nonprofit Sector

Some readers may want to know how this particular study fits within the Mellon Foundation's larger interest in the nonprofit sector. In certain respects, it is a direct outgrowth of the foundation's long-standing concern for the welfare of these specific libraries. As the recipients of substantial grants, they are of interest to us for this reason alone. But the decision to encourage Jed Bergman to conduct the research and record his findings in this form also reflects broader considerations.

From one perspective, the questions explored in this study are inescapable; those of us who work for grant-making foundations cannot help but "study" the prospective grant recipients that come to us in search of support. Understanding these organizations—their aspirations, problems, needs, and prospects—is, in fact, one of our most important responsibilities. Concern for their institutional health is especially appropriate at a foundation such as this one, which is committed to institution building and therefore seeks not only to support worthy projects but also, more generally, to strengthen key nonprofit organizations.

Success in undergirding the capacities of grantees depends on both detailed knowledge of particular institutions and an informed sense of trends in the relevant "industry." Needed, too, is a keen awareness of which forms of support will be of lasting value—accompanied by candid recognition that some kinds of foundation initiatives can have consequences that are not merely transitory but permanently harmful. For example, tightly restricted grants for purposes selected by the donor sometimes end up distorting the shape of an organization and weakening, rather than strengthening, its ongoing capacity to meet its basic obligations.

To be sure, grant seekers should have the brains and the courage to decline such "opportunities." But foundations should also avoid creating wrong incentives.

About three years ago, the trustees of the Mellon Foundation agreed that we should move beyond our "inescapable" interest in the welfare of particular nonprofits and launch a modest set of more systematic studies of this class of organizations. This decision was stimulated by experiences with the many nonprofits that, perfectly appropriately, appeared on our doorstep to ask for help. In discussing how to respond to several particularly poignant requests from institutions on the brink of extinction, we were struck by both the magnitude of the needs presented to us (which far exceeded levels of funding that any foundation, or group of foundations, could hope to provide) and the generic nature of the underlying difficulties these institutions faced. We thought that if we could understand more fully the origins of recurring problems, we might become better grant makers while simultaneously helping a wider range of nonprofits avoid traps that had ensnared some of their compatriots. Troubled organizations, it seemed to us, often need not just money but also encouragement and assistance in thinking through the issues that they confront.

It was equally clear that many of the problems that were so visible when institutions reached an *in extremis* state had been building for a long time. The crisis of the day often had deep roots, as it were, and it would obviously have been much better if impending problems had been recognized and addressed at a much earlier stage in the organization's life cycle. Even institutions seemingly "on a roll" are well advised to think hard about the longer-term implications of decisions made during what may prove to be a temporary period of prosperity.

In short, while the foundation has remained committed to providing direct, tangible assistance to organizations with demonstrated needs (including those poised to seize new opportunities), we decided to supplement our regular program of grant making with a research effort to understand more fully the evolution of nonprofits operating in areas familiar to the foundation. One goal was to see what lessons of general applicability might be derived from systematic examination of organizational histories—to learn from what in retrospect were brilliant insights or serious missteps along the evolutionary path.

We also wanted to make some contribution, if we could, to the burgeoning literature on the nonprofit sector. At the minimum, we thought that research might allow us—and others—to pose better questions in a timely way. The broad field of nonprofit planning and management remains seriously underdeveloped, and we thought it might be helpful if we were to join with others in trying various approaches to research in the field.

This is the second study of the nonprofit sector to be published by our staff since we began this research program, and the two illustrate very different ways of proceeding. In the fall of 1994, Jossey-Bass published a monograph examining the universe of charitable nonprofits [grant-seeking and grant-making organizations classified under section 501(c)(3) of the Internal Revenue Code].[3] Intended to frame the nonprofit landscape, this "macro" study provides a reasonably comprehensive analysis of what might be called *institutional demographics:* the number of charitable nonprofits and their distribution by field and geographic region, trends in institutional births and deaths, the ages and sizes of organizations, their characteristic revenue profiles, and broad trends in expenditures and funding patterns.

The present study, in sharp contrast, is focused much more narrowly—not on the half million entities that populate the universe of charitable nonprofits, but on just five of them! It illustrates the advantages (and, inescapably, the limitations also) of the case-study approach. Broad-based statistics on the changing numbers and types of libraries, historical societies, and museums are instructive in providing a broad picture of trends, but they can never tell us much about life inside any of these institutions. A case study, by contrast, allows for the development of in-depth understanding of an identifiable institution. The interplay of personalities, institutional processes, internal stresses and strains, and external forces can be studied. The institution's history can be mined for insights into the origins of present-day conditions. The dynamics of an institution's birth and maturation can be seen in all their richness. The two types of study are plainly complementary.

The Author and His Collaborators

I will say no more in this foreword about either the individual libraries studied here or the methods of analysis Jed Bergman uses as he will introduce both the libraries and his approach in the preface, where he will also describe the organization of the book.

But I do want to introduce the author himself. Jed Bergman came to work for the Mellon Foundation in June 1992, immediately after earning his bachelor's degree magna cum laude from New York University's Stern School of Business. One of his many virtues—particularly relevant to this subject—is that he combines exceptional analytical skill with a love of books, language, and ideas. Bergman has also proved himself to be a tireless worker, determined always to understand phenomena and then to explain them cogently. Over the course of the past two years, he has learned a great deal about both nonprofits in general and independent research libraries in particular. As one of my colleagues, Rachel Bellow, said about Bergman and another of our colleagues, Kevin Guthrie, who is doing a companion study of the New-York Historical Society: "We took two perfectly normal people and turned them into students of the arcane!" That may be something of an overstatement, but to the extent it is true, it is not all bad.

Bergman left the foundation to enter Columbia Law School in the summer of 1994, and those of us who have come to know him at the foundation are supremely confident that he will accomplish much in the field of law. We also believe that through this study, he has made a major contribution to the understanding of an important part of the nonprofit landscape. There are lessons here for everyone interested in the future of these irreplaceable cultural resources—and, more broadly, in the leadership and management of the many other nonprofit entities that contribute so much to our society.

Finally, I should provide a brief explanation of the collaboration that resulted in the final version of this manuscript and is referenced on the title page. When Jed Bergman entered law school, he had completed all of the basic research for this study. Also, he had finished writing Part One (the capsule histories of the individual libraries) and had prepared first drafts of all chapters in Part Two (the comparative part of the book). He did not have time, however, to rework the materials in Part Two, a task that Thomas Nygren and I subsequently undertook.

Our extensive interaction with Jed Bergman in the course of his own research, and our previous work in the nonprofit field (as coauthors, with Sarah Turner and Elizabeth Duffy, of the broader study of *The Charitable Nonprofits* referred to earlier in this foreword), made it much easier for us to pull together the remaining threads of the analysis than it would have been for anyone else. The editorial expressions in Part Two of the study ("we believe," "in our view," and so on) can properly be interpreted as the collective views of the three of us. We have worked so closely and have discussed these issues at such length that we could not disentangle our thoughts and assign personal responsibility for each one of them even if there were any point in trying to do so. We have enjoyed working together and would like to believe that the book in its final form has benefited from our varied perspectives and exchanges of ideas. It should be emphasized, however, that principal responsibility for the design, conduct, and writing of this study has rested with Jed Bergman from start to finish.

Princeton, New Jersey   William G. Bowen
August 1995   *President*
                                                            The Andrew W. Mellon Foundation

Notes

1. For an excellent discussion of many of these issues of private/public relationships, see Salamon (1987).
2. See Part Two of Bowen, Nygren, Turner, and Duffy (1994) for an extended discussion of these differences and of the relationship between the kind of output provided and funding patterns.
3. Bowen, Nygren, Turner, and Duffy (1994). There are also the so-called mutual benefit nonprofits, such as trade unions and chambers of commerce, which exist mainly to benefit their own members.

PREFACE

I never intended to write a book about independent research libraries. I began my employment as a research associate at The Andrew W. Mellon Foundation expecting to work on a broad study of the finances and governance of the nonprofit sector. Earlier experiences had piqued my interest in the field: I studied finance and management at New York University's Stern School of Business and conducted case studies and financial analyses while working part time at the Council of Jewish Federations, an umbrella organization of Jewish federations across the United States and Canada.

As time went on, though, my colleagues and I came to believe that a thorough understanding of a small set of institutions would be a valuable tool in coping with some of the problems afflicting the entire nonprofit sector. William G. Bowen identified the independent research libraries as useful candidates, for all the reasons enumerated in the foreword. Despite some skepticism (and relative ignorance), I commenced work; I quickly found myself becoming captivated. Independent research libraries are marvelous institutions; they hold great cultural treasures, offer neutral ground to scholars in a sometimes politicized academy, and form a living institutional link with our past. As the study progressed, I grew to love the look, the feel, and even the smell of rare books and of books generally.

Of course, I didn't write this book just to indulge my now-unshakable affinity for books and libraries. I wanted to contribute in some way to the nonprofit sector's understanding of itself, the forces that affect it, and the interplay between financial and programmatic considerations that is so crucial to long-term success. The difficulties enumerated in this study are by no means unique to independent research libraries. Many other institutions, including museums, humanities centers, and arts institutions, have encountered similar challenges over the past thirty years. The problems, and at least some of the solutions, are relevant to this broader set of institutions. I hope that the trustees and managers of those non-profits, as well as the growing body of scholars who make the nonprofit sector their field of endeavor, will read this book and find its lessons useful.

Outline of the Book

This book is divided into two quite different parts. Part One contains five individual case studies; one chapter is accorded to each institution. A brief introductory description of each library is presented here.

The *Huntington Library, Art Collections, and Botanical Gardens,* located in San Marino, California, is financially the largest of the five libraries in our set. This is due primarily to the fact that it also includes two art galleries and two hundred acres of botanical gardens. These features attract visitors on a scale unmatched by the other libraries. The Huntington's library collections are extensive, with strengths in British history, early American history, and the history of California. The collections and the estate, originally the property of Henry E. Huntington, opened to the public in 1927. In 1993, the Huntington's total expenditures were $17 million.

The *Pierpont Morgan Library,* originally the private collection of J. Pierpont Morgan, was founded as an independent institution in 1924. Located in New York City, the Morgan's collection is the smallest of the five libraries'. In terms of income, expenditures, and size of endowment, however, it is near the high end. The Morgan is commonly seen as having very strong museum programs, in addition to its activities as a research library. Expenditures in 1993 were $7.5 million.

Unlike the other libraries in this set, the collections of Chicago's *Newberry Library* were not acquired by the library's founder, Walter Loomis Newberry. A prominent citizen in Chicago's early history, Newberry left a provision in his will that called for the creation of a library if his two daughters died childless. The library was incorporated officially in 1892. The collections are vast: among the fifteen member institutions of the Independent Research Libraries Association (IRLA), the Newberry's collections are second in scale only to those of the New York Public Library. Because they were developed by professional librarians, the collections are focused more precisely on specific subject areas, which are mirrored in the Newberry's centers for research and educational programs. In 1993, the Newberry's expenditures were $7.6 million.

Located in Washington, D.C., just steps away from the Library of Congress, the *Folger Shakespeare Library* is the foremost collection of Shakespeareana in the United States and among the greatest in the world. Renaissance history, both English and Continental, are strongly represented as well. The Folger opened in 1932 and represented the culmination of twenty-five years of collecting by Henry Clay

Folger, chairman of the board of the Standard Oil Company of New York until 1928. The library, though a separate institution, is administered formally by the trustees of Amherst College, Folger's alma mater. In 1993, the Folger's expenditures were $5.9 million.

The *American Antiquarian Society* (AAS) is the oldest of the five libraries in our set. Founded in Worcester, Massachusetts, in 1812 by participants in the American Revolution, AAS's collections serve "to assure the preservation of the printed record of the American experience through the year 1876." AAS is financially the smallest of the five libraries; 1993 expenditures were $2.5 million. The collections, however, are about the same size as the Huntington's.

In presenting these five case studies, I hope to give a textured sense of the institutions that were studied. Also, readers will be able to note similarities (and some variations on common themes) in the paths followed by these libraries without the overlay of the more formal and statistical comparisons that comprise the subject matter of Part Two of this study. Questions to ponder while reading these brief histories include the reasons for growth, the interplay between the wishes of the founders and subsequent societal pressures, the changing roles played by individual directors, how the endowments were treated, the factors causing deficits to emerge, and then the ways in which the libraries responded as financial pressures intensified.

Why did we choose these five libraries specifically? The answer is simple and fairly prosaic. The libraries whose stories are told here are both among the largest members of the IRLA (after the New York Public Library) and the most similar in terms of history and scale of activities.[1]

Further evidence of their similarities is that in recent years, their directors have met yearly, in recognition of the challenges and opportunities that face them all. Furthermore, the Mellon Foundation has in the past supported these five libraries as a set. In 1991, as a precursor to a series of grants intended to endow and stabilize core functions, the five libraries participated in a preliminary process of financial analysis; it was this analysis that formed the basis of the current project.

Part Two, which brings together the threads of the individual stories told in Part One, analyzes commonalities and differences among the five libraries. Chapter Six examines trends in the growth of expenditures and programs. Next, in Chapter Seven, we consider shifts in funding profiles, which were driven in part by pressures from the expenditure side of the income statement and at the same time were themselves responsible for some of the spurts in spending. Investment income has been the most important (and most interesting) source of spendable funds; changes in the role played by endowments and in policies and practices concerning endowment management are treated in Chapter Eight. Ultimately, expenditures and revenues come together to determine whether an organization experiences a deficit or a surplus. This summary measure of an organization's financial status—and the dynamics that result when organizations seek to cope with deficits—are considered next, in Chapter Nine. The study's concluding chapter provides a synopsis of major points and some observations concerning changing patterns of governance and the evolving role of boards of trustees.

The dual approach of this book, with five chapters of history followed by five chapters of analysis and conclusions, may seem somewhat ponderous. At times, it did even to me. On balance, though, I believe that this structure is helpful. The detailed histories and in-depth examinations in the first part of the book are intended to inform readers who are not wholly familiar with these institutions; they lay the facts on the table. Part Two takes those facts and refines them to clarify and illuminate the lessons implicit in them.

Methodology and Sources

As just noted, this study integrates two different methodological approaches: it is part historical inquiry and part financial analysis. Both aspects are essential to understanding the events of the past thirty years and their effects on the libraries, and both parts of the study synthesize the two approaches. The financial work provided the metaphorical skeleton: changes in income and expenditures, growth in endowment, and the progression of surpluses and deficits revealed the factual outline of past events. To "put flesh on the bones," we turned to history: developing an understanding of the people, programs, and institutional cultures made the picture that much clearer.

The primary tool in the financial portion of the case studies was a spreadsheet, developed by the Mellon Foundation's research staff, which allowed us to analyze and compare different institutions' financial data. To obtain these data, we used audited financial statements, which have the advantage of being certified by external reviewers. We relied on the libraries' internal documentation when additional supplementary data were needed. Because the initial focus was on the 1980s, our analysis for that period was conducted in greater detail. Upon further reflection, we realized that an understanding of earlier events was essential, and we then compiled basic financial data for the period 1960 to 1980, again using audited statements wherever possible.

Of course, financial data cannot by themselves provide a complete picture. We augmented the financial portion of our analysis by reading annual reports, long-range plans, and books and articles about the five libraries and their fields as well as by visiting them. We interviewed each of the present directors and almost all living past directors. In some cases, we also met with key trustees or staff members.

One of the incidental effects of this study was the object lesson in historiography that it provided. The five libraries whose stories are told herein are repositories for the records and accomplishments of the past. Scholars who use these materials know that it is not enough for a given work or piece of information to exist; it must be accessible as well. The same is true of the historical materials on which this book is based. Unfortunately, the commitment to preservation, cataloging, and scholarly access that characterizes the libraries' operations has not always extended to financial and administrative data about the libraries themselves. In some cases, information was simply unobtainable. In others, it was buried and had to be excavated slowly and painstakingly.

Another lesson in historiography emerged from the analysis phase. I was forced continually to remind myself how substantial the changes at the independent research libraries have been. Thirty years ago, they existed in a different world. The scholars who used the collections were a smaller and more privileged group. The trustees who governed the libraries had less to do and could be characterized as more genteel. The founders' endowments paid for expenditures, and the fear of deficits was unknown; so, too, was the sometimes frenetic fundraising that is so common today. In light of these changes, vigilance was required in remembering that the directors, trustees, and scholars of bygone years saw things very differently. I tried wherever possible to keep in mind the dictum of the historian F. W. Maitland: "Always remember that events now long in the past were once in the future, and interpret those events in terms of how people expected them to come out, rather than how they did."[2]

Every book is in part a function of its limitations and of choices made concerning the allocation of time. This one is no different. Although I believe firmly that the book makes a real contribution to our understanding of the nonprofit sector, there is certainly more that could have been done. Undoubtedly, there are "missing pearls" in the libraries' archives or in the minds of experienced staff members. In most cases, it was impossible—due to time constraints or because information was buried—to gain access to these materials or to unearth the information. A decision was also made to concentrate on direct analysis of the available data. Hence I did not attempt to integrate this work fully with the vast and rapidly multiplying literature on the nonprofit sector and the field of libraries. Integrating the two might have enhanced my understanding of the subject matter and increased the utility of the book, but there simply was not time to review the entire field. When a source was directly on point, we included it. In general, though, a conscious decision was made to let this book stand on its own analytical feet.

Acknowledgments

As noted earlier, I did not come to the Mellon Foundation expecting to write a book about independent research libraries. In the interest of candor, I should confess that I had almost no idea what independent research libraries were, let alone how (or why) one would study them. This confession is not intended to be exculpatory: I performed the research reflected in this study myself, I stand by its conclusions, and all mistakes are my own. I mention my initial ignorance only to make the point as bluntly as possible that this book could not have been written without the goodwill, assistance, and patient tutelage of many people. I have attempted here to thank them all; I apologize in advance to those whom I have inadvertently omitted.

First on the list must be William G. Bowen, president of the Mellon Foundation. His guidance, constant willingness to listen and to teach, and persistent urging to "press on!" stand at the core of this venture. His later assistance in editing and rewriting was extremely valuable as well and is reflected in the formulation on the title page.

Tom Nygren, research associate at the Mellon Foundation, assisted in preparing Part Two. His name is on the title page, but I would like to thank him here as well. If the writing of this book was a marathon, Tom ran the last few miles.

Kevin Guthrie, my officemate and friend, played the crucial role of intellectual sounding board and late-night pizza companion. Whether the subject was fund accounting or the economics of the rare book market, he was always willing to think, to question, and to talk.

Richard Ekman, secretary of the Mellon Foundation, brought to bear his personal familiarity with the independent research libraries and with the National Endowment for the Humanities, as well as his passion for linguistic precision.

Joan Gilbert provided both encouragement and crucial assistance in our early analysis of the Folger Library.

Elizabeth Duffy, James Shulman, and Perry van der Meer taught me many important lessons, the most significant of which is that having a good editor (or two or three) can make all the difference.

Other foundation staff members were equally helpful, all in different ways. When my work habits turned the foundation into my home away from home, Ulrica Konvalin and Martha Sullivan became my surrogate mothers. Kamla Motihar proved once again that if something has been written, she can find it. Others, including (but not limited to) Dennis Sullivan, Alice Emerson, Elizabeth Breyer, and Stephanie Bell-Rose helped out, each in a unique way.

Sarah Turner, my predecessor as research associate, laid much of the groundwork for this study. She established the theoretical framework for our endowment analysis and was involved in the original collection of data for the foundation's 1991 grants to the five libraries.

The trustees of the foundation are to be thanked for allowing me to complete this study. Two merit special mention: Charles Ryskamp, former director of the Morgan Library, and Hanna Gray, president emeritus of the University of Chicago. They helped me understand events at the Morgan and the Newberry, respectively.

The other individuals whose cooperation was indispensable to this study were the directors, trustees, and staff members of the independent research libraries. They deserve credit as true collaborators in this venture: my questions were always answered, data were always provided (and sometimes even generated), and I was made welcome whenever I visited. Whether the questions were financial or programmatic, whether the person was a senior curator or an administrative assistant, and whether the information was readily accessible or buried in the archives, the staffs of the independent research libraries always did their best to help me.

In addition to the foregoing general acknowledgment, I must add an extra word of thanks to the past and current directors: Ellen Dunlap and Marcus McCorison of the AAS; Werner Gundersheimer and Philip Knachel of the Folger; Robert Skotheim, Robert Middlekauff, and James Thorpe of the Huntington; Charles Cullen of the Newberry; and Charles Pierce and Charles Ryskamp of the Morgan. Each took the time to review the chapter on his or her library, and all were willing to discuss with me their institutions, their environments, and their thoughts about the nonprofit sector.

Harvey Dale, professor of law at New York University, helped explain the mysteries of earned income and the unrelated business income tax.

Bevis Longstreth added his trenchant observations and knowledge of what the law is—and what it should be—to our discussion of endowment management.

Ronald Berman, former chairman of the National Endowment for the Humanities, gave us insight into events taking place "on the inside" at the time.

Ontrack Data Recovery deserves special thanks for saving my hard drive when it crashed. Without this company's disaster-recovery system, this book would literally have been lost.

My family and friends allowed me to forsake them for weeks on end, especially in the later stages of writing.

The final acknowledgment is to my wife, Jennifer Pepper. Her strength, support, and dedication (not to mention her willingness to eat dinner alone on a regular basis) were crucial to the completion of this study. I am eternally in her debt.

New York, New York   Jed I. Bergman
August 1995

Notes

1. The New York Public Library, in addition to being substantially larger, is financed differently; the city government covers the cost of key plant-related activities. Such arrangements, with which this book does not deal explicitly, represent another solution to the funding problems the independent research libraries face today.
2. Wheatcroft (1994).

THE AUTHOR

Jed I. Bergman received his B.S. degree (1992) in finance and international business from New York University's Stern School of Business. He held the position of research associate at The Andrew W. Mellon Foundation from 1992 to 1994. He is currently in his second year at Columbia Law School and is on the staff of the Columbia Law Review.

MANAGING CHANGE
IN THE NONPROFIT SECTOR

PART ONE

FIVE CASE HISTORIES

CHAPTER ONE

THE HUNTINGTON LIBRARY, ART COLLECTIONS, AND BOTANICAL GARDENS

The Huntington Library, Art Collections, and Botanical Gardens was founded in 1919 by Henry Edwards Huntington in San Marino, California. Set amid two hundred acres of lush, exquisitely groomed gardens, the Huntington is a cultural oasis, a place of learning and repose for scholars and visitors alike. As its name indicates, the Huntington is really three different institutions in one; each of its component parts could stand alone.

The Huntington Art Gallery houses such well-known masterpieces as Lawrence's *Pinkie* and Gainsborough's *Blue Boy*. British paintings from the Georgian period, acquired by H. E. Huntington, are particularly well represented. The American art collection, housed in the Virginia Steele Scott Gallery, is built around fifty American paintings drawn from the colonial period to the early twentieth century. The library's collections also include many fine prints and photographs, which are sometimes incorporated into gallery exhibitions.

The botanical gardens, which attract the most visitors, are varied and reflect the Huntington's evolution from a working ranch to a tourist attraction. The orange groves, for example, are a reminder of the early days, when income from the sale of produce was used to help pay for the upkeep of the gardens. Other popular parts of the estate are the Japanese Gardens, the Desert Garden, and the Shakespeare Garden, which contains only plants mentioned in Shakespeare's works.

The library, which is the part of the Huntington on which this chapter will focus most closely, has one of the most comprehensive collections of British and American books and manuscripts in the world. Among the library's particular strengths are British historical and literary documents from the late Middle Ages to 1900, American historical and literary materials from the nineteenth century to the present, and Western Americana.

What the average visitor does not perceive, and what is not always appreciated even by persons affiliated with the institution, are the Huntington's precarious financial underpinnings. Over the past thirty-five years, and especially during the 1980s, the Huntington faced a changing environment that undercut its financial strength. These difficulties were recognized by the Huntington's leadership belatedly. In the interim, serious financial problems developed, and these have been addressed systematically only during the past ten years.

Financially, the Huntington is the largest of the five institutions included in this study. In 1993, its expenditures were just over $11 million, while its endowment was valued at almost $83 million (see Table 1.1). Of the five libraries, it is the third best-endowed relative to expenditures.

The Huntington has evolved in many ways, and its financial history warrants study. Key questions of interest include these: How—and why—did this evolution occur? How was the Huntington's response to external circumstances affected by the organization's mission and governance? What provided the impetus for change? How effective were the institutional responses to a changing environment?

To answer these questions, it is important to have a sense of the Huntington's history, beginning with its founder, Henry Edwards Huntington, who was commonly known as Edward. Huntington's tastes and beliefs strongly influenced the institution that bears his name, as did the institutional culture and mode of governance that developed in the Huntington's early years. Without at least a cursory examination of these ideas and events, later institutional developments are difficult to understand.

Accordingly, the organization of this chapter proceeds generally along historical lines, with occasional digressions to examine specific issues and trends. The first portion of the analysis deals with Huntington himself and the founding of the institution. The second section describes briefly the first thirty years of the Huntington's history, during which it functioned as originally conceived and without financial difficulties. Section three considers the period from the late 1950s through the 1970s, which saw the Huntington's financial fortunes decline and its reserves depleted. Beyond describing these events, this section identifies the two broad sets of problems that lie behind the financial decline: a basic mismatch between income and expenditures and a set of perceptions and cultural assumptions that worked against changes in the Huntington's course. The final section analyzes the 1980s and early 1990s, when an acute financial crisis forced the leadership to address more seriously the underlying problems facing the Huntington.

Early History

Although Huntington was born in 1850 in Oneonta, New York, he spent much of his professional life in California. With his uncle, Collis P. Huntington, he helped

TABLE 1.1. SUMMARY STATISTICS FOR FIVE INDEPENDENT RESEARCH LIBRARIES, 1993.

	Income (thousands of $)	Expenditures (thousands of $)	Surplus/Deficit (thousands of $)	Endowment (Market Value) (thousands of $)	Capitalization[a]
Huntington Library	11,038	11,509	(471)	82,916	7.5
Pierpont Morgan Library	7,352	7,511	(159)	47,268	6.4
Newberry Library	5,280	7,261	(1,981)	32,733	6.2
Folger Shakespeare Library	6,233	5,937	296	57,604	9.2
American Antiquarian Society	2,483	2,368	115	25,871	10.4

Source: Audited financial statements for each library for fiscal 1993.

[a]Capitalization is the ratio of endowment to expenditures. It measures the extent to which an organization can rely on endowment income to fund its operations.

build the Southern Pacific Railroad. Later, he became a prime mover in the early twentieth-century development of Los Angeles. In 1903, three years after his uncle's death, Huntington bought the San Marino ranch that is now the Huntington. He later recalled: "When I went to California years ago, I traveled east, north and south from one end of the state to the other, even going off the beaten paths by team and studying every section carefully. I came to the conclusion then that the greatest natural advantages, those of climate and every other condition, lay in southern California, and that is why I made it the field of my endeavor. I have never for one instant lost faith in its unbounded possibilities and I am more sanguine today than I ever was."[1]

The placement of the Huntington in California, rather than on the East Coast like three of the four other libraries in this set, was thus a deliberate choice. Huntington was a firm believer in the future of southern California as the academic and cultural capital of the nation and thought that the intellectual development of the United States would parallel the country's political development. Although the physical frontier may have closed, as Frederick Jackson Turner had suggested in 1893, Huntington believed that the academic and cultural frontiers were still moving westward and would eventually reside in California.[2] It is perhaps fitting that Turner was the first senior research associate appointed at the Huntington; in this position, he was given the chance to explore Edward Huntington's own "new frontier."

The Huntington's location has affected the institution in many ways over its history, not all of which were foreseen by its founder. On the one hand, the nature of the Huntington's physical environment, specifically the existence of the botanical gardens, has made expansion of the physical plant far more economical than at other libraries, which are located in urban areas. On the other hand, Robert A. Skotheim, the current president of the Huntington, has suggested that historically, at least, it has been harder to raise money for endowment in southern California than in some other parts of the country. It has been suggested that there is less of a "service ethic" among southern California's wealthy, a difference perhaps traceable to the absence of the strong, often religiously rooted philanthropic tradition on the East Coast, and especially in New England.[3] Also, because of its location, the Huntington could not easily connect with potential supporters in England and Europe, who might have had a natural affinity for the Huntington's collections. (Of course, such questions of financial support were obviated for many years by Edward Huntington's own founding endowment.)

The focus of the Huntington's collection also reflects its founder's ideas and beliefs. Like the Morgan and the Folger, the Huntington's collection was developed primarily as a personal library. Consequently, its strengths are largely in areas that Huntington found of interest. (Independent research libraries differ in this regard from their university-based counterparts. The latter, because of the built-in demands of faculty and students, are expected to develop strengths in all fields of interest. Owing to the enormous "entry" costs and "exit" costs of having strong collections in a certain field, independent research libraries rarely change the foci of their collections, other than at the margins. Instead of adapting to changes in what scholars are looking for, it is the scholars who move, seeking out materials in which they are interested.)

Huntington was an avid collector who loved his books and was said to be on intimate terms with the contents of his collection, often spending mornings at the estate reading from a favorite work. Huntington also loved to buy books and artworks. As Max Farrand, the first director of the Huntington, recalled, "Mr. Huntington would talk business for only a few minutes at a time, and then would turn to show me some of the things he had under consideration with Duveen [the famous art dealer], or to read extracts from some manuscript or book in which he was especially interested."[4]

Huntington acquired books voraciously, often to the point where it was difficult to find liquid assets with which to pay for his purchases. His Los Angeles office, which was frequently called on to make payment, had a stock phrase for such situations: "We're feeling poor now." In the New York office, the comparable saying was "We're in mourning."[5]

By the time Huntington died in 1927, his library was among the greatest in the United States and, indeed, in the world. It had the largest collection of books in the *Short-Title Catalogue of Books Printed in England, Scotland, and Ireland, 1475–1640* in the United States. The authors of *Rosenbach*, a biography of the illustrious book dealer, went so far as to describe Huntington as the "greatest figure in the history of American book-collecting."[6]

Huntington's collecting, while avid and at times even feverish, should not lead one to believe that he was blind to the cultural and intellectual value of his library to the scholarly community at large. Far from it. As Huntington himself pointed out, "These books of mine in value to the world of thought are a great responsibility. The owner of these things is really little more than a trustee, and his responsibility is far greater than attaches to ownership of articles which there is some reason for regarding as purely personal."[7] Scholars were always welcome if they sought to pursue their investigations among Huntington's works. During the long and arduous process of moving the library from the Huntingtons' home in New York to California, boxes were even unpacked especially for particular scholars.

It appears that Huntington long intended to bequeath his collection to the public. As early as 1909, it seemed clear that the San Marino estate was going to be the location, for the architects were instructed to build the second floor of the house in a way that could withstand significant numbers of visitors. The library building, which was built in 1920, was considered the state of the art at the time it was built, and it is still in use today. An interviewer for a Los Angeles newspaper, after speaking with Huntington in 1919, wrote: "It is Mr. Huntington's intention to arrange for [these collections] eventually becoming in a way public institutions primarily for the use of literary scholars and painters, for nowhere else does such a wealth of material exist."[8]

Ray Allen Billington, a former senior research associate at the Huntington, has pointed out that a functioning research library requires three things: books, a facility, and money for staff, researchers, and acquisitions.[9] Huntington had already decided of his own volition to provide the first two. When it came to the need to establish a sizable endowment for the institution, however, Huntington had to be persuaded, even educated, as to the magnitude of the funds that would be needed.

Two men played important roles in this educational process: George Ellery Hale, the famous Mount Wilson astronomer and a member of the original board of trustees, and Max Farrand, the first director, who was originally titled director of research. Hale was an enthusiast when it came to the idea of a Huntington Library, and he expended much time and energy trying to convince Huntington that the best disposition of his collection would be in the form of an independent institution on the San Marino estate (which Huntington apparently believed already). Hale sent Huntington one proposal after another, some more realistic than others. One such proposal suggested that the facility should be an exact replica, in marble, of the Parthenon. (Huntington's tactful response was, "It is possible that you may have planted a seed." As James Thorpe, director of the Huntington from 1966 to 1983, put it, "Huntington saw to it that the seed was never allowed to sprout."[10])

Notwithstanding his fanciful dreams of a new Parthenon, Hale had very clear ideas as to what the new library should do. Using the scientific laboratory as his paradigm, Hale envisioned the Huntington as a laboratory for the humanities, a place where investigators could work, surrounded by all the tools of their discipline, furthering intellectual development by understanding the past advances and masterpieces of Western civilization.

Of course, paying the salaries of scholars and research associates, maintaining a library of secondary reference materials as well as of primary source materials, and publishing scholars' findings would be expensive endeavors. To help convince Huntington of this fact, Hale enlisted the help of Farrand, a scholar and administrator who was at the time the director of the education division of the Commonwealth Fund. Farrand was editing the autobiography of Benjamin Franklin and used this project to show Huntington how demanding scholarly research could be. "Research," explained Farrand, "is about the most expensive form of intellectual effort to encourage, and an independent institution, with adequate resources, can do more than the average university."[11]

Huntington proved a willing student, and when told by Farrand that a realistic budget would require an endowment of $7 million, promised it without reservation. Farrand, pressing his point (and perhaps his luck), went on to say that to create a truly first-class institution, an endowment of $17 million would be required. Huntington didn't know if such a sum was attainable, but he promised to try.

There is one more interesting twist to the story of the Huntington's creation. In the last few years of his life, Huntington began expanding his collections at a rate that scared Hale. Hale feared that the endowment, which was going to support the all-important future research efforts of the library, was being squandered on books and art. For all their value, books and art could hardly be used to pay salaries. Even though Hale probably underestimated Huntington's wealth, his fears were borne out in the end. Huntington's will, drawn up in 1925, had provided an additional $4 million for the library, in part to further the research function. A codicil added only weeks before Huntington's death, however, withdrew this benefaction, stating that this need had been met by recent gifts. Whether these "recent gifts" referred to books or money is unclear, but in any case the additional $4 million was not forthcoming. Attorneys at the time of Huntington's death estimated the market value of the endowment at $10.5 million.

From the start, endowment income was supposed to cover all of the Huntington's expenditures. Hale and Farrand had worked hard to ensure that the Huntington Library would be an endowed institution that did not have to raise money annually and could devote all of its time and resources to the scholars who came to it to conduct research. Although the original endowment was not as large as Farrand and Hale had hoped, it was more than adequate for the institution's needs at the time.

Although the library had been founded formally in 1919, and the trust indenture had contained a general statement of purpose, the research mission that is central to the Huntington today was not formalized until several years later. The original indenture described the Huntington as "a free public library, art gallery, museum and park, containing objects of artistic, historic, or literary interest."[12]

In 1925, the trustees developed, and Huntington signed, the "Policies Statement," which stressed the research mission for which Hale (and others) had argued so persuasively. The Huntington was to be a research library dedicated to the subject matter of the collections amassed by Edward Huntington, which revealed a "marked preference for books, manuscripts, and pictures illustrating the intellectual development of the English-speaking peoples."[13] American topics were to be an important focus of the research program, because "the establishment in California of a research institution like the Huntington Library shows how far America has encroached upon the duties of the Old World, but the long train of events leading up to this period from Colonial days has never been adequately studied and recorded."[14]

Finally, the implementation of this research mission would yield scholarship: "The international reputation of the Huntington Library and Art Gallery and its value to the world will depend chiefly on what it produces. Books, manuscripts and works of art are instruments of research, and they should be utilized in the most effective manner in advancing and disseminating knowledge."[15]

Equipped with vast collections, a comfortable environment in which to work, and a lofty mission, the Huntington was born as a fully endowed research library in the humanities. It opened to the public in 1927; in the first year alone, 140,000 people visited the institution. The dream for which Huntington, Hale, and Farrand had worked was realized. Farrand had the privilege of presiding over what must have seemed like a scholar's dream come true.

The First Thirty Years (1927–1957)

During the Huntington's first thirty years, it operated as originally intended. Income from the endowment was sufficient to cover expenditures. Year-end surpluses were used for acquisitions and for the establishment of reserves. The only major change in financial circumstances during this period was the establishment, in 1938 and 1939, of the Friends of the Huntington Library, a financial support group. Since the endowment provided more than enough money for operations, use of the Friends' gifts was restricted to acquisitions.

The Huntington's governance during this period was consonant with the general nature of the institution. Trusteeship was not a demanding activity that required a substantial commitment of time, energy, or money. The number of trustees was fixed by the indenture at five, and their terms were renewable. In many cases, this meant that trustees served for life; of the fourteen trustees appointed before 1957, all but four died in office. The trustees, and especially the chairman, were involved directly in the financial management of the institution. This was an extension of the role that Huntington had played while he was alive.

The director's responsibilities were less administrative and consisted mostly of publications and research. Thus when Farrand retired as director in 1941, he was not replaced until 1948, when Wallace Sterling was appointed. When Sterling went to Stanford University as president later that year, he too was not replaced until 1951, when John Pomfret was appointed.

It is not surprising that the Huntington's governance structure was relatively modest during its early history. In an ideal model, trusteeship and governance evolve to fit the needs of the institution, and the needs of the Huntington during its early years were served adequately by the arrangement outlined here. As a fully endowed institution, there was no need for a large board or for significant financial contributions. Moreover, since the Huntington's mission had been laid out in the Policies Statement, the board was not forced to grapple with major issues of direction or goals.

Programmatically, the Huntington continued to function on the two different levels implicit in its mission. On the one hand, the Huntington operated as a research institution. In 1929, the *Huntington Library Quarterly*, a scholarly journal, was published for the first time. The number of scholars working at the Huntington increased as well; by the early 1950s, about six hundred scholars a year were coming to the Huntington. On the other hand, the Huntington was also a "museum and park" open to the public. The Huntington's success in this regard was almost disconcerting. In the 1938 annual report, Max Farrand pointed out that Huntington "could not have foreseen the extent of public interest, which would at times tax the facility of the institution." At the time, approximately two hundred thousand visitors a year were coming to visit the Huntington, mostly the gardens and the museum. Because the stated focus of the Huntington was research, it was sometimes difficult to accommodate the huge numbers of people with the institutional resources available. The problem was not necessarily money; it was also people, facilities, and priorities. The indenture stipulated that the Huntington was to be a free institution; as a result, there was no obvious way to offset the costs related to the large number of visitors.

The Next Three Decades (1950s–1980s)

Circumstances began to change in the late 1950s, thrusting the Huntington into a decidedly less comfortable financial environment. Growth in costs and in the scale of activities accelerated rapidly; growth in the endowment, however, failed to keep pace. The disparate growth rates led to deficits, which over time eroded the Huntington's accumulated reserves. The impact of these trends, and how the Huntington's leadership dealt with the resultant difficulties, are the central themes of the second half of the Huntington's history.

It is instructive to have a rough sense of the Huntington's financial condition in the late 1950s, when circumstances began to change. Income in 1956 was $802,000. Of this, 99 percent came from the endowment. Expenditures were about $602,000. More than $2.25 million in reserves had been amassed since 1927; this was equivalent to four years' worth of expenditures and represents the extent to which the first thirty years had been "years of plenty." The market value of the endowment was $21.2 million.

Early Warning Signs

Figure 1.1, which shows surpluses and deficits from 1956 through 1993, illustrates the first manifestations of the Huntington's problems.[16] Between 1956 and 1960, expenditures increased to $991,000, an increase of 65 percent. Over the same three years, income increased only 19 percent, to $952,000. The result was a series of deficits in 1958, 1959, and 1960. These deficits, the first in the Huntington's history, were funded from the institution's substantial reserves.

Although these shortfalls may have seemed at first to be only a temporary problem, the clarity of hindsight demonstrates that this was not so. True, there were slight surpluses in the early 1960s, when cost-saving measures were put into effect. Even so, between 1964 and 1977, there was only one surplus. The particularly severe deficits of the early to mid 1970s no doubt resulted in part from the sharp rise in oil prices and the high general rate of inflation. The broad trend,

FIGURE 1.1.   SURPLUS/DEFICIT, HUNTINGTON LIBRARY,
1956–1993.

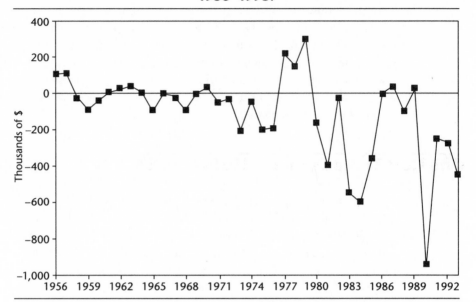

Source: Data from Tables B.1–1 and B.1–2 in Appendix B (operating fund series).

however, predated these years. Insufficient growth in the endowment, be it through reinvested earnings or new gifts, had rendered the original endowment-funding system inadequate.

This conclusion does not appear to have been understood by the Huntington's leadership at the time. From 1956 through 1966, an eleven-year period in which the Huntington incurred five deficits for the first time ever, the annual reports contained no mention of these financial difficulties. It is possible that this institutional silence reflected a decision not to discuss financial difficulties in a public forum. Still, it is unclear whether the underlying problems were recognized.

Potentialities for Service: James Thorpe's Directorship

The 1967 annual report, which was the first to be issued under the directorship of James Thorpe, was also the first to discuss the Huntington's budgetary problems. Essentially, the report tells us, growth in expenditures was too rapid. One indicator was the number of visitors annually, which by 1968 had risen to 398,000. This figure was seen by the trustees as the maximum that the Huntington could afford to sustain. The lack of an admission fee continued to exert pressure on the operating budget. The Huntington's revenues at the time came largely from a relatively fixed source—the endowment—which was not growing at the same rate as the expenses of serving visitors. Without an admission fee, there was no mechanism that would allow income to increase in proportion to the number of visitors. The growth in the number of visitors, coupled with growth in other aspects of the Huntington's activities, translated into increased pressure on the endowment, resulting in deficits.

In 1970, the following statement appeared in the annual report: "To continue the services of the institution at a high and undiminished level, the trustees have determined to embark upon a Development Program. It is apparent that the potentialities of the institution for service are far greater than we can exploit with our present funds." Here, finally, are the beginnings of a response to the Huntington's financial problems. The phrase "the potentialities . . . are far greater," however, indicates that the focus was on expanding the Huntington's programs rather than on funding existing activities. This reading is borne out by the activities of the following years: in 1970, the Huntington began a series of short informal dance, drama, and musical programs on a monthly basis, as well as twice-daily talks by staff members about aspects of the collection. In 1973, a library program of courses and discussions was begun for high school students in the morning and for the general public in the afternoon.

In addition to expanding its programmatic offerings, the Huntington also took steps to increase income. In 1970, a director of development was hired for the first time. Some steps were also taken to enlarge the circle of people affiliated with the Huntington and thus the pool of potential donors. While the number of trustees could not be increased without altering the indenture, an ancillary body called the Board of Overseers was created in the early 1970s. The twenty-three overseers provided the Huntington with financial support and served as a training ground for future board members. The latter function is particularly important, since a board with only five trustees cannot afford to make mistakes in its choice of members. Other support structures were created as well, including corporate sponsorships and the Society of Fellows, a broader support group than the Friends.

At first glance, it is somewhat mystifying that the gifts and grants reported in the annual reports of the early 1970s failed to solve the Huntington's budgetary problems. A closer examination of these figures is instructive because it illustrates the importance of distinguishing between operating and nonoperating support. In 1973, for example, gifts and grants were said to have totaled $1.4 million dollars, but there was a deficit of $193,000. This apparent contradiction can be explained as follows: of the $1.4 million, all but $778,000 consisted of gifts in kind, mostly books and artworks. Gifts in kind, although very important, obviously are not budget-relieving. Of the remaining $778,000, one-half million dollars was a grant from The Andrew W. Mellon Foundation to be used as an endowment fund and hence was not available for current purposes. Subtracting these in-kind and endowment gifts leaves about $300,000 in current support that actually could have been used to pay the bills.

Overall, the Huntington's efforts at increasing income through contributions and other ventures proved insufficient. The early to mid 1970s witnessed a series of deficits even more persistent and severe than those in earlier years. Although the "program of development" caused income to grow more quickly than it had in the past, expenditures grew even faster still. In other words, income failed to catch up.

In the late 1970s, though, the Huntington's efforts began to show a measure of success. Income matched expenditures, and there were even surpluses, probably as a result of grants from the National Endowment for the Humanities (NEH). (The NEH's role in the growth of independent research libraries is discussed in Chapter Seven.) Although these balanced budgets and small surpluses were only a temporary respite from financial distress, they are worth noting.

Another way to measure financial success or failure over a long period of time is by the degree of change in an organization's reserves. The Huntington, which by the late 1950s had amassed $2.25 million of reserves, was forced to spend much of this money to fund the recurring deficits of the period since the 1950s. Unfortunately, due to accounting changes, a usable time series of the level of reserves is unobtainable. A measure of the cumulative surplus or deficit, starting in 1956, is essentially the same thing; it represents the amount by which the reserves would have been depleted. As shown in Figure 1.2, this figure had reached $700,000 by 1976.

FIGURE 1.2.   CUMULATIVE DEFICIT, HUNTINGTON LIBRARY, 1956–1993.

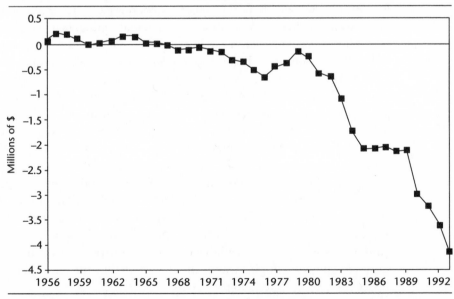

Source: Tabulations based on Tables B.1–1 and B.1–2 in Appendix B.

Root Causes of Financial Difficulties

This entire discussion seems to beg the question of why more was not done. Why was no action taken from the late 1950s until approximately 1970? Once the problem became too big to ignore, why were development efforts not more successful? The Huntington is located in one of Los Angeles's wealthier areas, and although the board was small, collectively it was quite wealthy. Was it truly impossible to take more successful action? At the very least, expenses should have been brought under control. The underlying reasons that explain the Huntington's problems can be subsumed under two general headings: financial conditions and perceptions and culture. Because the financial issues are the more proximate cause, they are discussed first.

Financial Conditions: A Harmful Mismatch

The central problem at the Huntington was a seemingly insoluble disparity in cost and income trajectories. The costs of the Huntington's activities, as well as their scale, grew more quickly than inflation. Due to various constraints (to be discussed shortly), income simply could not keep pace.

Some figures help to illustrate the problem. From 1956 to 1976, income increased at an average annual rate of 5.8 percent, while total expenditures increased at 6.4 percent.[17] This difference, although small, compounded over time, thus increasing the dollar disparity. Trends in later years exacerbated the problem. Between 1981 and 1993, total income increased by 7.6 percent per annum, while expenditures increased at an average annual rate of 9.4 percent. The differential between income and expenditure growth rates widened from 0.6 to 1.8 percentage points.

For most of the Huntington's history, the primary source of income was investment income. Some revenue was produced from orchard sales, a restaurant, and sales of publications and reproductions, but the endowment was clearly the main source of support. Like most endowment policies formulated in the 1920s, Huntington's original indenture limited spending from the endowment to interest and dividends. Because interest and dividends were needed for current income, there were practical limits on the extent to which the endowment could be invested in growth-oriented equities. As a result, the endowment principal could not realize fully the growth that equities would have provided.

Because of the provision limiting spending to interest and dividends, there were only two ways to increase the flow of investment income. One was to invest in higher-yield bonds or in stocks with higher dividend policies. Higher-yield bonds are inherently more risky and thus would not have been a prudent investment choice. As for companies with high dividends, the stock of such companies tends to appreciate less. Such moves on the Huntington's part would only have exacerbated the underlying problem, namely, the lack of growth in the endowment corpus. A second option would have been to increase the overall size of the endowment by soliciting capital gifts; this is the route the trustees have taken in the past ten years. Until the mid 1980s, however, the Huntington did not conduct a general campaign for unrestricted endowment funds. To summarize, until the 1980s, there were several real or imagined constraints on the Huntington's ability to increase investment income—its primary source of funds.

An admission charge, which could have become a source of income that grew with the number of visitors and with rising expenditures, was also deemed unavailable. Yet another way to increase income is the option that the trustees eventually elected in the 1970s: seeking contributions for current income. This strategy, although sound conceptually, was not executed optimally. By the time the trustees took action, the Huntington had already experienced twelve years of deficits. If adopted earlier, this approach might have closed the deficits.

If the Huntington's income was limited in its growth potential, the expenditure side of the ledger was a different story. The Huntington's expenditures grew rapidly, and both of the institution's principal activities, research and public programs, played a part. On the research side, such factors as the costs of books and periodicals and the need for increasingly expensive secondary reference materials led to cost increases. On the public side, the sheer volume of the Huntington's visitor flow appears to have exceeded the institution's ability to cope.

Perceptions and Culture

The second set of issues, involving "perceptions and culture," reflects the Huntington's history. When it was founded, the Huntington was a very wealthy organization, and it was almost inconceivable that it would be forced to solicit outside funds. Such features as the prohibition on an admission charge, the small size of the board, and the absence of any sort of membership or support group demonstrate this point. For the first thirty years of the Huntington's history, this wealth continued to exist. Even when the first support group was founded, the Friends had the luxury of limiting their support to acquisitions, as opposed to operating expenses. In those early years, the Huntington's great wealth was a matter of both perception and reality. The problem is that the perception remained after the reality had changed. Even today, it is difficult to believe when visiting the Huntington that its financial condition is less than robust. The perception of wealth, and the inability of the institution's leadership to dispel it, was part of the reason that the "program of development" was not more successful. As recently as the late 1980s, surveys revealed the persistence of this attitude among the Huntington's supporters.

After thirty years of laissez-faire governance, the board was slow to realize that the world was changing: as mentioned earlier, even though deficits began in 1958, financial problems were not discussed in the annual reports until the late 1960s, and a development officer was not hired until 1970. This inaction can be traced to the Huntington's organizational culture and to the prevailing set of assumptions—namely, that the money was there—that had been in place all along.

Another outgrowth of the "perception gap" was that the board's own giving was not on the scale that one might have expected. In all fairness, the trustees had never been asked to give. The idea of trustee giving, and the expectations that follow from it, were not part of the Huntington's culture. Even so, once the need arose, it does not appear to have been met as expeditiously as it might have.

In the late 1960s, soon after James Thorpe assumed the directorship, a "shake-up" of the board occurred that may have been linked to an attempted change in direction. In 1969 and 1970, four of the five trustees retired. A newly imposed age limit helped induce this series of retirements. Set originally at seventy-five, the limit was later lowered to seventy-two. Eventually, after all of the older trustees had stepped down, the limit was abandoned altogether. While the infusion of new blood appears to have been helpful in allowing the director more leeway in managing the institution, the changes were not substantial enough to alter the Huntington's course. The new trustees, although willing to make some of the institutional changes that were needed—creating boards of overseers and other support groups—do not appear to have grasped the full extent of the problem.

Part of the responsibility for the financial decline must rest with the Huntington's professional leadership as well. Although the board is ultimately accountable, the role of the director and the other administrators is to notice problems and suggest responses to them. One possible explanation for these oversights and omissions is the false sense of financial security that grew out of knowing how wealthy the trustees and local supporters of the Huntington were. The Huntington was regarded for many years as a jewel in the crown of Los Angeles's upper-crust, monied society. The annual Christmas party, held in the Huntington Art Gallery, was an important social event often written up in the *Los Angeles Times*. With all of that money in the neighborhood surrounding the Huntington, how could serious difficulties persist? This is perhaps the best example yet of the perception gap and the way it was perpetuated. The Huntington's staff believed that if the people of San Marino knew how serious the Huntington's problems were, they would come to its rescue. The people of San Marino, due to their own set of perceptions, apparently did not realize that the Huntington's fiscal problems were so serious. The trustees either failed to recognize the problem or were too circumspect in dealing with it. They failed to make the case persuasively, and the necessary funds were not forthcoming.

Financial Crisis: The 1980s

By the start of the 1980s, Thorpe and the board of trustees had achieved a limited measure of success. Despite the fact that investment income covered only two-thirds of expenditures, the budget appeared to be balanced, and the Huntington had maintained the scale and scope of its activities. A choice had been made: rather than cut expenditures to match income, income would be expanded (through fundraising primarily) to cover expenditures. While one might ask whether this represented a decision made actively or passively, it was at least a response to a growing problem.

In the years that followed, a series of events plunged the Huntington back into financial crisis. The immediate cause of this shift appears to have been the late 1970s renovation, which involved the addition of a pavilion wing and the creation of a parking lot. Although the renovation itself was paid for through a capital campaign, the associated expansion in activities and expenditures produced another series of operating deficits.

One positive outgrowth of the renovation was the initiation of a "suggested donation upon admission." The suggested donation was originally targeted to help pay for the parking lot but has grown into a major source of income. In 1981, suggested donations provided the Huntington with just $77,000. By 1992, income from this source had grown to $1.4 million. A voluntary contribution was one way to harness the giving potential of the large numbers of visitors without violating the indenture. (There are nevertheless real differences in the yield between mandatory and voluntary fees. In 1992, for example, the Huntington had about 578,000 visitors. The amount of money raised was $1.43 million. If a mandatory admission charge of $5 per person—equal to the suggested donation—had been in place, admission income would have been $2.9 million. Even if there had been a 20 percent falloff in attendance because of this charge, admissions income would still have been $2.3 million. Of course, imposing a charge would be predicated on obtaining the California attorney general's permission to modify the indenture.)

Figure 1.1 shows the timing of these events. In the early 1980s, deficits continued, broken only by a near surplus in 1982. In 1983 and 1984, as increased expenditures resulting from use of the newly renovated structure began to be felt, the operating deficits were about half a million dollars. In both percentage and dollar terms, these were the two largest deficits that had ever been incurred. Another way to appreciate the magnitude of these deficits is to realize that fully 11 percent of the Huntington's activities in those years had to be financed from operating-fund reserves.

The deficits of 1983 and 1984 came close to exhausting those reserves, which had dwindled steadily throughout the 1960s and 1970s. As large as these deficits were, though, they were prevented from becoming even larger by recourse to a high endowment spending rate. (As is explained in Chapter Eight, the term *spending rate* as used here refers to the portion of the total return on the endowment that is spent in a particular year, regardless of the form that return takes. Hence interest, dividends, and realized capital gains are all included.) Figure 1.3 shows the spending rates for the period 1956–1993. The "spike" in 1982 and 1983 is clearly visible. This strategy took money to fund the deficit from the endowment corpus

FIGURE 1.3.   SPENDING RATE, HUNTINGTON LIBRARY, 1956–1993.

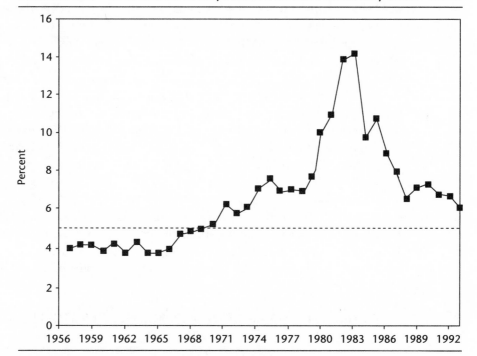

Source: Data from Tables B.1–1 and B.1–2 in Appendix B.

Note: Dotted line represents a spending rate of 5 percent, which is commonly regarded as prudent.

instead of from reserves; the only thing that changed was the pocket from which money was taken.

Balanced Budgets: Robert Middlekauff's Directorship

In 1984, the spending rate fell, even though the deficit was almost $600,000. One might ask why the spending rate dropped, since a higher spending rate would have made the deficit appear even smaller. A possible explanation is that as of 1984, the Huntington had a new director, Robert Middlekauff. The cut in the spending rate is a sign of Middlekauff's efforts to bring the institution's finances under control.

Middlekauff came to the Huntington from his position as provost of the University of California, Berkeley. A historian, he had conducted research at the Huntington in the 1970s and was familiar with the institution's scholarly resources and attractive environment. The ability to work in the library building itself and to conduct research with the Huntington's outstanding collections was very appealing after the administrative rigors of serving as provost.

Unfortunately, Middlekauff did not get a chance to enjoy the idyllic life of a scholar. Soon after his arrival, he was told that the "small budgeted deficit" that had been forecast for 1983 had ballooned into a $543,000 deficit. None of the preliminary inquiries that Middlekauff had made prepared him for this exigency. After discussions, the trustees and Middlekauff agreed that the problems called for serious action.

Middlekauff set about immediately to balance the budget. Operating income, which had been growing at an average annual rate of 8.8 percent in the last years of Thorpe's tenure, grew at 10.3 percent per annum between 1984 and 1988. This growth, furthermore, was accomplished without a sharp rise in the spending rate. Figure 1.4, which depicts the relative distribution of the Huntington's three main sources of income, shows that the increases were the result of increased gifts, grants, and earned income.

As part of his efforts to increase income, Middlekauff took several steps that represented a departure from the Huntington's culture and that of its supporters. For one thing, there was resistance to raising the "suggested donation upon admission." The Huntington was by indenture and long-standing practice a free insti-

FIGURE 1.4.   SOURCES OF INCOME, HUNTINGTON LIBRARY, 1981–1993.

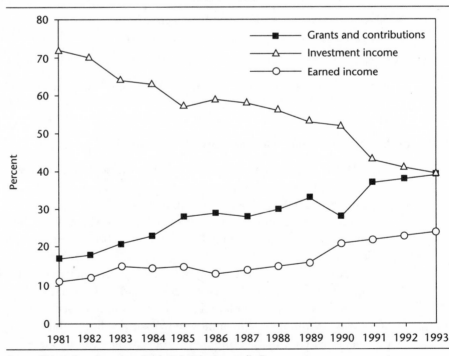

Source: Tabulations based on Table B.1–2 in Appendix B.

tution, and changing that status, even within the bounds of Huntington's indenture, went against the democratic ideals of the trustees.

Another point of contention was the broadening of the Huntington's support groups. The Huntington, like many other cultural and fine arts institutions, had long been patronized by the wealthy elite. There was a certain cachet to being involved with an institution as prestigious as the Huntington, a feeling that was bolstered by the quiet, genteel manner in which fundraising and other financial issues had been treated. The shift to a more aggressive, money-oriented approach engendered a degree of nostalgia for the old days, before fundraising drives and the constant need to recruit more supporters. The Christmas party could no longer be held in the Huntington Art Gallery—there were too many people associated with the Huntington. Only recently has this shift into the modern—some would say mercenary—age been fully accepted.

Whatever problems this transition caused, Middlekauff's efforts bore fruit. In 1982 and 1983, growth in operating expenditures far exceeded growth in operating income. These were the years that produced the large deficits discussed earlier. In 1984, Middlekauff's first full year at the Huntington, the rate of growth in income and expenditures were the same, and in each year between 1985 and 1987, income actually grew more rapidly than expenditures. By the mid 1980s, the budget had been balanced and the operating deficit eliminated, at least temporarily.

In addition to balancing the operating budget, Middlekauff took the important step of launching the first capital campaign targeted specifically toward unrestricted endowment. This move was important because it addressed an underlying problem: the lack of growth in the endowment and the resultant inability of investment income to cover expenditures. The increased endowment that came from the capital campaign meant that even though the spending rate continued to drop throughout the mid 1980s, the amount of investment income continued to increase. Although the capital campaign never reached its goal of $13.5 million, except in pledges and bequests not yet fulfilled, it did augment the endowment.

"Refinancing and Revitalizing:" Robert Skotheim's Directorship

Middlekauff left in December 1987, returning to Berkeley to conduct research and to teach. His successor was Robert A. Skotheim, the president of Whitman College in Walla Walla, Washington, and an American historian. The situation that Skotheim inherited posed different challenges from the ones Middlekauff had faced. In a sense, Middlekauff had stabilized the Huntington and solved its most pressing problems. Skotheim had the opportunity, and the responsibility, to address the situation in a more fundamental way.

This was a formidable task. Skotheim's plan was "to refinance the institution even as it [was] being programmatically revitalized."[18] A crucial component of this effort has been "consciousness raising": educating the board and overseers to the Huntington's long-term financial needs in much the same way that Farrand and Hale had educated Huntington himself. Since Skotheim's arrival, the development department has also been expanded and professionalized. This shift has resulted in greater efforts for both the annual campaign and the endowment. The Huntington's management of its endowment, still the largest single source of income, has also been revisited. The effort has consisted of three components.

First, a 6 percent spending rule (implemented in fiscal year 1987) has kept the draw from endowment lower than in previous years, although 6 percent is still a high spending rate by most standards.

Second, the focus on gifts to the endowment has been intensified. After watching the value of the endowment decline for so many years, the Huntington's leadership realized that true autonomy and financial stability will come only through increased endowment. Skotheim has pointed out that "endowment income alone allows institutional leadership to make decisions about program development without the kind of deference routinely required when funding is heavily furnished by the external environment. If an institution funded completely by its endowment is in danger of becoming arrogant, aloof and insensitive to external relations, it is also true that an institution completely dependent on annual giving and sales is in danger of losing its sense of internal direction."[19]

Third, the Huntington's investment strategy has been reexamined. As noted earlier, the asset allocation of the founder's endowment is constrained by its outdated restrictions on spending. Today, even though the "non–founder's portion" of the endowment is equal to almost half the value of the total, the endowment as a whole is still allocated in a way that is less than optimal. In 1993, the Huntington considered appealing to the California attorney general to relax that provision of the indenture; as of this writing, it is not clear what the outcome will be. Such a decision, however, would allow the Huntington to invest a greater portion of its funds in equities, thus realizing the higher gains that traditionally come with such a strategy.

The Huntington has also modified its governance structure. Three-year trustee terms have been introduced, with an absolute limit of five consecutive terms. An age limit has been reinstated; no trustee may be elected to another term if he or she has reached age seventy-two. So even though the board still consists of only five people, there will be more turnover, thus guarding against complacency through the provision of "new blood." It is hoped that now that the board is committed to the need for greater support, the trustees will help mobilize the broader segments of the Huntington's constituencies.

The relationship between senior staff and the board has also been "opened up." Until recently, the directors of the Huntington's divisions submitted their proposed budgets separately, and the board took it from there. Today, the process is more deliberative, allowing each division's director to work with a better sense of the institution's overall financial health and to understand the needs of other divisions more clearly.

This shift in attitudes did not come easily. According to Skotheim, in the first few years of his tenure, he faced significant resistance from the board and from the Huntington's other supporters. Surveys of the fellows, docents, and visitors to the Huntington show that some of this resistance still persists. Individuals have expressed resentment toward the "marketing" of the institution and the current focus on financial considerations. One of the fellows offered this revealing, albeit wholly anecdotal, perspective: "The nickel and diming of major donors is destroying the pleasure. We have in the past always taken pride in the Huntington and everything for donors has been done with taste and class. That, I fear, is fast disappearing, and the changes are not for the better."[20] On the whole, though, the Huntington's supporters appear to understand the need for change and have mobilized to support the institution and its mission.

There are still problems. The years 1991, 1992, and 1993 resulted in deficits, each bigger than the previous year. Although a balanced budget was forecast for fiscal 1994, the truth is that Middlekauff balanced earlier budgets as well, only to have the situation unravel after his departure. The spending rate remains higher than the 5 percent level normally considered prudent. The persistent recession in California has cut into the Huntington's ability to raise money. More ominously, there are unknown costs in the future. Such costs include conservation efforts, automation, and preservation issues related to the somewhat outdated library building.

After almost thirty-five years of financial difficulties, the trustees can look back with at least a measure of satisfaction on the progress the institution has made, especially in the past ten years. The leadership—volunteer and professional—is aware of the nature of the Huntington's problems and is committed to finding the resources to address them.

Notes

1. Thorpe (1969a, p. 333).
2. Thorpe (1969b, p. 304).
3. On this point, see the general discussion of geographic distribution in Bowen, Nygren, Turner, and Duffy (1994, pp. 25–31). A more modern perspective is provided in Greene, Millar, and Moore (1994). Also, Wolpert (1993) examines in some detail regional patterns of giving in America.
4. Thorpe (1969b, p. 298).
5. Thorpe (1969b, p. 299).
6. Fleming and Wolf (1960, p. 73).
7. Thorpe (1969b, p. 304).
8. Billington (1969, p. 354).
9. Billington (1969, p. 351).

10. Thorpe (1969b, p. 305).
11. Billington (1969, p. 361).
12. Huntington and others (1925, p. 1).
13. Huntington and others (1925, p. 1).
14. Huntington and others (1925, p. 2).
15. Huntington and others (1925, p. 1).
16. The data for the period 1956–1980 have not been subjected to the same level of analysis applied to the period 1981–1993.
17. To calculate these growth rates, we fitted a least-squares regression line to the natural log of the values in each year. This method constructs a data series that increases at a constant percentage rate and whose points match the underlying data as closely as possible. It therefore takes into account each year during the period, rather than just the first and the last. This methodology is used regularly in the subsequent analysis.
18. Skotheim (1993, p. 1).
19. R. A. Skotheim, letter to the board of trustees, Apr. 13, 1993.
20. Huntington Library internal marketing report.

CHAPTER TWO

THE PIERPONT MORGAN LIBRARY

The Pierpont Morgan Library's origin can be traced to its founder's earliest foray into collecting autographs and manuscripts: a signed letter from then-President Millard Fillmore, which Morgan received in 1851. Alternatively, it can be found in the churches and cathedrals of Germany, where the young J. Pierpont Morgan made his first art acquisitions: fragments of stained-glass church windows. The Pierpont Morgan Library evolved from these beginnings; as a research library and a museum, it perpetuates two related facets of Morgan's interests.[1]

The Morgan, which is located in New York City's historic Murray Hill district, became an independent institution in 1924. Designed by the noted architect Charles F. McKim, the library building was built in the early years of this century as Pierpont Morgan's private library. George Ellery Hale, the Huntington trustee whose fanciful hopes for a marble replica of the Parthenon are discussed in Chapter One (and who, interestingly, visited Morgan's library while the Huntington was still in the planning stages), would have been quite envious of the Morgan. McKim built the library in the manner of the ancient Greeks: dry masonry, with the blocks filed to perfect joints and the mortar placed invisibly in shallow grooves within. The Morgan resembles an Italian *palazzo*, emblematic of the Neo-Renaissance style that was common in New York around the turn of the twentieth century. Despite the additional cost of using dry masonry (said at the time to be $50,000), Morgan was apparently more than satisfied with McKim's creation.[2]

Our interest, of course, lies less in the buildings that house the collections than in the library itself. The collections, though smaller than those of the other four libraries, are superb. They consist of just under two hundred thousand items, of which roughly half are printed books and half are manuscripts, autographs, drawings, paintings, and artifacts. The focus is on Western Europe from the early Middle Ages to the end of the nineteenth century and on American history and literature from the colonial period forward. The Morgan boasts a carefully assembled collection of incunabula (books printed during the fifteenth century), including three Gutenberg Bibles. Six special collections are particularly strong: medieval and Renaissance manuscripts; drawings and prints; printed books and bindings; autograph manuscripts, letters, and documents; music manuscripts; and children's books. Like the other independent research libraries, the Morgan also has a collection of secondary reference works to facilitate scholarly research.

Programmatically, the Morgan functions both as a research library and as a museum. As a library, the Morgan maintains a reading room, open to qualified scholars year round, and a print room, available by appointment. In addition, library staff hold classes for graduate and undergraduate students from area universities in fields such as art history, medieval literature, and library studies. As a museum, the Morgan presents exhibitions, both drawn from its own special collections and on loan from other institutions. Docent-guided tours and introductory videos render the collections more readily accessible to the public. Since 1989, regular lectures by curators have been held as part of an effort to broaden public appreciation of the Morgan's holdings.

Financially, the Morgan is one of the larger libraries in this set. Table 1.1 in Chapter One gives a brief overview of the five libraries' financial positions in 1993. The Morgan is ranked second in income, second in expenditures, and third in endowment.

The Morgan is an instructive case study for two reasons. First, its historical development parallels that of the other institutions in its field. Like the other independent research libraries, the Morgan faced increasing costs and expanding programs but lacked the money to pay for them. The Morgan incurred deficits, although these were generally not as severe as those encountered by some of the other libraries. On the whole, the Morgan has been more successful than most in adapting to the changed circumstances of recent decades.

The second noteworthy aspect of this case study relates to the recent expansion of the Morgan's physical plant. An enlargement of the physical plant is often a risky endeavor for nonprofits. Because there is no easy way to raise capital, any nonprofit seeking to build or to buy a building faces a series of difficult choices. The Morgan's expansion appears to have been a success, at least insofar as it did not strain the library's resources to the breaking point. Here, too, there are useful lessons to be learned.

We begin with a preliminary discussion of Pierpont Morgan himself and his influence on the library. The biographical material is followed by a historical analysis of the library, its governance, and its finances. This analysis identifies the strengths and weaknesses of the Morgan's situation, as well as the external factors that have affected its development. The general discussion then narrows to an examination of the purchase of the Morgan House, the capital campaign that financed it, and related issues, such as debt and endowment management. The chapter closes by examining the Morgan's financial condition today and its prospects for the future.

The Morgan Family and the Founding of the Library

J. Pierpont Morgan

As a collector, Pierpont Morgan combined a voracious appetite with a discriminating palate. His collections, which included a vast array of paintings and other *objets d'art* as well as books and manuscripts, were assembled carefully. Even his habit of buying entire collections *en bloc* was indulged only when he was sure that the overall quality of the collection was high. From the 1890s through the 1910s, Pierpont Morgan pursued his avocation with a ferocity that matched his business reputation.

In contrast to Henry Edwards Huntington, whose focus was on California and the West, Pierpont Morgan was oriented toward Europe. He had been schooled in Europe, and throughout his life he maintained a city home and a country home in England, both of which he used frequently. Among his circle of friends and acquaintances were members of the English gentry and the European nobility. In fact, were it not for a timely change in the American tax code, it is entirely possible that a good part of Morgan's art collection would have stayed in England. Had the collections remained in Europe, the decision would have been based purely on financial considerations, not on personal ones. Pierpont Morgan was a staunch believer in the future of culture in America, as evidenced by his establishment of the library, his leadership of the board of the Metropolitan Museum of Art, and his eventual bequest to that museum.

It is not known precisely when Pierpont Morgan decided to bequeath his library to the public, but a passage in his will was quite clear on the subject: "I have been greatly interested for many years in gathering my collections . . . and it has been my desire and intention to make some suitable disposition of them . . . which would render them permanently available for the instruction and pleasure of the American people."[3]

Morgan's books formed the core of the library. Morgan chose not to create a museum of his own, as Huntington had done; most of his art collection went to the Metropolitan Museum of Art, on whose board Morgan had served since 1888. Unfortunately, because some of the most valuable objects had to be sold at the time of Morgan's death for tax purposes, the library is the only portion of Morgan's collections still intact today. While the library's collections have grown, the assemblage of books, drawings, and manuscripts that Morgan acquired is still at their heart.

J. P. (Jack) Morgan

At the time of Pierpont Morgan's death in 1913, responsibility for the library passed to his son J. P. (Jack) Morgan, Jr. He was assisted in this task by Belle da Costa Greene. Pierpont Morgan's nephew had "discovered" Belle Greene while the latter was a young assistant in the Princeton University Library; Greene became the elder Morgan's librarian and confidential art secretary in 1905. She played a crucial role in building the collections, and when the Pierpont Morgan Library was incorporated formally, she became its first director.

In the years after his father's death, Jack Morgan continued the process that Pierpont Morgan had begun. Despite the pressing concerns of his father's estate and his financing of the Allied cause during the First World War, Jack Morgan enriched the library's collections tremendously through acquisitions. In 1924, having decided that the library had become too important to continue as a family holding, Morgan created the institution formally. He transferred it to a board of trustees and provided an endowment to fund the library. The Regents of the State of New York chartered the new institution as a public reference library. Together, these events marked the beginning of the Pierpont Morgan Library as an independent institution.

Of the five libraries in this study, the Morgan is the only one that can truly be called a family institution. Henry C. Folger had no children; the American Antiquarian Society, as an elective body, is an intellectual inheritance rather than a familial one; Henry E. Huntington's son and nephew both served on the board of trustees, yet they were never involved deeply in the life of the institution; and the Newberry, as we shall see, came into existence only because Walter Loomis Newberry had no grandchildren.

Although the library is legally separate from the Morgan family, the fact is that it bears the Morgan name and thus commands a high degree of loyalty. Every president of the board until the 1980s was a descendant of the founders, and the Morgan name is also prominent on the wall of the library's Garden Court, which honors individuals who have made substantial contributions to the library over the years. In this sense, the commitment of the Morgan family is a living bequest from the library's founder.

The Early Years (1924–1969)

Belle Greene

During the years after the library's founding, it became apparent that its new public role required additional space. An annex was built in 1928 on the site of Pierpont Morgan's old house, effectively doubling the available space. Among the facilities included in the annex were an exhibition hall, a reading room for scholars, staff space, and stack space for reference books.

Belle Greene remained at the Morgan's helm until 1948, bringing her years of service to a total of forty-three. In addition to the seminal role that she played in the library's founding and the acquisitions that were made under her tenure, Greene also left a bequest, which today is worth over $1 million. Jack Morgan died in 1943, signifying the end of an era at the Morgan. Although the chairmanship passed to Junius S. Morgan, Jack's son, the family's ties to the institution were no longer quite as close.

Frederick Adams

Frederick B. Adams, Jr., the second director of the library, was appointed in 1949. The Morgan's circumstances had begun to change; postwar inflation had diminished the earning power of the library's bonds, and high taxes had impinged on the disposable income of the Morgan family. At the same time, the number of scholars wishing to avail themselves of the Morgan's resources was increasing.

In 1949, Junius Morgan convened an advisory council to discuss the future of the library and its activities. According to the council's report, "The Library, as a collection of original records of man's creative achievements, has no real limits of city or country or century. [As a national institution], the public no longer expects it to be the exclusive concern of a single family."[4]

To provide a vehicle through which the broader community could support and be involved with the Morgan Library, the council proposed the establishment of a national organization of Fellows of the Morgan Library, whose purpose would be "to provide funds for exceptional acquisitions, and to encourage the use of the collection by financing publications and making grants-in-aid to scholars."[5]

The formation of the Fellows was a crucial development in the Morgan's history. The Council of Fellows is something of a cross between other support groups that were in existence at other libraries, including the Huntington's Friends and the AAS's Society. Like the Friends of the Huntington, the Fellows' primary purpose is financial support. Like the American Antiquarian Society, membership is elective; this device serves to limit the size of the association and to lend it an air of collegiality and exclusivity.

To be sure, an organization whose primary purpose is raising money should not necessarily be small or exclusive. In fact, recent developments have led to the expansion of the Fellows. On the whole, however, the approach seems to be successful. One of the Morgan's distinguishing characteristics is its relationship with moneyed individuals in the United States and abroad. This association is probably due to the Morgan family's connections, as well as to the library's location in New York, a city with large artistic, financial, and cultural elites. Whatever the reason, the Council of Fellows is the vehicle through which the support of wealthy individuals has been mobilized. In 1991, for example, the Fellows contributed over $1 million for operations and acquisitions to the library.

Like the other early supporting organizations, the Fellows raised money chiefly for acquisitions. When the Council of Fellows was established in 1949, the institution was no longer as wealthy as it once had been and was looking to outside sources to augment its resources, but the Fellows still had the luxury of targeting support primarily to acquisitions. The top-dollar acquisitions that had come from Pierpont Morgan and Jack Morgan were not going to recur, and the contributions from the Fellows ensured that the collections would continue to grow.

Another important change in the library's financial circumstances occurred in 1959. Once again, the library's programs, collections, and staff had outgrown the available space. To raise money for an addition, the National Development Committee was formed, and a capital campaign for $3 million was inaugurated. Half of the proceeds were to pay for an expansion of the library, and the other half were designated for endowment. The campaign was a success, raising just over $3 million from 665 donors. The resultant expansion included a climate control system, electronic fire-detecting apparatus, private offices for the curators, a new and larger print room, a bindery and conservation laboratory, and additional stack space for reference books. The 1960 campaign marked the first time that external fundraising had been conducted for any purpose other than acquisitions.

The need for more space has been a recurring theme in the Morgan's history, as evidenced by four separate expansions over the past seventy years. Although Pierpont Morgan considered his collections a public trust, he probably did not expect the public to come traipsing through his library *en masse* to see them. Also, it is not clear that he anticipated the extent to which the library would be professionalized or the degree to which its public role would ultimately expand. And it certainly would have been difficult to foresee the extent to which the collection would grow, through acquisitions, gifts, and bequests. Since 1960, the Morgan has expanded its physical plant again twice: once in the mid 1970s and again in 1987 with the purchase of the Morgan House.

Adams served as director until 1969. The Pierpont Morgan Library under his direction was very different from the library of today. For one thing, it was smaller. Income in 1968 was $762,000, compared with $7.6 million in 1993. Another difference is the extent to which the library's operations were funded by its endowment. Investment income in 1968 was $551,000, or about 72 percent of the total. In 1993, the comparable figure was 30 percent. Also, the Morgan had an operating surplus, with income exceeding expenditures in every year but one from 1963 through 1968. Acquisitions expenditures were relatively low, averaging $109,000 between 1963 and 1968. The market value of the endowment was $14.3 million.

Although the Morgan may appear to have been financially sound, several problems did exist that are not apparent from these figures. A good deal of deferred maintenance had accumulated over the years. Also, salaries were apparently out of line with those in comparable New York institutions. In short, there was work to be done.

Charles Ryskamp's Directorship (1969–1987)

In 1969, Charles A. Ryskamp was appointed director of the library. Serving through 1987, he presided over far-reaching changes at the Morgan, some taken at his initiative and others dictated by external circumstances. To a very real extent, Ryskamp made the Morgan the institution that it is today.

New Directions

Between the mid 1970s and the mid 1980s, the Morgan broadened its public outreach efforts. This shift came primarily in the form of exhibitions, which were both bigger and more frequent than at any time in the past. Several exhibitions from other collections around the world were arranged, including some shown only at the Morgan. These exhibitions raised the Morgan's public profile and brought many new people through its doors. These projects were also very expensive, especially the traveling exhibitions. Costs such as insurance and travel increased rapidly, making it difficult to mount the sort of "blockbuster" exhibitions that were most successful in bringing in large audiences. Even when exhibitions were funded externally, the Morgan was often responsible for the indirect costs.

Changes were also made in the Morgan's scholarly and library programs. Classes were offered for upper-level undergraduate and graduate students from local universities, using original materials from the special collections. Internships were developed for students interested in careers in museums and libraries. In the late 1970s, the Public Programs Department was organized within the Public Affairs Division to manage docent-guided tours. These programs were supported in part by grants from the National Endowment for the Arts and the National Endowment for the Humanities, each of which made a challenge grant of $150,000 to the Morgan during the 1970s.

Another feature of Ryskamp's leadership was a sustained increase in spending on acquisitions. This increase reflects growth in both the price of rare books and the extent of acquisitions. Figure 2.1, which expresses acquisitions as a percentage of total income, shows that a greater portion of the library's income was committed to acquisitions during Ryskamp's tenure (29 percent) than during that of his predecessor, Frederick Adams (16 percent), or his successor, Charles Pierce (13 percent).

Of course, these differences cannot be attributed entirely to the directors' appetites or even to the board's. Most of the Morgan's funding for acquisitions consists of donated funds that are restricted to that purpose. Until recently, acquisitions were also the primary purpose for which Fellows' contributions were spent. Thus an observed increase in acquisitions does not necessarily come at the expense of other aspects of the operating budget; rather, it means that restricted giving for

FIGURE 2.1.   ACQUISITIONS AS A PERCENTAGE OF TOTAL INCOME, PIERPONT MORGAN LIBRARY, 1963–1993.

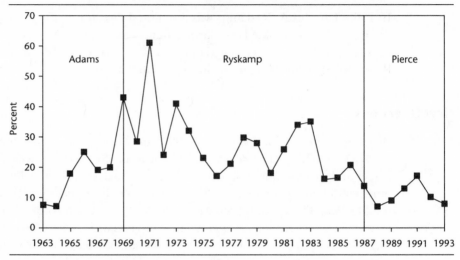

Source: Tabulations based on Tables B.2–1 and B.2–2 in Appendix B.

acquisitions is increasing. In this sense, spending for acquisitions is unrelated to spending for operations.

This sharply drawn distinction—between acquisitions funding and operations funding—is only valid once the gift has been made. When the money is still in the donor's pocket, it is theoretically available for operations or acquisitions. This is what makes the role of the director so important. While certain donors may not be willing to shift their gift from acquisitions to operations under any circumstances, others may be more flexible. In the latter instance, if the director or the board feels that operations is the more pressing cause in a given year, there may be room to maneuver.

The presence of substantial acquisitions funding, coupled with more general budgetary problems, prompts the question of whether gifts could have been reoriented toward operations. There is some historical evidence that such a strategy can be pursued successfully. Figure 2.2 depicts the total dollar amount contributed by the Fellows between 1985 and 1993. During these years, the Fellows were asked to target part of their contribution to operations and part to acquisitions—a change from the historical purpose of the Fellows.

Because 1988 and 1989 were the years during which the library's capital campaign was at its peak and because current giving was artificially low, it is difficult to draw conclusions from those years. We cannot, for instance, determine whether the call for gifts for operations "cannibalized" gifts for acquisitions or brought in new money. What is clear is that in the period 1990–1993, the relative share of gifts for operations increased, suggesting that management can influence the pur-

FIGURE 2.2.   FELLOWS' GIFTS,
PIERPONT MORGAN LIBRARY, 1985–1993.

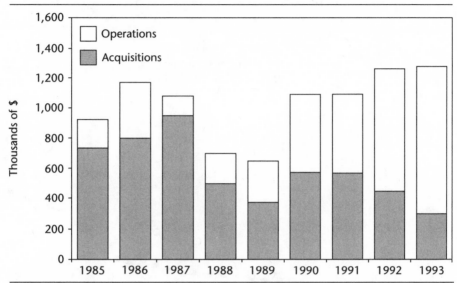

Source: Audited financial statements of the Pierpont Morgan Library, 1985–1993.

pose for which gifts are made. Charles Pierce, the current director, has observed that the Fellows would prefer to be able to give more to acquisitions. Their present willingness to target funds to operations probably reflects their awareness of the library's urgent financial needs, rather than a long-term shift in their interests.

The Cost of Growth

The growth in the scale and scope of the Morgan's programs during the 1970s required money. Additional funding came primarily from increased gifts and contributions, as shown in Figure 2.3. The figure depicts the level of investment income and other income (gifts, grants, and earned income) from 1963 to 1993. Gifts, grants, and earned income have increased more rapidly than investment income; since 1972, gifts and grants have outpaced funding from the endowment as the largest source of income.

Much of the Morgan's success in fundraising is attributable to Ryskamp's efforts. He conducted almost all of the fundraising himself, especially the solicitation of major gifts. As time went on, though, the amounts of time and energy required to raise money began to impinge on other aspects of the director's role. The burdensome need for constant fundraising is a recurring theme in the annual reports. In his January 1981 report to the trustees, for example, Ryskamp wrote: "In one way or another, I estimate that about three-fourths of my work for the

FIGURE 2.3. INCOME BY SOURCE, PIERPONT MORGAN LIBRARY, 1963–1993.

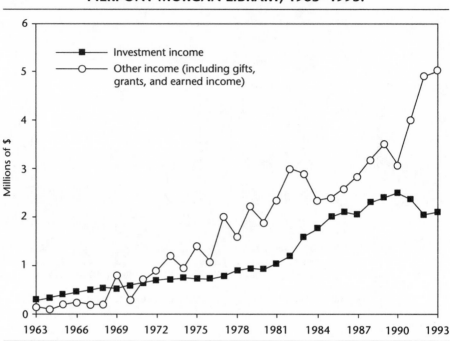

Source: Data from Tables B.2–1 and B.2–2 in Appendix B.

library during the last year was given to that purpose. The pressure of the financial problems meant also that three-fourths of my weekends were spent on Library business, and at least half of the time when I was supposed to be on vacation. . . . There is, alas, no time to think about where we are going, and my personal, private life has almost ceased to exist."

Despite the Morgan's success in attracting contributions and earned income during the 1970s and 1980s, income was not always sufficient to cover expenditures. Although deficits were not as pronounced, or as common, as at some other institutions, there was a developing imbalance between what the library wanted to do and what it could afford. Figure 2.4 depicts the imbalance between surpluses and deficits for the period 1963–1993. Between 1970 and 1987, the total value of surpluses was just under $1.1 million, while deficits totaled almost $3 million. Overall, it is fair to categorize this period as one in which, despite valiant efforts, the Morgan began to fall behind.

The financial difficulties that the Morgan encountered were also related to a lack of growth in the endowment. Figure 2.5, which tracks the market value of the endowment, shows that the endowment declined both in nominal and in real dollars during the period 1973–1980. This trend was due to several

FIGURE 2.4.   SURPLUS/DEFICIT,
PIERPONT MORGAN LIBRARY, 1963–1993.

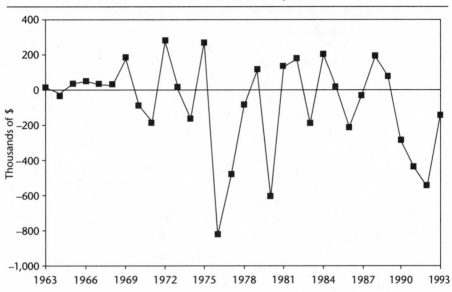

Source: Data from Tables B.2–1 and B.2–2 in Appendix B.

FIGURE 2.5.   MARKET VALUE OF ENDOWMENT,
PIERPONT MORGAN LIBRARY, 1963–1993.

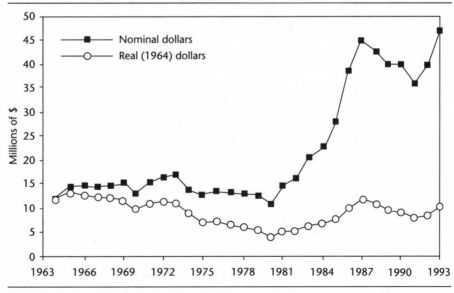

Source: Data from Tables B.2–1 and B.2–2 in Appendix B.

economic factors, primarily the high inflation and poor returns that characterized the 1970s. On an institutional level, the rising spending rate (Figure 2.6)
and the use of endowment funds to help pay for a renovation in the late 1970s
played a role as well.

The value of the endowment dropped during the 1970s; at the same time, the
cost of operations rose. As a result, much of the Morgan's fundraising was the
institutional equivalent of treading water. With the amount of investment income
falling, more outside money would have been needed even if the scale of the
library's operations had remained constant. Because new programs were also
begun during this period, the need for external funding was even more pronounced.

Rising expenditures also led to increased spending from the endowment. In
the 1960s, investment income alone could have covered the library's expenditures,
which is why the spending rate was relatively low (Figure 2.6). During the 1970s
and 1980s, when expenditures grew far more rapidly than the endowment, the
board resorted to a higher level of spending in order to shield the operating budget from massive deficits. Even this shift, however, failed to resolve the problem.
The library was forced increasingly to rely on annual fundraising to support its
operations.

FIGURE 2.6. SPENDING RATE, PIERPONT MORGAN LIBRARY, 1963–1993.

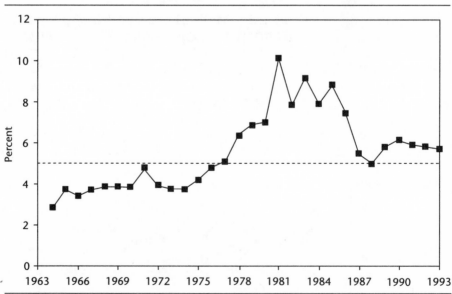

Source: Data from Tables B.2–1 and B.2–2 in Appendix B.

Note: Dotted line represents a spending rate of 5 percent, which is commonly regarded as
prudent.

Deficits and Deeper Problems

It is worth noting that many of the problems documented here are not specific failings of the Morgan Library but rather the results of an adverse economic climate. A falloff in the ability of endowment funds to pay for operations was a common occurrence in the 1970s. The poor performance of both the equity and the bond markets depressed returns, and inflation brought rapidly increasing costs across the board. Economic "stagflation" defeated the endowment's ability to grow with the economy.

In theory, the share of returns on an endowment that is not spent in a given year is reinvested, allowing the corpus to grow, thus producing more income the following year to meet rising costs. During the 1970s, such accumulation was simply not possible. An endowment fund, even if its performance matched the S&P 500 or the Lehman bond index, and even if spending never exceeded 5 percent, would have been hard pressed to grow with inflation.

In addition to its financial difficulties, the library had once again outgrown its physical space; by the 1970s, this was recognized as one of the main problems affecting the library. The developing constraints on expenditures over the previous ten to fifteen years had led to the deferral of much-needed maintenance. Also, programmatic expansions had exhausted the available space. In 1975, the board approved various structural improvements and additions: a photographic department, an enlarged conservation bindery, a three-story underground vault, and more office space. The total cost of these renovations was about $3.5 million, of which about $2 million was covered by gifts. The remainder was taken from the endowment, either as income from the operating budget or as capital transfers.

By the early 1980s, the falloff in endowment income had become a serious problem. In his annual reports to the board of trustees, Ryskamp stressed repeatedly the need for a campaign to augment the endowment and to alleviate both the constant pressure to raise money and the attendant inability to focus on broader concerns. In the 1981 report to the trustees, for instance, he recommended considering "a possible full-scale drive for endowment funds. Discussion of such a drive and the finances of the library generally will be the principal matter of business for our winter and spring Board meetings."

The need for an endowment campaign, and later the campaign itself, were significant issues for the board over the next few years. Although the campaign did not start formally until 1987, efforts were made throughout the 1980s to augment the endowment through gifts (see Figure 2.7). Between 1981 and 1987, the average level of gifts to endowment was $2 million.

Such a high degree of support, especially for the operating endowment, was a relatively new phenomenon. Charles Ryskamp exerted much effort to persuade the board to increase its financial support. Through his efforts, Ryskamp helped begin a shift in the board's role—from lending names and prestige to the institution to active involvement in fundraising and institutional advocacy. As in the

FIGURE 2.7. CAPITAL GIFTS,
PIERPONT MORGAN LIBRARY, 1981–1993.

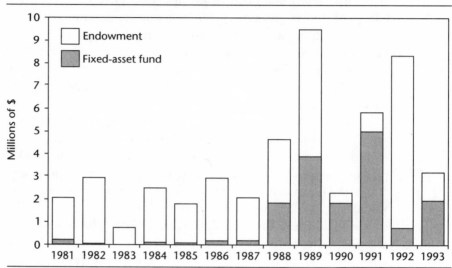

Source: Data from Table B.2–2 in Appendix B.

Huntington's case, the board members did not always embrace this change. To date, at least one Morgan board member has resigned, expressing discomfort with the degree of support expected of trustees.

Notwithstanding the need for a larger endowment, the Morgan was able to balance its operating budgets during the early 1980s.[6] As seen in Figure 2.4, there were even small surpluses from 1981 through 1984. The Morgan's situation was not comfortable or completely stable, however. Problems existed, although they were merely less pressing than at other institutions. The endowment was not big enough, much of the staff was underpaid, and space was again in short supply. This shortage was in many ways the library's most vexing problem. The staff was crowded into basement offices, and one curator had no office at all. In the mid 1980s, when Gordon N. Ray bequeathed his collection to the library, even the remaining vault space was completely overwhelmed.

As explained earlier, one of the ways that the Morgan balanced its budgets, despite the rapid growth in expenditures and the lack of comparable growth in endowment, was by spending a greater share of the returns on the endowment. This policy can be seen clearly in Figure 2.6, in which the slow rise in the spending rate during the second half of the 1970s, as well as the peaks in the early 1980s, are indicative of the greater pressure on the endowment that was produced by rising expenditures.[7] If the spending rate had stayed in the 5 percent range, which is now normally considered a prudent upper limit, the 1980s would have seen a string of deficits (or the trustees, Fellows, and other supporters might have given more money).

In 1984 and 1985, concrete progress was made toward a capital campaign. Cambridge Associates, a financial consulting firm for nonprofits, conducted an analysis of the library's financial equilibrium and prepared a fundraising report.[8] The report identified several problems confronting the Morgan. Expenditures were increasing more rapidly than income, the spending rate was too high, and there were physical-plant issues which needed to be addressed. Also, cost controls were less stringent than they should have been, many employees were underpaid, and the director was said to be spending an "unsustainable" amount of time on fundraising. Cambridge Associates recommended a six-year capital campaign for $20 million, which would augment the endowment, improve the library's facilities, allow for an increase in compensation, and eliminate the operating deficit.

The campaign, however, had a difficult start. In the 1986 report to the trustees, Ryskamp wrote:

> At this time last year I wrote that "although there are again signs of improvement in various aspects of the finances of the institution, the forecast for us is bleak unless a major endowment drive is undertaken as soon as possible." For the second year in a row I gave up a leave of absence in order to raise money for the Library, particularly endowment funds, and to attempt to find a chairman for this campaign. During the past fiscal year, $2,000,000 was added to the endowment funds, but we still have not launched our endowment drive and have no chairman for such a campaign. The situation for the Library, and for me personally, remains critical; our most urgent concern must be to find such a leader and to start a campaign, which should have begun months ago.

By this time, the Morgan's underlying problems had come to the surface. Figure 2.4 charts the Morgan's descent into deficits during 1985, 1986, and 1987. During those years, expenditures grew rapidly while endowment income was almost flat, the latter perhaps due in part to efforts to spend less from the endowment (Figure 2.6). Among the different expenditure categories, spending for public programs grew rapidly; in 1986, it became the single largest expenditure category.

Charles Ryskamp resigned in 1987 and was replaced temporarily in April of that year by the assistant director, Francis Mason. The principal reason behind Ryskamp's decision to leave was the board's unwillingness to assist in fundraising. It appears that by leaving, Ryskamp finally communicated the message he had tried to convey for so long. Since 1987, the board has become substantially more involved in all aspects of the institution. This involvement has included increased financial support, as well as an expanded committee structure and governance role. Seen from a historical perspective, there may have been a practical limit to the degree to which a single director could encourage the board's evolution. Beyond that point, there was a need for a governance "revolution," which was accompanied, and effected in part, by a new director. Charles E. Pierce, Jr., a professor of English at Vassar, was appointed the fourth director of the Morgan in May 1987; he assumed his duties in September of that year.

Soon after Ryskamp's departure, the endowment campaign was finally begun, with trustee Betty Wold Johnson at its helm. In April 1987, the campaign goal was set at $25 million. At the time, the market value of the Morgan's endowment was $45 million, of which $41 million was earmarked for operations. At a 5 percent spending rate, endowment income could cover just under half (46 percent) of the $4.4 million operating budget. If the endowment were to grow by $25 million, the portion of expenditures that would be covered by investment income would increase substantially. Such a situation would take pressure off the director, allow the Fellows more leeway in their choice of giving, and ease the financial burden under which the library and its staff had been operating for some time.

Charles E. Pierce and the Morgan House (1987–1993)

The Morgan House: A Daunting Opportunity

The change in directorship and the start of the endowment campaign had substantial implications for the library's future. Both were overshadowed, however, by a series of events that took place later that year. In September 1987, the building known as the Morgan House came on the market. The Evangelical Lutheran Church, which owned the building at the time, moved its headquarters to Chicago, making the property available.

The "property to the north," as it was known at the Morgan, was a very attractive site. First, it had historical significance, having been Jack Morgan's residence. Second, it was a rare opportunity to acquire property that was directly adjacent to the library building. Third, the four-story brownstone, with a small five-story office building attached, was large enough to address the Morgan's need for additional space and still leave room for growth well into the next century.

In October 1987, an internal study examined the various courses of action available to the library in relieving the shortage of space.[9] Five options were studied:

1. Purchase all or portions of the Morgan House
2. Purchase a brownstone in the Murray Hill area
3. Lease office space in the Murray Hill area
4. Build underground vault storage
5. Build off-site vault storage

The purchase of the Morgan House was the most appealing choice. Each of the other options fell short on either cost or proximity. The daunting factor about the Morgan House, however, was its price. It was estimated that it would cost between $13 and $15 million just to buy the site, before any development. At a time when the library was already conducting a capital campaign, the thought of having to raise an additional $20 million or more would have given pause to even the most self-assured fundraiser.

Several means of financing this endeavor were explored. The board looked into two potential joint ventures: one with the Italian government, which wanted to build an Italian cultural center, and the other with Oxford University Press. The board also considered using the air rights to both the library and the Morgan House and building an office tower, the proceeds from which would pay for the entire venture. Because the planning took place near the peak of New York's 1980s real estate market, this plan must have been especially appealing at the time. A final option, which was not explored at great length due to a general aversion to external debt, was the use of tax-exempt borrowing.

In the end, the board decided to go it alone. In a vote taken on January 21, 1988, the board of trustees of the Pierpont Morgan Library decided to try to acquire the Morgan House. In March of that year, following negotiations, the purchase price was set at $15 million. To accommodate the expanded needs of the library, the goal for the endowment campaign was increased to $40 million. Of this amount, $15 million was for the purchase price of the House, another $15 million was for renovations, and the remaining $10 million was for the endowment. Considering that the market value of the library's entire endowment was in the $40 million range, the campaign's goal was exceedingly ambitious.

Even if the campaign were successful, the proceeds would not be available for some time; in the interim, the library would have to borrow money to pay for the acquisition. During fiscal year 1989, when the Morgan House was actually bought, the $15 million purchase price was funded with an $8 million bank loan and a $7 million internal loan from the endowment. It was intended that both of these loans would be repaid with the proceeds of the capital campaign. During 1989, $4.5 million of the $8 million bank loan was repaid from contributions to the capital campaign. The remaining balance was paid off in 1990 through an additional transfer from the operations endowment. The capital campaign reached its goal in gifts and pledges during 1991. As cash receipts have come in, the endowment has been repaid, and after the repayment, all gifts will be used to augment the endowment.

After buying the Morgan House, Pierce and the board had to address the question of how to join the house and the library. The solution, as designed by Voorsanger & Associates, was an enclosed garden court. This space, covered by an arching glass and white-steel roof, has become a quiet haven in the midst of Manhattan. The Garden Court can also be used for entertainment and has increased the Morgan's attractiveness as a site for corporate functions. The addition has won several awards, and, as Charles Pierce put it, its open structure "communicates our desire to open and make more accessible this institution, its magnificent holdings, and the pleasure and learning they promote."[10]

Impact on Operations

The purchase of the Morgan House placed great strains on the operating budget. Figure 2.8, depicting operating income and expenditures from 1981 to 1993, shows the severity of those strains and suggests that the deficits of 1990–1993 were caused more by income shortfalls than by expenditure growth. In 1990, income fell further than expenditures, causing an operating deficit that has not yet been closed fully. Each of the Morgan's sources of income (investment income, gifts and grants, and earned income) behaved differently during this period, and a closer look at these trends can help clarify the broader ramifications of the Morgan's physical expansion.

Investment income was affected most directly, and most adversely, by the purchase of the Morgan House. During 1989 and 1990, there were transfers from endowment equal to about $17 million. Although there were some inflows of cash from the capital campaign, these funds did not for the most part materialize until 1992 and 1993. Figure 2.3, which tracks the various sources of income, shows that investment income declined in 1990, 1991, and 1992. This drop reflects both the reduction in the size of the endowment and the efforts to lower the spending rate in 1992 and 1993. As cash payments from the capital campaign continue to come in, the endowment will grow. At the end of fiscal year 1993, the value of the operations endowment fund was about $38 million. Using the 6 percent spending rule that was put into effect during 1993, the endowment will produce about $2.5 million in spendable income in 1994. As long as the pledges from the capital cam-

FIGURE 2.8.   OPERATING INCOME AND EXPENDITURES, PIERPONT MORGAN LIBRARY, 1981–1993.

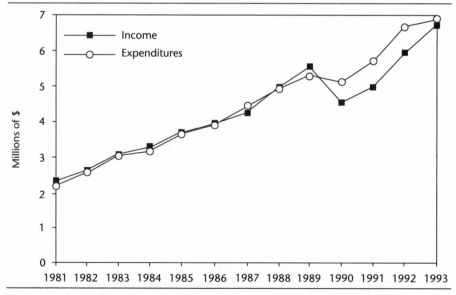

Source: Data from Table B.2–2 in Appendix B.

paign are paid off, endowment income should recover most of the ground that it has lost.

Contributed income, which is now the library's primary source of operating funds, declined in 1989 and 1990. This drop is probably attributable to the capital campaign's competing demands on the same donor pool. In 1991, 1992, and 1993, however, contributed income increased substantially. This increase is probably the result of two different factors. First, the end of the capital campaign increased the availability of operating gifts. Second, steps have been taken to increase revenues from the library's various support groups. These steps are discussed in greater detail later in this chapter.

Earned income is the third part of the Morgan's revenue structure. It has also increased since 1990, as the expanded facility created new opportunities for earned-income ventures. As mentioned, the Morgan is now a more attractive place to hold outside events, the funds from which are used as operating income. Also, the bookshop has been moved to the Morgan House and given a separate entrance on Madison Avenue, thus making it accessible to a wider audience. The bookshop has been placed under professional management, and efforts are being made to increase the shop's earnings and profitability.

Contributions upon admission, a subcategory of contributed income, have not figured prominently in the Morgan's finances. Unlike the Huntington, whose botanical gardens and art galleries draw hundreds of thousands of people a year, the Morgan's visitorship has not reached the scale where it can provide substantial funding. During the 1980s, for example, the average level of admissions income was just $148,000. In 1992 and 1993, after the expansion, the figures for admission were somewhat higher, averaging about $215,000. Nonetheless, it does not appear that this source of income will play a major role in supporting the library's activities.

Because the Morgan's original indenture requires it to be a free institution, the library's policy is to request a contribution rather than to charge an admission fee. In 1993, the library appealed to the New York State attorney general to allow a change in the indenture and to permit the library to charge a fee. The basis for the argument was that Pierpont Morgan and his son, Jack Morgan, had not foreseen the extent to which the library would become a public institution. The prohibition against charging an admission fee was meant to apply to scholars, not to the public at large. As long as admission remained free for scholars, the reasoning went, the conditions of the trust would be fulfilled. The attorney general has approved the Morgan's request, although at present there are no plans to begin charging a fee.

Prospects for the Future

Although the capital campaign and the time, effort and resources that it required were at least partly responsible for the deficits of recent years, they are not the only factors at work. As William M. Jackson, the associate director of the Morgan, pointed out in the 1991 report to the trustees, "These [1991 budgetary] figures, and our projections for next year, make it clear that we cannot assume that the end of the construction project will bring our operating budget back into balance. The board, the Finance Committee, and the administration have therefore set themselves the goal of beginning to reverse these increasing deficits. Efforts both to increase income and control expenses have been initiated."

Since that time, concrete steps have been taken toward tighter budgetary control. Budgeting has been performed more rigorously and on a departmental level. In 1992, the library switched health plans in a successful attempt to slow the increase in health care costs. Additional board committees have been established to facilitate better governance. A new computerized accounting system has been installed as well. In short, the financial management of the institution has become more professional, providing improved ability to control costs.

Pierce and the library staff have also made efforts to increase the Morgan's revenues. The Fellows program has been reevaluated, and the number of participants is to be increased to one thousand. The dues structure was also increased. Other development vehicles have been introduced, including the Director's Roundtable, a group for high-level corporate sponsors. A formal spending rule has been adopted, limiting expendable endowment income to 6 percent of the average market value of the endowment over the past three years. As mentioned earlier, the staff is also taking a more business-oriented approach to the library's earned-income ventures.

It is still too early to judge the success or failure of these efforts. Some of the pledges for the capital campaign have yet to be paid in full, there is still an operating deficit, and it is not yet possible to get a real sense of the library's cost structure in the new space. The early signs, however, are promising. The capital campaign appears to have achieved its goal, and most of the pledges have been paid already. The library's internal systems have been improved immensely, thus allowing for better cost controls. Contributions are up sharply; if the new levels of giving prove sustainable, operating deficits should not continue beyond the next few years. In both 1992 and 1993, income grew more quickly than expenditures, and the deficit declined, indicating, at least provisionally, that the Morgan Library is moving in the right direction. If these trends continue, Charles Pierce and the board of trustees will be able to congratulate themselves on overcoming an enormous hurdle and preserving for another generation the treasures of the Morgan Library.

Notes

1. For an interesting discussion of the relationship between libraries and museums, see Gundersheimer (1988).
2. Andrews (1957, pp. 5, 12).
3. Taylor (1957, p. 39).

4. Adams (1964, p. 14).
5. Adams (1964, p. 14).
6. The various funds in the Morgan's accounts are aggregated into operations funds and acquisitions funds, each of which is a self-balancing accounting entity. Thus it is possible to speak of the operating surplus or deficit and to exclude acquisitions. If acquisitions were funded from the operating budget, it would be proper to include them with (operating) expenditures.
7. These figures are rough calculations and are useful primarily for their depiction of the overall trends. It is difficult to adjust precisely for such issues as the timing of gifts and the distinction between operations funds and acquisitions funds.
8. 1985 director's report.
9. Pierpont Morgan Library (1987, p. 4).
10. Pierce (1993, p. 3).

CHAPTER THREE

THE NEWBERRY LIBRARY

The Newberry Library, founded in 1887 in Chicago, has the curious distinction of being the only library in this book whose founder died without having any idea whether or not it would ever be built. In fact, it was only through an unlikely string of family deaths that the Newberry came into existence. Its untoward origins notwithstanding, the Newberry Library has evolved over the past century into one of America's premier independent research libraries, in many ways a paradigm of programmatic development.

Because the Newberry's founder, Walter Loomis Newberry, left a cash bequest and not a collection, the Newberry's holdings have been built over time by its librarians. The collections are very broad, with several defining themes. In light of this variety, the Newberry has been described as "an uncommon collection of uncommon collections."[1] The size of the collections is formidable, consisting of almost 1.5 million volumes and approximately 5 million manuscript pages. The emphasis of the Newberry's collecting through most of its history has been the humanities, broadly defined. In addition to the general collection, there are a number of special collections, including the Edward E. Ayer Collection, which is concerned with the history of the American Indians and their early contacts with Europeans; the William B. Greenlee Collection, focused on Portuguese and Brazilian history; the Everett T. Graff Collection of Western Americana; and the John M. Wing Collection in the history of printing. The world's largest collection of Herman Melville editions is located at the Newberry, as are the archives of the Pullman Corporation. In addition, the Newberry has major medieval and Renaissance collections, very extensive genealogical and family history holdings, and large collections of historical maps and midwestern literary manuscripts.

The Newberry has taken great strides in the past thirty-five years toward becoming a research and education center in addition to being a world-class library. Under Lawrence W. (Bill) Towner, director from 1962 to 1986, and Charles T. Cullen, director since 1986, the Newberry has devoted itself to promoting the "effective use" of the collections. The extent of these efforts is attested to by the prodigious growth in the programs budget: from $20,000 in 1962 to $1.8 million in 1991.

The Newberry's research and education offerings are varied, ranging from pure scholarship to public programs. A fellowship program for advanced research brings about sixty scholars a year through the Newberry's doors. The Chicago public is served most directly by the Center for Public Programs, which offers exhibits, the musical programs of the Newberry Consort, and seminars that attract over one thousand adults on an annual basis. Four research and education centers offer fellowships, sponsor major research and publication projects, develop scholarly tools such as bibliographies and atlases, and offer summer institutes and term-time seminars for university faculty, secondary school teachers, and graduate students on a more permanent basis.[2] The centers, conceived and created under Bill Towner, are akin to academic departments in the ongoing nature and specific orientation of their activities. The fields on which the four centers focus— the history of cartography (founded in 1971), the history of the American Indian (1972), family and community history (1974), and Renaissance studies (1979)— correspond to the traditional strengths of the Newberry's collections.

Financially, the Newberry's size puts it somewhere about the middle of the five libraries in this set. According to Table 1.1, the Newberry ranks fourth in income, ahead of the American Antiquarian Society, and third in expenditures, behind the Huntington and the Morgan. It is presently less well endowed relative to expenditures than any of the other four libraries.

The Newberry makes for a particularly interesting case study. Many of the issues that are addressed in this study—a declining share of endowment funding, rising cost structures, space problems, and governance issues—have figured prominently in the Newberry's history. Of the five libraries, the Newberry's problems have arguably been the most serious. Due to a combination of factors, which will be analyzed in detail in this chapter, the Newberry in the 1980s encountered significant difficulties that at points threatened the ongoing operations of the library. In recent years, the trustees and staff have realized the acute nature of the Newberry's plight and have undertaken substantial efforts to remedy the situation. The burden under which they are laboring, however, is comparatively great. So, too, is the didactic value of their experiences.

This chapter is divided into eight sections, which are ordered chronologically. Because the Newberry is considerably older than most of the other libraries, the entire history of the institution is not discussed in detail. Instead, the first section deals briefly with the founding of the library and related issues. The remaining sections describe and analyze the events of the past thirty-five years, including the Newberry's expansion, the renovation of its building, and the financial difficulties that ensued.

The Founding of the Library

Walter Loomis Newberry, the library's founder, was born in 1804. He made his fortune in banking and real estate. When Newberry came west to Chicago in the 1830s, it was a small town of about four thousand hardy pioneers; by the time he died in 1868, it had become a major city, with more than three hundred thousand people. During the intervening years, Newberry's wealth grew with the city itself; he was numbered among Chicago's civic leaders and held posts ranging from acting mayor to president of the school board.

In his will, Newberry provided that should his two daughters die without children (the Newberrys had already lost two infant sons), half of his estate should be used to found a free public library in Chicago. At the time, his daughters were in their teens, and the creation of a library must have seemed little more than a remote possibility. Tragically, both of Newberry's daughters died young and childless: Mary in 1874 and Julia in 1876. The trustees of Newberry's estate, Eliphalet Wickes Blatchford and William Henry Bradley, were therefore charged with the establishment of "a free public library in Chicago's North Division."

Because the Newberry Library was founded with money, rather than an extant collection, Blatchford and Bradley had great leeway in deciding what sort of library it was to be. These decisions were affected by the local environment. Since Chicago already had a public library, the Newberry became a noncirculating institution with a research orientation. In 1894, when the John Crerar Library decided to focus its collecting on the sciences, the Newberry limited its field of endeavor to the humanities.

The trustees hired William Frederick Poole, librarian of the Chicago Public Library, to be the Newberry's first librarian. Poole was an eminent figure in the library field; he was one of the founders of both the American Library Association and the American Historical Association and was the founding librarian of the Cincinnati and Chicago public libraries. Because Poole was hired before the Newberry existed, he played an influential role in its creation.[3]

Poole's thinking had a profound impact on the physical structure that was to house the Newberry. At the time the Newberry was built, the prevailing model of library architecture was changing. Traditionally, a library had consisted of a series of rooms in which scholars could work, with books easily accessible on the shelves. The newer approach relied on a bookstack and separate reading rooms (a model still common today). Poole argued forcefully in favor of the old approach and won. This decision was to have significant repercussions in later years and was directly related to the Newberry's decision to build a separate book storage facility in the 1970s.

Prior to the construction of the so-called Cobb Building (after its architect, Henry Ives Cobb), the Newberry rented space in other buildings around Chicago. The library building was built in the Romanesque fashion and was intended to form one side of an eventual quadrangle. In 1891, its building built, the Newberry Library was incorporated officially under a special act of the Illinois legislature, titled "An Act to Encourage and Promote the Establishment of Free Public Libraries in Cities, Villages, and Towns of this State."

It is worth noting that $2 million, which comprised half of the Newberry estate, furnished all three components of the research library—the building, the collections, and the endowment. It is to the credit of the Newberry's early librarians and trustees that they were able to leverage these funds to the extent that they did. The Huntington and the Morgan each started out with a building, a collection, and a larger endowment, yet by the early 1960s, the Newberry had become the best-endowed relative to expenditures of the five libraries in this set. Part of this growth is obviously related to the Newberry's age, which allowed reserves to accumulate for a longer period of time. Nonetheless, the success of the Newberry should not be underestimated. During the first sixty to seventy years of its history, it grew from a backup provision in a will to one of the largest and best-endowed independent research libraries in the country.

From the start, education was an important component of the Newberry's activities. In 1887, even before the library itself existed, a lyceum program of lectures and classes was established. In 1891, the library was reputed to have attracted 16,802 readers, although it is not clear how the number of visitors was counted. The first exhibition was organized in 1896, featuring samples of the library's earliest acquisitions.

When Poole died in 1894, the essential elements of the Newberry Library were already in place: the building was built; the acquisition of books, maps, and other materials had begun; and the Newberry's strong tradition of educational programs had been launched.

The 1950s: Independence Reaffirmed

The story of the Newberry's growth from its founding through the 1950s appears to be one of financial stability and growth in the collections. Gifts and bequests brought large collections within the Newberry's walls; acquisitions, particularly in Europe after the Second World War, played an important role as well. The library, especially its genealogical collections, was used extensively both by scholars and by local residents. During the 1940s, for example, the number of readers was said to be as high as fifty thousand people a year.

The Newberry's growth also brought problems. One problem encountered in the 1950s was that the number of people using the Newberry was rapidly outpacing the ability of the staff to provide services. Many college students were using the Newberry to do research; it was felt that the library's resources could be used more effectively if access to the collections was limited to a smaller, more advanced group of scholars. Thus in 1960, a more restrictive admissions policy was adopted. During December of that year, thirty-five applicants for reading cards were turned down per day, a higher than normal number of refusals.[4]

Another problem that the library faced could not be addressed as easily: its building was inadequate in a number of ways. First, the building's age meant that it was not as resistant to fire and other environmental forces as it should have been. Second, the collections had outgrown the stack space in the building. Third, the building's design, which reflected the old model of libraries, was outdated and complicated efforts to guard against deterioration and even theft.

To consider possible solutions to these problems, the Committee on the Future of the Library was established in 1958. The librarian at the time was Dr. Stanley Pargellis. Pargellis, a historian and "bookman" trained at Oxford and Yale, had served in that post since 1942. The committee examined the problems the library faced and delved into its history in an effort to understand the root causes of those difficulties.

The Committee on the Future of the Library soon discovered that the shortcomings of the building had long been recognized. In 1943, for instance, Pargellis had outlined to the trustees his proposed plans for the Newberry Library. As described in the committee's report, his goals in 1943 had been to make the library a

1. Reference library in humanities for the Chicago metropolitan area
2. Research library for the scholar
3. Center for certain kinds of literary and educational activity

Pargellis had also called attention to the limitations of the library building. At the time, it had been "the consensus . . . that the board should develop a policy which would seem adequate to pursue in the future development of the Library."[5]

As early as the 1940s, then, and perhaps even earlier, the trustees had recognized the shortcomings of the library building and the need to define the Newberry's precise mission and niche. As the Committee on the Future of the Library recognized in 1960, though, it was easier to call for change than to effect it: "So far as the committee can tell, there has not been much discussion of the development of a policy as recommended in 1943. The board's minutes of October 9, 1950, make reference to a meeting of a Special Library Policy Committee, consisting mostly of outsiders but which does not appear to have resulted in any action by the board."

The committee noted that policy changes, and what today is called strategic planning, generally had not been the board's strength: "The library appears to have gone on for a good many years without defining its aims. It has been in the fortunate position of having no financial wolves scratching at the door. The purchases of books have unquestionably improved the collections, though with certain exceptions, it is not clear that they have greatly increased its stature in the eyes of scholars generally."

In its report, the committee pointed out that it would be prudent to consider the broader issues of the Newberry's future before deciding on the best way to proceed with the building. These issues included questions of audience and clientele, strengths and weaknesses of the collections, the appropriateness of the education program, and the possibility of some sort of merger or collaboration with a local university or library.

The last point is an important one. At various points in the Newberry's history, the trustees have considered merging the Newberry with another institution. The list of potential partners has included Northwestern University, the University of Chicago, the Chicago Public Library, and the John Crerar Library. (The last two options, incidentally, would involve a merger like the one between the Astor and Lenox libraries, which created the New York Public Library, the largest member by far of the Independent Research Libraries Association.) In 1960, for instance, there were discussions between the University of Chicago and the Newberry about the possibility of combining the two institutions. Timing considerations prevented the merger from being consummated, and the Newberry's board voted instead to remain independent. This decision set the stage for the events of later decades.

Acting on the committee's recommendations, the library was renovated in the summer of 1961. Among the additions and improvements were air conditioning, air filtration, additional fire precautions, and two elevators.[6] This renovation was among the less drastic options under consideration; some of the more far-reaching ones were the aforementioned merger with the University of Chicago, the destruction of the library building and the construction of another one in its place, and the addition of a separate wing to house the most valuable collections. The renovation was not "root and branch," so to speak, and therefore many of the same problems that faced the committee in the late 1950s resurfaced in the 1970s and 1980s. In hindsight, it appears that the decision of the committee, like the board's earlier decision in the 1940s, left essential issues unresolved.

The 1960s: Years of Growth

Bill Towner

In 1962, Stanley Pargellis stepped down as librarian. To replace him, the trustees appointed Lawrence W. (Bill) Towner, who was at the time the editor of the *William and Mary Quarterly,* the prestigious journal of American history. Towner arrived in Chicago on August 28, 1962, with his wife, then pregnant with twins, and their four other children crammed into a 1957 Chevy. The Newberry would never be the same.

Bill Towner was to prove central to the changes at the Newberry over the next twenty-five years. He has been described by many as a man with a vibrant, charismatic personality who could accomplish much by sheer force of will. Almost single-handedly, he took the Newberry into the modern era and made it into a top-flight institution for scholarship and learning. He also played a national role. When some independent research libraries were deemed ineligible for federal funding under the Higher Education Act of 1966 and then threatened with classification as "private foundations" after the tax reforms of 1969, Towner was active in the campaign to reverse those decisions and in the resultant creation of the Independent Research Libraries Association (IRLA).[7] The sole shortcoming mentioned in the course of discussions with several people who knew him and worked with him is that Bill Towner did not have a solid grasp of financial issues.

What was Towner's vision of the Newberry Library? It can be summed up in a single succinct phrase, one that he used frequently to describe the Newberry's mission: effective use. To Bill Towner, a library without a vibrant educational program was nothing more than an inert mass of books. By the same token, a community of scholars with no resources at its disposal could not engage in scholarship. The Newberry already had a collection; Towner saw his challenge as creating a community of scholars.

New Acquisitions

In 1964, two years after Towner took office, the Newberry acquired the Louis H. Silver collection, which consisted mostly of English and Continental first editions, primarily from the Renaissance. The story of its acquisition is emblematic of Bill Towner's drive and determination, as well as his relative lack of financial expertise. It also marked a sea change in the Newberry's financial situation.

Louis Silver was a Newberry trustee, but when he died, he did not bequeath his collection to the library. From the Newberry's perspective, the Silver collection was attractive; it fit well with the Newberry's areas of collecting and contained many works that conceivably would never come on the market again, at least not at an affordable price. According to the *London Times*, Silver had assembled "the most distinguished collection of English literary first editions formed by a private collector in our times."[8] It was clear that it would be an enormous boon to the Newberry to acquire it. The only problem was the cost. The purchase of the Silver collection was guaranteed to strain the Newberry's finances, especially because the library had just spent $1.4 million on renovations. Nevertheless, Towner and the trustees decided to go ahead with the purchase, with the expectation that part of the purchase price would be recouped through the sale of duplicates and out-of-scope materials and that the rest would be raised from the Newberry's supporters. The Newberry's offer narrowly beat out an almost-consummated deal between the Silver estate and the University of Texas, which involved an agent; Towner offered to eliminate the middleman and split the difference. The final price was $2,687,000.

Coming on the heels of the 1961 renovation, the Silver purchase forced the Newberry to change its financing. Unlike the Huntington, where the drop in investment income was a long-term trend that made itself felt slowly, the purchase of the Silver collection was a seminal event that put an abrupt end to the Newberry's days of full endowment funding. The Newberry Associates, a financial support group, was formed in 1965 as part of the first general fundraising drive in the Newberry's history.

Of course, one should not infer that buying the Silver collection was ill-advised or imprudent. The $13 million present value of the purchase price would not pay for the collection today, even if those works were to become available again. The broader point, which transcends the question of whether the acquisition might have been "cheaper" today, is that buying books is part of what research libraries do. Hoarding money at the expense of collection development is not the goal. In this case, the purchase price was recouped through gifts and the sale of duplicates (but see Towner's essay in *Past Imperfect*, a 1993 collection of Towner's writings in which he implies that the "proceeds" were used to buy more books rather than to replenish the endowment). The broader importance of the Silver purchase is that it marked the end of the Newberry's dependence on endowment and the beginning of its "modern period."

The acquisition of the Silver collection was followed by other prestigious, large, and often expensive acquisitions, including the Novacco and Sack cartography collections and the Deering collection of early Americana. By the late 1960s, the Newberry was more firmly ensconced in its fields of collecting than ever before; likewise, Bill Towner was the institution's unchallenged leader. The board of trustees was duly impressed with the man who had shaken up the quiet, sedate, often dusty confines of the library world. According to most accounts, the trustees were more than happy to let their visionary librarian lead the way.

New Programs

During the 1960s, Towner began to broaden the Newberry's educational and scholarly offerings. In 1964, the Associated Colleges of the Midwest began to hold seminars at the Newberry; this program, now joined by the Great Lakes Colleges Association, continues to this day, bringing about seventy-five students a year from affiliated colleges to the Newberry for seminars using primary source materials. In October 1964, the endowed Kenneth Nebenzahl Jr. Lectures in the History of Cartography also began, and the Newberry Library Renaissance Conference, founded during Stanley Pargellis's tenure, continued to bring scholars to the institution.

Conservation also gained prominence during the 1960s. Much of the library's collection, especially in the field of genealogy, was on acidic paper printed after 1850. This paper, which becomes brittle and corrodes with age, was a source of great concern to the Newberry's staff, and the problems were exacerbated by the poor environmental controls in the library. Books were stored all over the Newberry, and the humidity and temperature were more suited to people than to books. Paul N. Banks, the library's first conservator, was hired in 1963; he eventually went on to head the first graduate program in conservation at Columbia University. While at the Newberry, Banks photocopied the genealogy materials, supervised the addition of protective chemicals to restore and strengthen leather bindings, and started the Newberry's conservation program, one of the first of its kind in the country. In 1966, he visited Florence twice to assist in the massive restoration efforts that followed the flooding of the Arno.

All of these conservation efforts amounted to little more than stopgap measures as long as the collections remained scattered about the library building. Although air conditioning had been added in the 1960 renovation, the temperature and humidity conditions in the building were far from optimal. The trustees understood that as stewards of the collection, they would at some point have to address the storage issues in a more fundamental way.

Another set of changes that occurred during the 1960s can be described generally as the professionalization of the library. In 1963, the position of librarian became "director and librarian," and the office of treasurer was created by the trustees. Although the latter was a board position, it reflects an attention to financial needs that was not present before. In the same year, the position of associate director was created, combining responsibilities for acquisitions, research, and publications. The position of associate librarian was established shortly thereafter. A broader step came in 1967, when the library surveyed its staff with the intent of writing job descriptions, revising personnel policies, and reexamining fringe benefits and pensions.

New Money

As would be expected, the Newberry's expansion cost money. Figure 3.1, which shows income and expenditures at the Newberry from 1960 to 1980, illustrates this growth. During the period 1960–1969, income grew at an average annual rate of 3.7 percent. At the same time, expenditures grew at 7.9 percent. Clearly, there was a mismatch.

Until the 1960s, the endowment provided most of the Newberry's income. The only exceptions to this rule were gifts for acquisitions and income on real estate owned by the library. Beginning with the 1965 formation of the Associates and the first campaign, gifts began to play a role as well. These contributions, which in theory should have made up the difference between investment income and rising expenditures, failed to do so. Figure 3.2 illustrates the shift from operating surpluses to deficits between 1960 and 1980. As late as 1969, despite the fact that expenditures were growing more rapidly, income remained higher, thus producing a surplus. By 1970, however, the differential in growth rates had put the Newberry into an operating deficit position.

FIGURE 3.1. INCOME AND EXPENDITURES, NEWBERRY LIBRARY, 1960–1980.

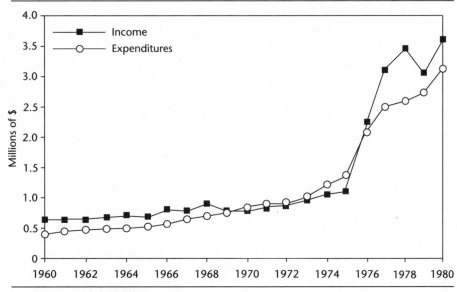

Source: Data from Table B.3–1 in Appendix B.

FIGURE 3.2. SURPLUS/DEFICIT, NEWBERRY LIBRARY, 1960–1980.

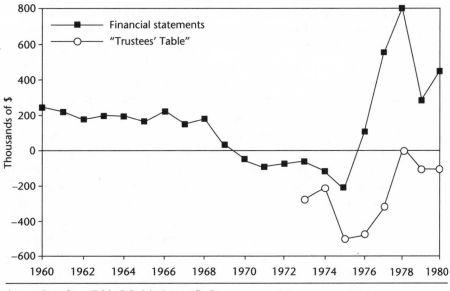

Source: Data from Table B.3–1 in Appendix B.

The Plan for the Newberry Library

In the late 1960s, Bill Towner began to spell out his long-term vision for the Newberry Library. We have already encountered some of his coinages: "an uncommon collection of uncommon collections," "effective use," and the absolute necessity of "a community of scholars," not just "an inert mass of books." His *Plan for the Newberry Library,* a draft of which is reprinted in *Past Imperfect,* paints a clear picture of Towner's aspirations for the Newberry.[9] The document as it appears in *Past Imperfect* is version number 4.9, dated 1971; it was reworked many times, reflecting a consensus-building process that included staff, trustees, and scholars. At its heart, however, was always Bill Towner's vision.

At the risk of oversimplification, it is possible to describe the plan's two overarching themes as follows:

1. A move toward the creation of "a community of scholars," working both on short-term projects with a specific focus and in more permanent subject-specific centers. One possible name for such an environment would be an "Institute for Advanced Study in History and the Humanities."[10]
2. A building program that would deal definitively with the inadequacies of the present library building. This initiative would consist of two parts: the construction of a state-of-the-art bookstack building that contained nothing but books and the renovation of the old building to accommodate the activities described in point 1, as well as increased public programming.

Different sections of the plan dealt in detail with issues of collection development, access to the collections, and the specific focus of the library's research efforts. The building program was a central element and addressed the conservation issues that were important to the Newberry. Due to the building's age and layout, the collections were stored inefficiently, subject to deterioration and threatened by fire, water, pollution, and theft. As described in the plan, Poole's design had led to "books located in thirty-four separate locations behind twenty-four locked doors on six different floors and stored in dark and gloomy stack areas with great amounts of wasted space between stack and ceiling."[11]

In response, Towner proposed two bold strokes. The first was "the erection of a modern, fireproof, air-conditioned, and efficient stack building adjacent to the present building." Once the safety of the collections was ensured, the next set of priorities related to the extant library building; a reallocation of space would be facilitated by the addition of "a combined exhibition hall, lecture hall, dining facility, staff lounge, and reader's lounge."[12] The physical expansion would be both the capstone of the Newberry's past and the foundation of its future: without it, little could be accomplished; with it, the Newberry would stand proudly in the front ranks of libraries and academic institutions. The Newberry's commitment to conservation, effective use, and all levels of scholarship would be realized.

It was clear from the start that the Plan for the Newberry Library would cost an enormous amount of money. In 1971, when the version in *Past Imperfect* was drafted, the rough estimates were in the range of $10 to $15 million—a large sum considering that the Newberry's annual income at the time was under $1 million and the endowment's market value was about $21 million. The amounts to be raised, though large, did not seem inconceivable. With Bill Towner and his proven fundraising skills at the helm, the Plan for the Newberry Library could well become a reality.

The 1970s: The Plan for the Newberry Made Real

Centers and Seminars

Even before Bill Towner had articulated fully his goals for the library, he had begun putting them into effect. The programs described earlier were the first steps toward the creation of a critical mass of scholars. Another step was taken in 1971 with the creation of the first center at the Newberry, the Hermon Dunlap Smith Center for the History of Cartography. "Dutch" Smith had been a trustee of the Newberry since 1943 and was president of the board from 1964 to 1975.

The Center for the History of Cartography combined a collection, a research program, and money. The Newberry's map collection was well established by the time Towner arrived in 1962, and it had also been augmented with the acquisition of the Novacco collection (1967) and the Sack collection (1968). In the mid 1960s, the first two parts of the center's eventual research program had been established: the Kenneth Nebenzahl Jr. Lectures in the History of Cartography and a publication program in concert with the Society for the History of Discoveries. Funds allocated by the board helped bring the Atlas of Early American History project to the Newberry, along with its own funding. During this time, Dr. David Woodward joined the Newberry, serving first as a research fellow, then as a consultant, and finally as curator and director of the cartography center. The financial piece of the center came with "Dutch" Smith's gift of a $600,000 endowment.

The other centers, founded throughout the 1970s, followed similar patterns. They built on established strengths of the library's collections, established an ongoing research program, and attracted substantial outside gifts for restricted endowment funds. In June 1972, the Center for the History of the American Indian was established. This center held a special resonance for Bill Towner, whose dissertation adviser had been Ray Allen Billington, himself a student of Frederick Jackson Turner. Billington had studied frontier history from the Eurocentric perspective (a minor anachronism); the Newberry's newest center would take a different perspective and facilitate the American Indians' search for a "usable past."

Other programmatic expansions came quickly, including two new centers before the end of the decade. In 1972, The Andrew W. Mellon Foundation Fund for Research and Education, a restricted capital fund, was established. In 1973,

Richard H. Brown was appointed to the newly created post of associate director for research and educational programs, thus institutionalizing some of the programmatic changes. In 1974, the Great Lakes Colleges Association joined the Associated Colleges of the Midwest, bringing to twenty-five the number of schools affiliated with the Newberry's Program in the Humanities. Also established was the Center for Family and Community History, formalizing the Newberry's long-standing prominence in that field. In 1977, the Chicago Metro History Fair, a program for high school students, was initiated by the Newberry with cosponsorship from groups including the Chicago archdiocese, the Chicago public schools, the Chicago Historical Society, and the Chicago Public Library. And in 1979, the Center for Renaissance Studies was established, after more than twenty consecutive years of the Newberry Library Renaissance Conference.

Money and Oversight

Unfortunately, the Newberry's ability to raise operating funds did not keep pace with its growth. According to many people, Bill Towner was a fundraiser *par excellence*, able to wheedle money out of almost anybody. His talents, however, were employed mostly for the funding of specific projects that attracted his attention, such as the centers. Figure 3.2 depicts the string of deficits that the Newberry incurred in the early 1970s.[13]

The apparent surpluses in the mid to late 1970s are misleading. For many years, the Newberry did not differentiate between capital and current gifts. It is therefore almost impossible to determine from the data what the true operating balance was. One piece of evidence that sheds light on this period is a chart of selected financial data, the "Trustees' Table," prepared for the trustees' meeting of September 1982. The table compares operating income (with capital gifts excluded) with operating expenses. These figures are far from authoritative: not only are they unaudited, but they also do not match the audited financial data. (This discrepancy in itself is further indication of the poor financial control systems at the Newberry.) In any case, the numbers are clearly worth considering, if only because they allow us to see what the trustees saw and hence what they acted on. As the "Trustees' Table" line in Figure 3.2 indicates, there were deficits through most of the 1970s.

Figure 3.1 illustrates clearly the Newberry's growing expenditures over an extended period of time and the resulting imbalance between income and expenditures. The sharp increase in the Newberry's programmatic offerings that took place during the mid 1970s is visible, as is the extent to which income failed to cover expenses (bearing in mind the Trustees' Table). These divergent trends trigger an obvious question: were the trustees aware of the situation? In 1973, following changes in the relevant Illinois legislation, the number of trustees was increased from twelve to twenty-five. Yet this seems to have had little impact on trustee oversight. Trustees who were on the board at the time have recalled that the Newberry's financial problems did not begin in earnest until the 1980s, with the renovation of the library building. Even if we make allowances for imprecise recollections with the passage of time, and even if we adopt a strict definition of "in earnest," it would seem that a series of deficits that ran from 1970 to 1975, which averaged 7 percent of expenditures, should have been cause for concern. Yet apparently this was not the case.

The board's apparent inattention cannot be understood without returning to our discussion of Bill Towner and his relationship with the board. Once Towner had established himself in the mid 1960s as a visionary leader who could get things done, the trustees basically sat back and let him run the show. If trusteeship can be seen as a delicate balance between doing too little (neglect) and doing too much (meddling), then it is possible with hindsight to say that the board erred on the side of passivity. Because financial management was not Towner's strength, the Newberry's financial status was perhaps the single area where it was imperative that the trustees exercise their full authority and responsibility.

Another factor was more mundane but no less important: the Newberry's accounting systems were not as useful as they should have been. Budgeting was not done successfully, cost allocations were performed somewhat haphazardly, and the operating budget was forced to absorb the costs of, among other things, the full-time staff member who coordinated the Associates program. (Because all Associates gifts went to acquisitions, this cost fell on the operating budget.) So even if the trustees had tried to monitor the Newberry's finances more closely, doing so would have been difficult or impossible. One of the Newberry's trustees has stated that if at the end of the year it looked like there was going to be a deficit, Towner would just go out and raise the money. Whether the funds raised were capital or current gifts, whether they were restricted or unrestricted, and whether or not they were program grants that would incur additional overhead costs do not appear to have been at issue.

Planning and Building

During the 1970s, as the Newberry moved toward the programmatic goals that Bill Towner had outlined in his Plan for the Newberry Library, discussion continued over the best way to renovate the library and how to pay for it. In 1974, a new Committee on the Future of the Library was created. In 1975, the committee received and approved a ninety-eight-page staff draft titled "The Newberry Library: A Plan of Development."

The report of the Committee on the Future of the Library outlined the nature of the renovation and its anticipated costs. As originally discussed in Towner's Plan for the Newberry Library, there would be two parts to the Newberry's expansion. The first was the construction of the bookstack building. The building was designed to be a state-of-the-art book storage facility with appropriate temperature and humidity settings. Unlike the old building, whose steel beams could melt at high temperatures, the bookstack building would consist entirely of poured concrete, with no windows; it was often referred to as a "Thermos bottle." The estimated cost of the bookstack building was $6.5 million.

The second part of the physical expansion was the renovation of the Cobb building, which would restructure and augment the space freed by the removal of the collections. The renovations were to include an auditorium, electrical and mechanical systems, an entrance for the disabled, partition removal, and other improvements. The estimated cost of this portion of the building project, although less firm, was about $6 million.

In addition to the $12.5 million cost of the expansion and renovation, the committee outlined a second phase of the Program for Development. The broad goal of the second phase was to complete the Newberry's transformation into a humanities center and to institutionalize and fund those changes. It was recognized that the second phase would have to wait until after the first one and that it was perhaps less likely to be realized in its entirety. This portion of the plan included such goals as additional funds for acquisitions, housing for visiting scholars, funds for staff travel and sabbaticals, and publication endowments. The attached dollar figure, although clearly somewhat abstract, was $18 million. Thus, all told, the Newberry intended to raise about $30 million. The fundraising was supposed to take nearly ten years.[14] Even the irrepressible Towner recognized that their target was a highly ambitious goal: "Even the three million dollar average in gifts that it would require is twice the amount we have raised in one year at the Newberry for capital (1964–5) and equally double the highest yearly amount we have raised in a combination of capital and program grants."[15]

In 1975, the Committee on the Future of the Library submitted its report to the board, which approved it. A development office was established for the first time in the Newberry's history. The trustees created the separate Centennial Fund (so called because of the expectation that the renovations would be completed by 1987), which would be the vehicle used in raising money for the renovation. The Plan for the Newberry Library was one step closer to becoming a reality.

The Renovation: Bold Venture or Towner's Folly?

The Building

By 1980, when the trustees voted to build a bookstack building, there was a degree of urgency to the proposal. Problems in collection storage were no longer abstract—leaks in the roof had been discovered, the library had literally run out of shelf space, and it was apparent that something had to be done. Failure to act would have been a dereliction of duty.

Well before the board gave its approval, an in-depth planning process, supervised by Newberry staff member Joel Samuels, had considered the details of the proposed expansion. By the time the board gave the final green light, almost two years' worth of planning had been done, considering every possible way to build the building. The extent of the planning was such that the trustees even considered moving the building by distances as small as five feet in order to see how the cost and utility of the addition would be affected. One trustee remarked that there had been more planning for the bookstack building than for any other project in his recollection.

As designed by Harry Weese and Associates, the Chicago architectural firm that had supervised the 1961 renovation, the bookstack building had two parts: a seventy-seven-thousand-square-foot, ten-story storage structure and a twenty-thousand-square-foot "link" building connected to the original library. The bookstack building incorporated state-of-the-art systems to guard against theft, fire, and decay. Access to the building was through an electronic card-controlled entry system. Each floor was sealed, and the materials used in construction had the highest possible fire rating. A Halon fire extinguishing system (which does not use water) was included in the rare-book vault, which would be used to store the most precious portions of the collection.

Groundbreaking came soon after the approval, on September 16, 1980. Due in no small part to the building's fairly simple structure—there were no windows, no pipes or other plumbing, and almost no internal partitions—as well as to the degree of planning, the bookstack building was completed ahead of schedule and under budget. The completion of the bookstack building was a source of justifiable pride to the trustees, Bill Towner, and all who were affiliated with the Newberry. The old library building, with its inappropriate temperature and humidity, its unsafe storage in open areas, and its leaky roof, would no longer threaten the Newberry's collections. Moving them to the new building, a massive undertaking in its own right, began on March 29, 1982.

The second phase of the Newberry's physical expansion was the renovation of the original building, which was also to be undertaken by Harry Weese and Associates. The "new Newberry" was to include

> a multi-purpose conference center capable of seating more than 300 people for a variety of events, . . . two large exhibit galleries, and a reader/visitor lounge . . . , an enlarged Main Reading Room, with an entire room devoted to microfilm reading, and a new area for reserve readers. . . . The card catalog and 18,000 reference books will be moved to the middle three sections of the floor to create a Reference and Bibliographical Center, which will be available to readers and staff all hours the Library is open. The fourth floor will house the Special Collections Department, the Research & Education Centers, and fellows' carrels. The fifth floor will house the Conservation Department, Word Processing, Internal Services, a staff lounge, the Business Office, and a computer room. We will also increase the number of meeting and class rooms, improve restroom facilities, and make the Newberry more accessible to the handicapped.[16]

The cost of the renovation was budgeted at $6 million. Joel Samuels, director of planning, was again responsible for working with the architects and implementing the planned renovation. Unlike the bookstack construction project, the renovation was slower and far more expensive than originally intended.

The Newberry's financial statements provide a sense of the overruns. Figure 3.3 shows the expenditures of the Centennial Fund from 1981 through 1986. The cumulative expenditures during this period were just over $19 million. Subtracting from this figure the $6.5 million that the bookstack building was said to cost yields $12.5 million for the renovation—more than double the original cost estimates.

The Campaign

The other side of the equation was funding. On March 3, 1981, the trustees launched a capital campaign on a scale unprecedented in the Newberry's history. The Campaign for the Newberry Library, as it was called, began with pomp and circumstance, including a declaration by Chicago Mayor Jane Byrne of "Newberry Library Development Day." At its inception, the campaign's goal was set at $12.5 million. This figure reflected the expected cost of the addition and the renovation, not an assessment of the Newberry's fundraising potential. According to the recollections of Richard Brown, director of the Newberry's research and education division, a fundraising consultant at the time had predicted that the Newberry should be able to raise about $6.5 million from a capital campaign.

FIGURE 3.3. INCOME AND EXPENDITURES, NEWBERRY LIBRARY CENTENNIAL FUND, 1981–1986.

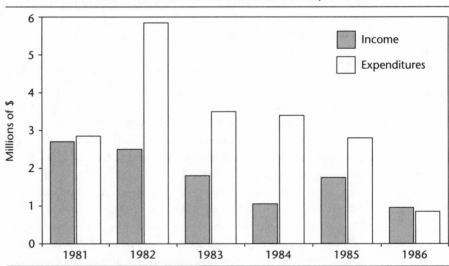

Source: Data from Table B.3–2 in Appendix B.

Nevertheless, in light of Bill Towner's track record, the trustees believed that the higher figure was attainable.

From the start, the trustees had understood that there would be short-term cash flow difficulties. After all, even if the capital campaign were successful, the expansion and the renovation would have to be paid for before the bulk of the proceeds materialized. For the Newberry to build immediately, while the campaign was being conducted, the trustees took out a bank loan of $5 million in short-term funding; the loan was to be repaid between 1984 and 1988 as pledges to the campaign were paid off.

By 1984, though, the library's problems were of a different order of magnitude than had been foreseen. According to the 1983 audited statements, almost $11.5 million had already been spent, yet no end to the renovations was in sight. It was estimated that as much as $8.5 million would still be needed to finish the renovation. The capital campaign had bogged down and seemed unlikely to meet its original goal, let alone the $18 to $19 million that would be needed to pay for the overruns. The Newberry Library was in a quandary.

What Happened?

What went wrong? Why was the cost of the renovation so grossly underestimated? Why did the capital campaign fail to attain its goals? The actions and attitudes of at least three players or sets of players—Towner, the staff (and the architects), and the trustees—need to be explored to understand the difficulties.

First, Bill Towner. The bookstack building and renovated library were to be twin edifices that perpetuated Towner's legacy at the Newberry Library. By all accounts, Towner was an energetic, committed man who knew what he wanted and would do what was needed to get it. O. B. Hardison, former director of the Folger Shakespeare Library in Washington, D.C. (and a good friend of Towner's), described him as "crafty and ruthless, but not in a pejorative sense. He just never takes 'no' from anybody when he wants something."[17]

Of course, ruthlessness and drive are not necessarily bad qualities; in fact, it was precisely these attributes that made Bill Towner the visionary, activist, trailblazing librarian that he was. The success that Towner achieved was due in large part to his ability to challenge the institution, to stretch expectations, and then to achieve the seemingly impossible. Was the expansion and renovation matter a case of hubris? It is difficult to say. One of the reasons the renovation and the capital campaign did not succeed as planned is that Bill Towner became ill and was unable to remain as involved and energetic as he had been earlier. Had he remained healthy, it is at least possible that he would have raised the money and kept tighter control on the cost of the renovation.

If we are willing to consider the possibility that Bill Towner's vision outstripped plausibility, we must turn next to the people whose job it was to question management's assumptions: the trustees. The trustees signed on to a $12.5 million expansion, renovation, and capital campaign and understood that ultimate responsibility for the institution lay with them. Was their endorsement of the Plan for the Newberry Library realistic? With the clear vision that hindsight often provides, the answer appears to be no, on three counts. First, the trustees failed to plan adequately for the renovation. The bookstack building, which was subjected to extensive, even exhaustive planning, came in ahead of schedule and under budget. If a similar level of scrutiny had been applied to the original building, then at the very least a better estimation of the costs would have been made. It has been suggested that the board should have recruited or hired someone with extensive building experience. Such an individual could have brought the expertise that the board lacked. Chalkley J. Hambleton, chairman of the board from 1979 to 1982, summarized the lesson succinctly: "If we'd had a model to emulate, we could have done better. We could have saved some money."[18]

Second, there was apparently little consideration of the feasibility of raising so much money. According to one trustee, the campaign goal was a function of what Towner believed was needed, not a function of what the fundraising "market" would bear. The safety of the collections was increasingly at risk, and action was required. Towner had always raised the money in the past, and the trustees apparently believed that he would do it again.

The third point is less definite but worth mentioning nonetheless. According to several sources, the board's giving was not what it should have been. In this the Newberry was far from unique; the "old model" of trusteeship did not include substantial giving as a prerequisite. In recent years, as the Newberry's financial situation deteriorated and the board became more aware of its responsibilities, the attitude toward fundraising has begun to change. This change is exemplified best by the leading gift of Charles C. Haffner III, chairman of the board, who has pledged $6 million to the library.

Staff problems also played a contributory role. A specific difficulty, which was structural as well, was the position of development officer. Until 1975, the Newberry simply did not have one; Bill Towner did all the fundraising himself. When the position was created, as one of the precursors to the Campaign for the Newberry Library, it did not carry a "normal" job description. According to Richard Brown, Towner felt that a successful development officer needed two qualities: (1) the ability to raise money and (2) the ability to understand what sort of institution the Newberry was. In Towner's opinion, the latter was harder to teach. So when the time came to hire somebody, Towner looked for someone who understood the Newberry, with the assumption that he could teach that person how to raise money.

According to several accounts, the library's first development director did not get along well with the Newberry's leadership. Although the accuracy of this categorization cannot be established definitively, the fact that she left the Newberry in 1981, just as the all-important capital campaign was getting under way, may be telling. After her departure, the Newberry's development office foundered, as it was led by a series of directors who served only for short periods of time and never truly achieved consistent success. This confusion, coupled with Bill Towner's illness, undoubtedly contributed to the failure of the capital campaign.

The staff also bears some responsibility for the cost overruns. We have already noted the fundamental problem: the planning process was inadequate.[19] Bill Towner's illness played a role here too. Beyond that, poor control over costs—on the part of both the Newberry's staff and Harry Weese and Associates—led to the overruns.

The Next Phase: Damage Control

Despite the difficulties, the trustees resolved to finish the renovation. To stop halfway, even if it were possible, would have meant a loss of momentum that might never be recovered. Rather than give up, the trustees decided to jettison some of the more costly portions of the renovation, such as the auditorium, and to proceed with the rest.

The trustees took three steps to fund the renovation and to address the operating deficit. First, they renegotiated the $5 million loan. The repayment of principal, originally scheduled to begin in 1984, was deferred until 1988. This move bought time, during which the Newberry could complete the renovation and raise the funds to repay the bank loan. Second, the trustees authorized borrowing by the Centennial Fund from the unrestricted fund. Third, the trustees voted to put the entire portfolio into bonds. This move, although arguably misguided, was intended to lock in a fixed level of income and guard against the possibility of a stock market crash.

The difficulties with the campaign and the renovation, coupled with the trustees' decisions, touched off a financial crisis at the Newberry. We have already noted an imbalance between operating income and expenditures dating back to the late 1960s. Also, based on the Trustees' Table, deficits appear to have persisted through the late 1970s. Figure 3.4, which shows overall income and expenditures for the period 1981–1993 (which have been analyzed in depth), indicates deficits in 1981, 1982, and 1983. During these years, the capital campaign and the renovation had some effects on the operating budget, but these effects were apparently modest. Overall, through the 1970s and early 1980s, the library operated in a mildly negative but fairly stable financial position.

The decisions made in 1984, however, upset this precarious balance. Figure 3.4 suggests that the budget was balanced in 1984 and 1985. However, Figure 3.5 reveals the truth behind this apparent balance. The two panels of the figure, which separately track income and expenditures for the unrestricted and restricted funds, show that the unrestricted fund was in a deficit position from 1981 to 1993, for a cumulative loss of $13 million. The apparent increase in income during 1984 and 1985 consisted almost entirely of "restricted dollars."

FIGURE 3.4. CURRENT INCOME AND EXPENDITURES, NEWBERRY LIBRARY, 1981–1993.

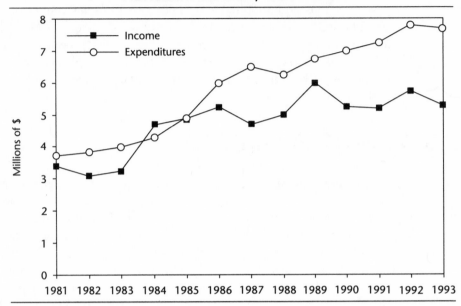

Source: Data from Table B.3–2 in Appendix B.

Restricted funding, be it from an endowed restricted fund or from a restricted grant, can be spent only for a specific purpose. A surplus in the restricted fund is therefore of limited utility because by definition, the funds must be spent in later years for the same purposes or else reinvested. In either case, the "restricted dollars" cannot relieve the unrestricted budget, which must cover all other expenditures. In other words, an organization could run million-dollar surpluses in its restricted fund for twenty-five years; if the unrestricted fund ran out of money, however, the organization would have to close its doors, its "wealth" notwithstanding. (If the organization is raising restricted funds to cover core expenditures, as the Newberry did in recent years, then the share of total expenditures that is funded by restricted dollars should increase. Restricted fundraising notwithstanding, this has not been the case at the Newberry.)

If 1984 was the watershed year in which the Newberry's difficulties came to a head, then the period between 1985 and 1987 was one in which the consequences of earlier actions became apparent. Unrestricted expenditures increased rapidly, due in part to higher operating costs associated with the newly renovated and expanded Newberry. Another factor was the absence of strict cost controls, which made it impossible to rein in expenditures.

Meanwhile, unrestricted income stayed flat, widening the Newberry's operating deficit. Figure 3.6, which shows unrestricted income broken down by category, helps explain the shifts over time. The increase in 1984 was due almost

FIGURE 3.5A. UNRESTRICTED INCOME AND EXPENDITURES, NEWBERRY LIBRARY, 1981–1993.

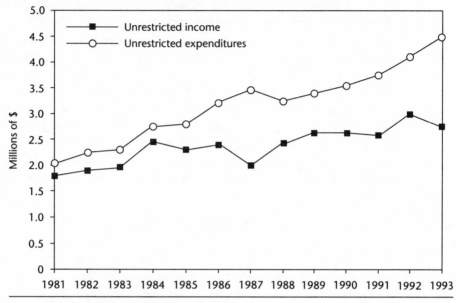

Source: Data from Table B.3–2 in Appendix B.

FIGURE 3.5B. RESTRICTED INCOME AND EXPENDITURES, NEWBERRY LIBRARY, 1981–1993.

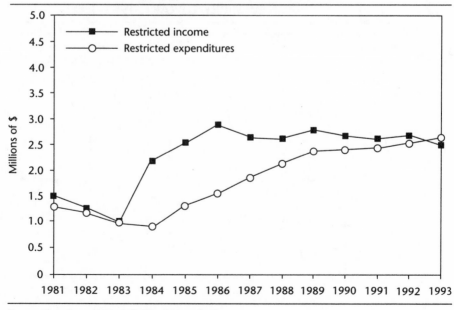

Source: Data from Table B.3–2 in Appendix B.

entirely to the extra investment income that resulted from the move into bonds. From 1985 to 1987, however, investment income dropped. Each deficit had to be funded from the unrestricted endowment, as did the overruns in the renovation. These outlays drew down the endowment, which in turn meant that less income was produced. Also, because almost all of the endowment was invested in bonds, the endowment was denied the substantial capital gains of the mid 1980s.

Contributed income, which had traditionally furnished a fairly small share of unrestricted income, was down in 1985 and down sharply in 1987. The most likely explanation for this falloff is that as Towner's illness worsened, he was increasingly unable to raise money. Whatever energies Towner could bring to bear appear to have been focused on restricted grants, which increased substantially during this period. Also, as mentioned earlier, the development office was in a state of disarray, further complicating efforts to place the operating budget on a secure footing.

New Leadership: Charles T. Cullen

On August 31, 1986, Bill Towner retired and was named president and librarian emeritus. His successor was Charles T. Cullen, a Ph.D. in American history who came to the Newberry from the editorship of the Thomas Jefferson papers at Princeton University. Cullen stepped into a difficult situation, to say the least. The renovations of the Cobb Building, which were concluded officially

FIGURE 3.6.   UNRESTRICTED INCOME BY SOURCE, NEWBERRY LIBRARY, 1981–1993.

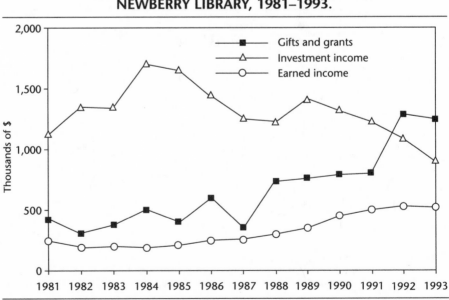

Source: Data from Table B.3–2 in Appendix B.

on August 29, 1986, had finally been financed by a "loan" from the unrestricted endowment of almost $5 million. Each passing year that this "loan" was not repaid meant the loss of investment returns; the compounding effects magnified this opportunity cost. Also, the repayment of the $5 million bank loan cast its own shadow. In 1988, the Newberry issued bonds worth $5.8 million to repay the loan and to rebuild reserves depleted by deficits; repayments are not scheduled to begin until 2002. Because the interest rates on the loan are lower than the earnings on the endowment, this action bought time at a lower cost than borrowing from the endowment. (In fact, were it not for the fact that $5.8 million was the legal limit, the Newberry might have been well advised to borrow all of its money externally.)

The problems caused by the renovation continued to upset the operating balance. In 1986, the last year of Towner's regime, the overall operating deficit (excluding depreciation) was $134,000. The deficit in the unrestricted fund, however, was $1.1 million, the equivalent of 50 percent of unrestricted expenditures. A quick look at trends in income and expenditures reveals the magnitude of the underlying problems. During the period 1981–1987, income grew at an average annual rate of 8.9 percent, while expenditures grew at an annual rate of 10.5 percent. For the unrestricted fund, income grew at an average annual rate of 3.1 percent, while expenditures grew at 8.4 percent.

Since his arrival in 1986, Cullen has taken several important, albeit belated, steps to address the basic problems the Newberry Library faces. First, he and the board have engaged in the "consciousness raising" that has occurred at the Huntington and the Morgan as well. One manifestation of these efforts has been increased board giving. The development of a mission statement and a long-range plan in 1993 was an important element in this process because it encouraged the board to develop a shared vision of the Newberry. One of the difficulties that the board has encountered in the past was that because the Newberry is both a research institution and a collecting library, there has been a divergence of views as to what was wheat and what was chaff. Different trustees have accorded primacy to different parts of the institution, making it difficult to set priorities.

Another set of changes has centered on the Newberry's financial control systems. We have alluded several times to the inefficiencies of those systems during Towner's administration. In 1986, for example, the library's auditors pointed out several instances of miscommunication between the development office and the accounting department. Budgeting also was not done in a consistent, useful manner. In 1984, the auditors reported that the deviations between budget and actual results were so wide as to render budgets almost meaningless.[20]

Under Cullen's administration, the Newberry's systems have been upgraded and brought into the modern era. A new computer system has helped the Newberry implement more accurate cost controls that for the first time will allow management to have an accurate sense of where costs are incurred, an impossibility in the past. For many years, for instance, there has been an ongoing debate

at the Newberry over whether the research and education programs are net pro-
ducers or consumers of income. Only in the past two years has it been possible
even to begin addressing this issue.

Problems of financial information and control are not unique to the Newberry. Nonprofits have historically been "behind the curve" in adapting new
technology, with real implications for budgeting and decision making.[21] As the
independent research libraries continue to upgrade their facilities, they will
become better able to predict their future needs and, it is hoped, meet them.

There have been financial changes as well. The Newberry launched a second
capital campaign on January 1, 1987. Unlike the Centennial Campaign, which
was targeted toward the twin goals of expansion and renovation, the second capital campaign's goal is to raise $12.5 million for general endowment. In reality, the
second campaign is a necessary step to undo the damage wrought by the failure
of the first campaign and the cost overruns of the renovation. By 1993, the Newberry had received $9.3 million dollars in capital gifts; if pledges are included, the
campaign has met its goal.

How has the Newberry fared financially in recent years? Figure 3.7 shows the
overall deficit without depreciation and the deficit for the unrestricted fund. The
results are troubling. In 1988, once the new administration gained a solid footing,
the deficit was cut. Since then, however, it has increased almost every year. In 1993
(admittedly an atypically bad year), the Newberry lost $1.7 million. One way to
put this figure in context is to think of its future value. Assuming a 5 percent spending rate, the $1.7 million that had to be withdrawn from the endowment to fund
the deficit would have produced $85,000 in current income next year. To balance
the budget next year, the Newberry will have to raise an additional $85,000 in cur-
rent gifts. In this way, each successive drawdown makes it more difficult to balance
the budget in the following year. Yet another way to put it is that $34 million in
new endowment would be required to produce income sufficient to close the $1.7
million gap between income and expenditures. By any standard, the data are
not encouraging.

Is there hope for the Newberry? The answer is unclear, but there are several
promising signs. The board has committed itself to a more balanced endowment portfolio and a lower spending rate, which should help reduce the drain
on the endowment. According to Charles Cullen, there is still about $15 million
in capital gifts "in the pipeline." If these gifts materialize, and if the flow of capital gifts continues thereafter, the Newberry may be able to rebuild its endowment.
Also, if the recent growth in the annual campaign can be maintained, less endowment will have to be raised in the immediate future.

The other element that is essential if the Newberry is to regain a solid footing is control over expenditures. Since 1987, expenditures have increased at an
average annual rate of 4.3 percent, while income has grown only at 0.2 percent. The unrestricted figures are only slightly less discouraging: income has
grown at an average annual rate of 3.5 percent, while expenditures have grown

FIGURE 3.7.   SURPLUS/DEFICIT, OVERALL AND UNRESTRICTED, NEWBERRY LIBRARY, 1981–1993.

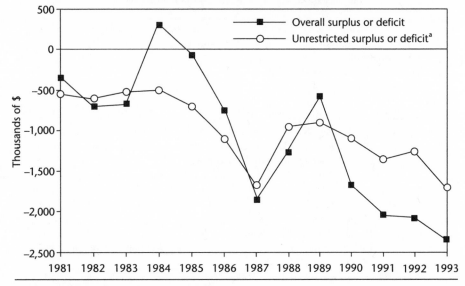

Source: Data from Table B.3–2 in Appendix B.
[a]Includes expenditures for acquisitions.

at 7.0 percent. Expenditures are growing more slowly than they have in the past, but they are still outpacing income. Given the size of the gap between income and expenditures, these rates must be reversed—quickly. If each passing year brings substantial deficits, in effect cutting the endowment and raising the hurdle for the following year, it will not be long before the Newberry's endowment is consumed.

For now, though, the Newberry's doors remain open. Charles Cullen and the board of trustees are aware of the problems they face and are committed to tackling them. Improved systems will make it possible to monitor and control expenditures, and the new development staff have increased the effectiveness of the annual campaign. Thanks to the renovations of the early 1980s, the physical plant is in excellent condition and will serve well for many years to come. The end of the Newberry saga is not yet written.

Notes

1. Achilles (1987, p. 17).
2. Cullen (1991, p. 8).
3. For more information about Poole, see Williamson (1963).

4. Achilles (1987, p. 88).

5. Uncredited quotes in this chapter are drawn from the minutes of various board and committee meetings on file at the Newberry Library.

6. Achilles (1987, p. 88).

7. For a useful summary of the IRLA's background, and the independent research libraries generally, see Buddington (1976) and Towner (1993).

8. Griffin (1985).

9. Towner (1993, p. 148).

10. Towner (1993, p. 151).

11. Towner (1993, p. 164).

12. Towner (1993, pp. 164, 166).

13. In 1974, the Newberry altered its fiscal year, resulting in an eight-month year. Rather than depress the totals artificially, we assumed that the eight months were representative and extrapolated to a whole-year rate.

14. Towner (1975, p. 2).

15. Towner (1975, p. 1).

16. Towner (1982, p. 7).

17. Griffin (1985).

18. Phone interview with Hambleton, January 5, 1994.

19. Readers with a greater interest in the "nuts and bolts" of planning library buildings may wish to consult Metcalf (1986).

20. Auditors' memos, 1984, 1986.

21. Herzlinger (1977).

CHAPTER FOUR

THE FOLGER SHAKESPEARE LIBRARY

In 1879, a young man named Henry Folger bought a ticket, for twenty-five cents, to a lecture by Ralph Waldo Emerson. Folger, who at the time was a student at Amherst College, was fascinated not only by Emerson, then old and rather frail, but also by his subject, Shakespeare. For the remainder of his life, Folger would devote significant shares of his time, energy, and treasure to collecting the works of Shakespeare and related materials. Shakespeareana was his passion; it was shared by his wife, Emily Jordan Folger, whose love of the subject predated her relationship with Folger. Emily Folger wrote her master's thesis at Vassar on the subject of differences in the various volumes of the first folio. Today, the Folger Shakespeare Library numbers among its collections seventy-nine copies of the first folio. These works are a testament to the insights and scholarly pursuits of Emily Jordan Folger and her husband's bibliomania.

The Folger Shakespeare Memorial Library, as it is formally known, is located in Washington, D.C., just around the corner from the Library of Congress. Founded officially on April 23, 1932, the library is governed by the trustees of Amherst College. Despite this unusual governance arrangement, the Folger is not a part of Amherst College; the board acts as the governing body of two separate institutions.

The Folger's collections are more focused than the other libraries in our set, and its Shakespeare materials form the largest and most comprehensive collection of its kind in the world. In addition to the aforementioned first folios, the library has the only known original copy of the first quarto of *Titus Andronicus* and a total of 196 copies of the four folios. Overall, the collections contain about 250,000 volumes and about 55,000 manuscripts.

Although Shakespeare's works are the primary focus of the collection, it is not the only one. Since the late 1930s, the Folger has at various points widened its acquisitions policy. Materials are collected in the field of English history during the Tudor and Stuart periods, and the library's holdings include an estimated 50 percent of the titles listed in the *Short Title Catalogue* of books published in English before 1640. Among the Folger's Continental materials, Italian and Reformation works are especially well represented. A collection on theater and art history extends through the nineteenth century. The Folger also holds documents (including a 1325 copy of the Magna Carta), manuscripts, objects, paintings, sculptures, tapestries, and videotapes.

The Folger's scholarly and public activities are varied, reflecting a commitment to scholarship and learning in all forms. The library is the publisher of *Shakespeare Quarterly*, the top scholarly journal in its field. The Folger Institute sponsors seminars in coordination with thirty universities in the eastern United States. Approximately one thousand scholars per year conduct research at the Folger, and twenty fellowships are awarded annually to scholars who wish to work at the Folger for longer periods of time. For younger audiences, there are school tours, the annual Student Shakespeare Festival, and educational outreach programs that bring more than ten thousand students a year in contact with "Bill's Buddies." Furthermore, the Folger has developed teacher training courses and materials that render the works of Shakespeare more accessible and more clearly relevant to high school students.

From a financial perspective, the Folger falls somewhere near the low end of the spectrum relative to the other institutions in this study. Its income in 1993 was $6.2 million, its expenditures were $5.9 million, and the market value of its endowment was $58 million. The Folger is our second-best-capitalized library, behind the American Antiquarian Society (see Table 1.1).

The Folger is an instructive case study. Like the other libraries in this book, the Folger has made the difficult transition from full endowment funding to a more variegated income profile, with deficits along the way. The Folger's leadership has grappled with many of the issues that have figured in other case studies: governance, inadequacies of the physical plant, control over rising costs, and the rest of the now-familiar litany of problems and challenges.

A particularly relevant aspect of the Folger's history is the need to strike a balance between pure scholarship and public programming, which was a major issue at the Folger during the 1970s and 1980s. Reevaluating this balance was one of Werner Gundersheimer's first tasks when he assumed the directorship of the Folger in 1984. The leadership of the Folger was forced to make hard choices and to think clearheadedly about the resources at its disposal and the manner in which it chose to allocate them. In studying the Folger, we may be able to discern a paradigm that other institutions can follow, or at the very least from which they can learn.

This chapter, like the ones that precede it, is organized chronologically. The first section describes Henry Folger and the circumstances that surrounded the library's founding. The second section considers briefly the period 1932–1969, during which the Folger evolved from a repository of Shakespeareana to a functioning research library with a broader range and an active commitment to scholarship. The remaining sections of the chapter analyze in greater detail the events of the 1970s, 1980s, and 1990s. During this time, the Folger solidified and expanded its scholarly efforts and developed an expansive "public side," exemplified most clearly by a theater company. This growth led to financial problems, which were addressed in the 1980s through a process of programmatic retrenchment and reorientation.

Henry Folger and the Founding of the Library

Henry Clay Folger was born in 1857 in New York City. After graduating from Amherst College and Columbia Law School, Folger took a job with Standard Oil, where he was to remain for the rest of his working life. In 1885, Folger married Emily Jordan, who shared his love of Shakespeare and was influential in the creation of the library. Folger's chairmanship of Standard Oil notwithstanding, the Folgers were never as wealthy as the Huntingtons or the Morgans. In fact, for most of their lives, the Folgers did not even own a home.[1] Because they were childless, though, whatever funds were available could be spent in pursuit of their shared passion—collecting.

Like the other collectors we have encountered, the Folgers collected obsessively. The extent of Folger's obsession, which sometimes overtook his professional commitments, once caused A.S.W. Rosenbach, the illustrious collector and book dealer whose name figures prominently in the histories of Huntington, Morgan, and Folger, to boast that he was "perhaps the only bookseller ever to interrupt a meeting of the Executive Committee of Standard Oil Company."[2] At the time of Folger's death in 1930, he had book debts outstanding of almost one-half million dollars. Also, because the Folgers were not as wealthy as some of the other collectors, they could not house their collections in a library building. As books were bought, they were packed away in sealed boxes in fireproof warehouses, an act derided by some as miserly and antithetical to scholarship.

Folger was less forthcoming about his intentions to create a library than either Huntington or Morgan. He once explained his penchant for discretion by saying, "I have persistently avoided all publicity, feeling that book-buying could be done more cheaply and successfully if there was no advertising."[3] A hint of Folger's desire to create a research library can be read between the lines of a message he sent to Henry E. Huntington when the latter founded the Huntington Library and Art Gallery in California. Folger wrote that the Huntington was "an inspiration and a guide for others who may wish to do something of the same sort, only much more modestly."[4]

When the time came to choose a site for the eventual home of the Folgers' collection, several were considered, including Stratford-upon-Avon (Shakespeare's birthplace), several major American universities, and Amherst College. In the end, Washington, D.C., was chosen as the location, with Amherst the legal recipient of the trust. Although his wife's roots in Washington doubtless influenced this choice, Folger explained his decision in the following way: "I did think of placing the library at Stratford, near the bones of the great man himself, but I finally concluded I would give it to Washington, for I am an American."[5]

Like J. Pierpont Morgan and H. E. Huntington, Henry Folger was enamored of America and had great faith in its future. In placing the library near the Library of Congress, he expressed the clear hope that the two institutions together could advance culture and learning in American society. On a more prosaic level, Folger realized that the Library of Congress would provide the full range of research tools with which scholars needed to work. Although one was private and the other a governmental agency, the two libraries were said to fit together so well that if the Folger had not been created, the Library of Congress would have had to put it there.

The Folger's location in Washington has been a mixed blessing. On the positive side, the Folger's proximity to the Library of Congress has been a boon to both institutions and to scholars working there. The numerous universities in the area have presented opportunities for partnerships, especially in later years as the Folger has expanded the scope of its academic programs. Finally, the Folger in recent years has been the recipient of substantial government funds, as well as publicity; for example, two separate events were held at the Folger during Inauguration Week in January 1993.

On the downside, Washington does not enjoy some of the fundraising advantages of other cities. The wealthy do not constitute as large a group in Washington as they do in New York, Chicago, or even San Marino, the Huntington's home. Washington has attracted comparatively few corporate headquarters, and until recently, the city's cultural life did not match that of other prominent eastern cities. Of course, when Henry Folger chose Washington as the site for his library, none of these limitations were relevant; the Folger was to be an endowed institution, working in tandem with the Library of Congress.

The cornerstone for the Folger Shakespeare Library was laid in 1930, only two weeks before Henry Folger's death. The news that Folger had bequeathed his collection to the trustees of Amherst College came as a surprise, even to the trustees. According to the will, they were directed "to maintain said library . . . as a separate and distinct library under said name . . . for the promotion and diffusion of knowledge in regard to the history and writings of Shakespeare."

Even before it opened to the public, the library faced financial problems. Due to the stock market crash of 1929, Folger's Standard Oil shares were worth less than they were at the time he drew up his will. After repaying Folger's debt, administering the will, making payments to various members of the Folger family, and finishing the building, it was estimated in 1931 that the value of the Folger fund was about $1.6 million. At a 5 percent yield, this sum would have produced income of $80,000 per annum. According to Folger's will, the costs that stood against these revenues included $76,000 a year to be paid to Amherst College and $85,000 in annuities to his beneficiaries. The cost of keeping the library open was estimated at $100,000 a year. To save the library from being stillborn, Emily Jordan Folger donated $3 million of her own funds. This gift, along with some financial concessions on the part of Amherst College, is the reason that the Folger Library exists today.

The Folger Shakespeare Library opened officially on April 23, 1932, the 368th anniversary of Shakespeare's birth. Emily Folger was in attendance, as were the trustees of Amherst College, dignitaries and scholars, and President and Mrs. Hoover. The opening ceremonies were conducted in the replica of an Elizabethan theater that is part of the library building. Thanks to Henry Folger's single-minded pursuit of Shakespeare materials, as well as his generosity and that of his wife, the Folger Shakespeare Library had become a reality.

The Early Years (1932–1969)

Building the Collections (1932–1946)

The first director of research at the Folger Library was Joseph Quincy Adams, a Shakespeare scholar and former professor of English at Cornell University. In the library's earlier years, he shared responsibility with William A. Slade, the first librarian. In fact, the two were essentially co-directors, a state of affairs that proved unwieldy from an administrative standpoint. By 1934, Slade had returned to the staff of the Library of Congress, and Adams had become the acting director. Emily Folger urged the trustees to appoint newly unseated President Herbert Hoover, book collector (and Huntington Library trustee), to the directorship, but the board did not follow her suggestion.

In recognition of the complexities involved in running a research library, a special committee of the Amherst board was established to deal with the Folger. In 1938, the practice of holding one of the board's meetings in Washington was initiated. Earlier, in 1933, the board had moved to sell Folger's Standard Oil shares and to invest the proceeds in a balanced portfolio. This was the first example of how the library has benefited from the institutional knowledge and expertise of Amherst College.

In the late 1930s, the Folger acquired a series of collections that extended its holdings into Elizabethan literature and into other fields not as closely related to Shakespeare. The most significant purchase was the Harmsworth collection, one of the great private libraries remaining in England. The purchase of the

Harmsworth collection was described in *Publishers Weekly* as "the outstanding bibliographical event of the season."[6] The collection contained more than 11,000 of the 26,143 items listed in the *Short Title Catalogue,* placing the Folger in the first tier of research libraries in this field, along with the Huntington, the Bodleian, and the British Museum.

The first generation of Folger administrators ended in 1946. Adams died in 1946, as did Harlan Fiske Stone, chairman of the Folger committee; also, Stanley King stepped down as president of Amherst College. King had been instrumental in the creation of the library and had personally conducted the negotiations for the Harmsworth collection.

Adams's death capped an extraordinary period of growth for the Folger Library. If we recall that Henry Folger's bequest was insufficient even to allow the library to open and that in its early years the focus of the collection was almost exclusively on Shakespeare, then the amount of progress made by Adams, the Folger staff, and the Amherst board's Folger committee is clear. The value of the endowment in 1946 stood at $6.9 million. Expenditures were $240,000 and income was $290,000, for an operating surplus of roughly $50,000. The total asset value of the library, including the building, the endowment, and the book value of the collections, was estimated at $11.6 million.

For all its strength, the Folger Library in 1946 was not viewed unanimously as living up to the lofty ideals set out by Henry Folger. For one thing, even advanced scholars did not feel welcome. With one or two exceptions, readers were excluded from afternoon tea. The guards carried pistols, and there was a shooting range in the basement.[7] The credential-checking process by which readers were admitted was considered by most to be unreasonable. At one point, the Modern Language Association (MLA) considered filing a formal protest about the way the Folger was being run. A Massachusetts congressman threatened the Folger with a loss of its tax-exempt status unless it did something to appeal to the public. If the Folger was to flourish, rather than simply survive, it would have to do more.

A Working Research Library: Louis B. Wright

To succeed Adams, the trustees named Louis B. Wright, who came to the Folger from a position as research professor at the Huntington Library. At the time he was hired, the Amherst trustees charged Wright with making the Folger into a fully functioning research institution. As the trustees wrote in a letter to Wright upon his appointment, "It is clear that the time has come to take a further step in the Library's Development in order that it may become a more effective research institution and take a more active part in historical study."[8]

Wright, who had furthered the Huntington's acquisitions, fellowship, and publications programs, took great strides in making the Folger a modern research library. A critical first step was assembling a collection of reference works, including encyclopedias, journals, books of history and criticism, and microfilms. The fellowship program was also expanded during Wright's administration, and he initiated both a publications program and a series of scholarly conferences. Of course, acquisitions were not ignored. During Wright's tenure, more than nineteen thousand sixteenth- and seventeenth-century English works were added, and the Folger's collection of Continental Renaissance materials was begun; more than twenty-two thousand European books were bought as well.

Wright also took several steps to improve the utility of the library building. When he arrived in 1948, the reading room was not even air-conditioned. Anyone who has visited Washington in the summer knows that such an environment is hardly conducive to productive research. The fact that most academic research is conducted during the summer increased the seriousness of the problem. Wright had air-conditioning installed. Other improvements made to the physical plant under Wright's tenure included the creation of additional vault space in the basement, office space and an art department on the third floor, and a roof garden.

Finally, the overall feel of the Folger was changed. The velvet rope was removed from the door of the reading room, a receptionist was hired, the strictness of the credential-checking process was reduced to a reasonable level, and readers were finally invited to the Folger's afternoon tea sessions. These steps, although small individually, sent an important message to the scholarly community: the Folger was a place where scholars were welcome, rather than one where they were merely tolerated.

In the 1960s, the Folger initiated a range of public programs intended to broaden its appeal and utility without undermining its central commitment to scholarship. The library began to hold public lectures, became involved with various governmental and private institutions that sought to improve teaching in secondary schools, and increased the number of exhibitions.

Wright retired in 1968, after overseeing twenty years of progress at the Folger. In his final reports to the Amherst board of trustees, he urged them to maintain their focus on the three areas he had emphasized during his tenure. First, he felt that the library must continue to collect in its fields of interest; it should not be seen as having completed its "buying phase." Second, he saw the fellowship program and the Folger's various publications as the main ways in which the institution influenced knowledge and society; consequently, it was important to continue these activities in an uninterrupted fashion. Third, Wright pointed out the absolute necessity of hiring, training, and retaining top-flight professionals. Only if the Folger remained strong in each of these areas could it hope to live up to the hard-earned reputation it had developed over the previous twenty years.

Programmatic Expansion (1970–1977)

The Theater: A Radical Step?

O. B. Hardison, a professor of English and comparative literature at the University of North Carolina, Chapel Hill, was chosen to replace Wright as the director of the Folger. Like Towner at the Newberry (with whom he was good friends),

Hardison believed that institutions such as the Folger should not be the sole preserve of curators and advanced scholars. The cultural treasures with which the Folger was entrusted were the inheritance of all Americans, whatever their level of education, income, or background. Under Hardison, the Folger Library continued and eventually expanded on the changes made in the mid 1960s. Although some of these activities may have seemed new at the time, their broad outlines had been envisioned even before the library came into existence. A quotation from Paul Cret, the architect who designed the library building, suggests that they were integrated into the building's design:

> The problem was to provide for the housing of (1) a world famous library, (2) collections of painting, sculpture, and curios constituting a small museum, and (3) a small theater to be used for the presentation of Shakespeare's plays in their original staging, and for lectures and concerts. Accordingly the following division in three distinct sections was adopted:
>
> A. The library, with a main reading room . . .
> B. The exhibition gallery, open to all visitors and to be used for the display of paintings, sculpture, books and manuscripts, musical instruments, costumes, etc. with an entrance lobby and coat rooms . . .
> C. The theater, a reconstruction of a Shakespearian playhouse, with dressing rooms, property rooms, a lounge for the public, and a separate entrance.[9]

The first new program initiated under Hardison was the establishment in 1970 of the Folger Theater Group. Although scholars are not in agreement on the exact dimensions or characteristics of the original sixteenth-century Globe Theater, or for that matter any theater at the time, the Folger's small theater was designed to convey the feeling of an Elizabethan theater. (However, instead of the "pit," there is a gently sloping floor with cushioned seats.) Until 1970, the theater had not been used for the staging of plays. Lectures and ceremonies had been held there, but the formation of the Folger Theater Group marked the first time that an organized, sustained attempt had been made to use the theater.

The formation of a theater group represented a departure from long-standing practice at the Folger. When the Folger was built, permission had been granted by the district government to include a theater only with the understanding that it not be used to stage plays. Operating a theater would have required substantial changes in the materials and design of the theater, mostly for fire prevention purposes. Furthermore, the institutional ethos that had characterized the Folger in its early years was resistant to such activities, which would inevitably detract from the primacy of the rare book collection and from scholarship. This attitude was expressed well by Louis B. Wright:

> Periodically during the past twenty-five years, someone, in a burst of enthusiasm for amateur Shakespearean drama, has insisted that the Folger ought to go

into the theater business. And from time to time my predecessor and I have summarized the reasons why that is an impossibility. Even if it were legal for us to use the model stage we could not do it without closing the Library for other purposes. We have a choice of running a research library or running an amateur theater at an enormous monetary loss, but we cannot do both. The operation of a theater and a research library are impossible in the same small shell, as Mr. Folger realized and took care to forbid.[10]

Hardison obviously felt otherwise. The 1970 annual report described the changes made to the theater that allowed it to be used for performances and pointed out that "the most important new public program at the library is the Folger Theater Group."

Widening Circles

The title of an introductory booklet about the Folger that was prepared during Hardison's tenure summarizes well the way the Folger was perceived at the time. The book's title, *The Widening Circle,* can be understood as referring to the focus of the collections, which had broadened from Shakespeare to Tudor-Stuart England, the Continental Renaissance, and theater history (on both sides of the Atlantic). A widening circle would also be an apt description of the Folger's constituencies, which under Hardison came to include local schoolchildren, teachers nationwide, ever-increasing numbers of scholars, and the theatergoing and museumgoing public.

The new theater group was but the first of many new programs in the Folger's widening circle. The annual reports issued during Hardison's tenure, especially in the early 1970s, are notable for the amount of activity they describe. In the years between 1970 and 1975, the following programs were started at the Folger:

- The Folger Institute, a cooperative venture whose founding partners were the library, American University, and George Washington University. The list of participating universities has grown yearly and stands today at about thirty.
- The Folger Theater Group, mentioned earlier.
- A volunteer docent program, which allowed the Folger to offer a full schedule of tours and lectures for the first time in its history. Between mid October and December 1970, more than thirteen hundred high school and college students were given tours.
- An expanded fellowship program.
- Publication of the *Shakespeare Quarterly,* which was transferred to the Folger from the Shakespeare Association.
- The library's *Catalog of Printed Books* in twenty-eight volumes and *Catalog of Manuscripts* in three volumes, published in 1972.
- An annual acquisitions benefit, with readings from Shakespeare by famous individuals such as Charlton Heston.

The list could be continued, but the point is clear: like so many other institutions in the 1960s and 1970s, the Folger democratized, expanded, and took on a new role.

One aspect of the Folger's circle was far from wide enough: its physical plant. The annual reports alluded with increasing urgency and desperation to the need for more space. This was not the first time that space problems had surfaced at the Folger. In 1948, the library's basement had been altered to allow rare books and manuscripts to be stored there. In 1958, the A and B levels of the stacks had been extended. By the 1970s, however, all of this additional space had been exhausted. In the 1971 annual report Hardison wrote: "The chief problem now facing the Folger Library is that of space. Current needs are being met and as growth continues some additional demands can be met by locating certain activities outside of the present building. . . . In two areas, however, the Library cannot locate activities outside of the present building, nor can it limit growth without changing the role which it has maintained with brilliant success ever since its doors opened in 1932. These are book acquisitions and reader services. . . . In short, additional space must be provided or the central activities of the Folger will be compromised."

The need for more space was to be a recurring theme in the annual reports. Fortunately, the Folger's space problems did not have the urgency that they did at the Newberry, where a "waterfall of ice" was once discovered inside the roof. In the 1960s, the Folger had bought adjacent property on which it could build when the time came, thus preempting the need to raise money for land and a building simultaneously. Even so, with each passing year, it became increasingly difficult to house books and readers in the available space.

Yet another widening circle was the set of individuals, corporations, and foundations that provided the Folger with financial support. The Folger's new programs required additional funds, a situation that led to the creation of a fundraising apparatus. The first step was taken in 1970, when the Friends of the Folger Library was founded. This group grew yearly, from 175 members in 1972 to over 600 by 1977.

The creation of a "friends" group was even more important at the Folger than at the other libraries in our set. Because Henry Folger intended the library to be an endowed institution, he probably never thought about the need to raise money when considering the library's governance. Whatever its overall merits, one of the downsides of the Folger's unique structure is that until the 1970s, the board consisted solely of individuals who were members of the Amherst board. Although this does not mean that the library was governed carelessly, it does mean that the Folger committee's members had a primary financial commitment to Amherst. The Friends provided a vehicle to mobilize financial support specifically for the Folger.

In 1972, the Folger committee voted for the first time to include public members on the committee in addition to the members who were on the Amherst board. It is not clear whether or not Hardison urged this change on the board, but he must have been thankful when it happened. The inclusion of public members was an important step in the Folger's evolution. It accorded greater prominence to the Folger as a significant institution in its own right. It allowed the board to play a more active role in financial development. And it created a vehicle for the appointment of individuals with specific qualifications or areas of expertise that were related to the Folger. Like the expansion of the Newberry's board and the creation of the board of overseers at the Huntington, the expansion of the Folger committee helped create a structure that could further the goals of the institution more effectively.

The Folger's staff underwent changes as well, reflecting the shift from an endowed institution that regularly earned more than it needed to a library with a diversified revenue profile that had to scramble, sometimes unsuccessfully, to balance its budget. A development office was founded in 1972 and was eventually expanded to target individuals, foundations, and corporations. In 1973, the Folger's accounting department was reorganized in order to allow for tighter control over expenditures.

The Widening Deficit? Paying for Growth

The growth that marked the first half of the 1970s was not without its price. Rapid inflation diminished the relative size of the endowment, even while the cost of new programs swelled the operating budget. Figure 4.1 illustrates the rapid growth in the Folger's operations (this section focuses on the "with theater" series; the differences between the two series will be discussed shortly). Over the period from 1972 through 1978, income and expenditures both increased at an average annual rate of 14 percent. To be sure, these years were also marked by high inflation; still, the average annual rate of growth in real dollars during the period 1973–1978 was 5 percent. Despite the Folger's apparent success at matching income and expenditure growth, there were deficits, as depicted in Figure 4.2.

Like the other institutions discussed in this book, the Folger was caught in something of a vise: the share of income drawn from the endowment was dropping, and the cost of new programs was increasing. Like other endowed institutions, the Folger's endowment in the 1970s was unable to provide the same share of funding as it had in the past, forcing the Folger to seek revenues elsewhere. Figure 4.3 shows the shift in the Folger's revenue profile, with current income divided into investment income and noninvestment income such as gifts, grants, and earned income. During the period under discussion, 1973 to 1978, investment income grew at an average annual rate of 4 percent, while other income grew at 35 percent per year. By 1978, the endowment provided only 50 percent of the Folger's income.

The shift in the Folger's revenue profile was accelerated by the increasing importance of the theater (included in Figure 4.3), expenditures for which grew from $108,000 in 1974 to $719,000 in 1979. Because the theater was supposed

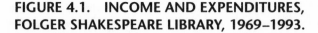

FIGURE 4.1.   INCOME AND EXPENDITURES,
FOLGER SHAKESPEARE LIBRARY, 1969–1993.

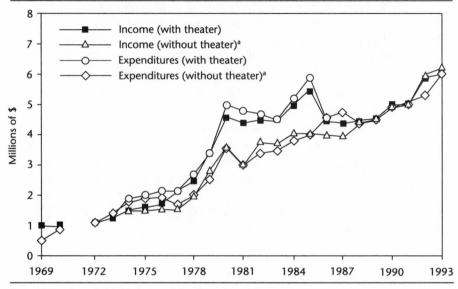

Source: Data from Tables B.4–1 and B.4–2 in Appendix B.

Note: Data were not available for 1971.

[a] See note 15 for an explanation of the "without theater" series.

to raise all of its funds from a combination of earned income (ticket sales) and gifts and grants, these income sources became responsible for a greater portion of the Folger's overall budget. The growth in gifts and grants was insufficient to cover the entire cost of the Folger's new programs, resulting in the deficits shown in Figure 4.2.

The Renovation (1977–1982)

The Folger's budgetary difficulties, troubling as they were, were forced to take a backseat to space problems. The collections, and the number of scholars using them, had completely outgrown the space available. Beyond the problems facing the Folger at the time, there was also an expectation that future growth would be even more rapid. As Hardison saw it, the vastly increased enrollments at universities would result in a general shift at those institutions away from research and toward teaching. In the sciences and social sciences, this shift had already led to the development of independent organizations such as the Institute for Advanced Study at Princeton, the Brookings Institution, and the Center for Advanced Study in the Behavioral Sciences, all of which afforded scholars a chance to conduct

FIGURE 4.2.   SURPLUS/DEFICIT,
FOLGER SHAKESPEARE LIBRARY, 1969–1993.

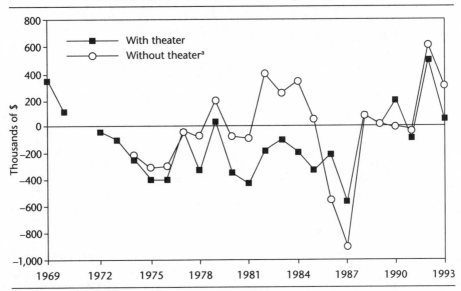

Source: Data from Tables B.4–1 and B.4–2 in Appendix B.

Note: Data were not available for 1971.

[a] See note 15 for an explanation of the "without theater" series.

research in an environment that was largely free of organized teaching and the other pressures of university life. As Hardison explained, "The Folger and institutions like it have already evolved significantly toward becoming centers for advanced study in the humanities in response to the needs of the academic community. It seems very likely that the evolutionary process will accelerate as these needs become more pressing and more explicit."[11]

With each passing year, space problems became more acute. In 1972, a "space study" was prepared, in consultation with the staff and the architectural firm of Harbeson & Hough, descendants of the firm of Paul Cret (the architect who had executed the design for the original building). The annual report for that year reflected the optimistic possibilities that attached to the idea of a new "humanities center." Hardison wrote: "The opportunity to create a striking new building on Capitol Hill, three blocks from the Capitol itself, and one block from the Supreme Court and the Library of Congress, is exciting both in itself and in terms of the national statement which such a building can make about the importance of humane values in American culture."

In 1974, the Folger moved from exploratory studies and bright hopes to action. According to the annual report, the library was "actively searching for a major donor or group of donors" who would assist in the provision of resources for a

FIGURE 4.3.   INCOME BY SOURCE (INCLUDING THEATER),
FOLGER SHAKESPEARE LIBRARY, 1973–1993.

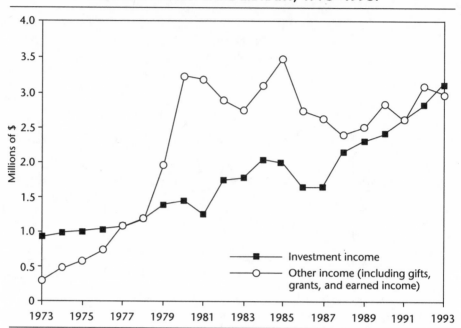

Source: Data from Tables B.4–1 and B.4–2 in Appendix B.

new building. Despite difficulties in the operating budget, which led to retrenchment during 1974 and 1975, the trustees in 1976 directed the architectural firm
of Hartman & Cox to prepare a feasibility study of the minimum expansion
needed to solve the Folger's problems. The director estimated the cost of a renovation at $5 million; with another $5 million to augment the endowment, a $10
million campaign would be required. The feasibility study progressed to detailed
plans that were approved by the appropriate authorities and, later, given an award
by the American Institute of Architects. The campaign was announced formally
in April 1976, with the official goal of $5 million. By October 1977, the Folger
had reached the halfway mark of the campaign, thanks in large part to the trustees,
who contributed collectively $1.5 million.

Building commenced in 1978. The program as a whole was divided into three
phases, each of which could be carried out independently. Phase one involved the
creation of a two-story underground vault beneath a parking lot, which would add
about fifteen thousand square feet for rare book storage and would allow all of the
Folger's books to be stored in one place, facilitating access, security, and conservation. The vault incorporated security features and a Halon gas fire extinguishing system, which, as Hardison put it, provided "improvements of several orders

of magnitude in security and fire prevention."[12] Phase two was the renovation of the original building. Because of the risks posed to books by ongoing construction, phase two could not begin until phase one was completed and all of the Folger's books locked away. Phase three was the construction of a new reading room, designed to alleviate the overcrowding that had become increasingly problematic in the original space.

In the 1979 annual report, Hardison reported proudly on the Folger's progress. Phase one was complete, and phase two was under way. The balance of the building fund was $4.8 million. It is worth noting that phase three, the new reading room, was clearly seen as an independent project that would be started only if the funds, or at least the pledges, were in hand. The contingent status of this phase is illustrated by Hardison's explicit statement that "whether or not it [Phase III] will be possible depends on the progress made on Phase II funding and the generosity of our funding sources."[13] Dividing a construction project into discrete components, with the ability to stop after any one of those components, appears to provide a judicious means of limiting the risks inherent in a renovation, expansion, or move.

Although dividing the renovation into three independent phases was a helpful device, the problem of raising the money remained. The difference between gifts and expenditures was funded by transfers from endowment, which were not repaid fully until 1987. As we have seen, this is hardly an uncommon pattern; capital campaigns often extend over a longer period than the renovations.

By 1981, the first two phases of the renovation were complete. The Folger reopened its doors to the public on April 23 (Shakespeare's birthday). The Folger's fiftieth anniversary year, 1982, saw the last major piece of the renovation's funding fall into place with a $1 million bequest from Theodora Sedgwick Bond. With the addition of the new reading room, it seemed that the Folger had solved its problems.

The 1980s: Financial Problems Come to a Head

The end of the renovation, which should have been a time of relief for the Folger's staff and board, brought a whole new set of difficulties. Returning to Figure 4.1, we can see a sharp escalation in both income and expenditures in 1979 and 1980. During this time, income increased by 98 percent, while expenditures increased by 94 percent. Effectively, the scale of the Folger's operations doubled. Even if we discount the effects of inflation, we arrive at two-year growth rates of 57 percent for income and 53 percent for expenditures.

What did this expansion represent? The bulk of the increase in 1979 consisted of spending on administration, fundraising, and the physical plant—in other words, operating costs. "Grant activities" increased substantially as well, probably reflecting the resumption of normal grant-seeking activities.[14] Although the direct costs of grant activities are fully funded (by definition), the full extent of indirect costs is rarely covered.

In 1980, fully 83 percent of the increase in expenditures was in three program areas—central library, grant activities, and the theater. Most of the increase in the "central library" category was linked to efforts to increase earned income, including a mail-order catalog; these ventures lost $77,000 in 1980. The increase in grant activities is self-explanatory. The increase in the theater's expenditures was caused largely by the addition of two programs at the Kennedy Center and by administrative costs that were higher than expected.

The years from 1980 to 1982 were especially problematic for the Folger, as shown in Figure 4.2. A comparison of the two series shown on the figure (the lower series includes the theater; the upper does not) reveals an interesting phenomenon.[15] Although both series indicate deficits in 1980 and 1981, the "without theater" series shows surpluses from 1982 to 1984. In other words, with the theater excluded, the Folger was taking in more money than it spent. Of course, what actually happened was that this "surplus" was used to fund the theater's deficits. Werner Gundersheimer, the Folger's current director, has commented that during the period in question, the Folger's other programs were being "starved." One illuminating example is funding for acquisitions, which was $100,000 in 1972 and hardly increased at all until the mid 1980s, despite the general level of inflation and increases in rare book prices.

One of the ramifications of the financial squeeze affecting the Folger was increased spending from the endowment. The spending rate, which is represented in Figure 4.4, increased in the early 1980s to the 8 to 10 percent range. As noted elsewhere, 5 percent is considered today to be a prudent rate. Even with income heightened artificially through a high spending rate, and even with aggressive fundraising, the Folger continued to run deficits.

Late in 1983, Hardison notified the trustees of his intention to resign, effective January 1, 1984. In the words of Philip Knachel, long-standing associate director and acting director after Hardison's departure: "The task he had begun in July of 1969 was, he said, essentially complete, and he wished to return to teaching and to research at Georgetown University. Certainly the 14 and a half years of his tenure at the Folger had been filled with accomplishment. He had brought to successful conclusion an eight and a half million dollar renovation and expansion of the physical plant, . . . the Folger theater was born, a Public Programs Department was established, . . . an Academic Programs Department was created . . . [and he] organized the Folger Institute for Renaissance and 18th Century Studies."[16]

At the time of Hardison's departure, the Folger faced a difficult financial situation. Deficits had been run in every year but one from 1979 to 1984, averaging 4.5 percent of expenditures. The spending rate was higher than it should have been. And except in 1983, the theater had not balanced its books.[17] On the income

**FIGURE 4.4.   SPENDING RATE,
FOLGER SHAKESPEARE LIBRARY, 1970–1993.**

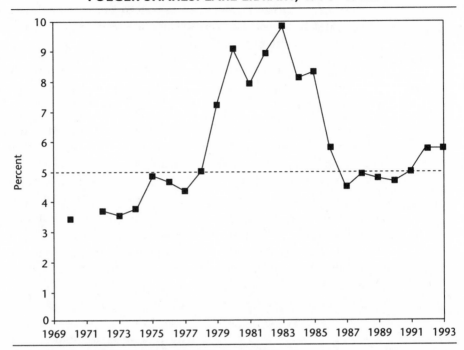

Source: Data from Tables B.4–1 and B.4–2 in Appendix B.

Note: Data were not available for 1971. Dotted line represents a spending rate of 5 percent, which is commonly regarded as prudent.

side, the value of the endowment had dropped relative to the Folger's expenditures. The earned income ventures—the museum shop and the mail-order catalog—appeared to be producing substantial income but in fact were operating at a loss. A general way to characterize the Folger's financial situation would be as follows: much had been built, but the foundations were in need of shoring up.

Werner Gundersheimer (1985–1993)

"A Number of Surprises"

The job of repairing the foundations fell to Werner Gundersheimer, who took office as the Folger's new director in July 1984. Gundersheimer, a graduate of Amherst College and Harvard University, came to the Folger from a professorship at the University of Pennsylvania. In the 1985 annual report, Gundersheimer described his first year at the Folger:

In the year that has gone by, it has been my privilege to learn how deep the Folger's resources are, in terms of its collections and programs to be sure, but above all, in terms of its people, a large category including a dedicated, highly talented staff; a devoted concerned circle of Friends and volunteers; and an imaginative and supportive board.

All of these great assets were called into play in the course of the transition, and none were found wanting. My first month in office began with a number of surprises. . . .

One such surprise was the largest deficit yet encountered by the theater. As Louis B. Wright had pointed out years ago, the finances and problems of a theater differed from, and were sometimes at odds with, those of a research library; the Folger could not run both types of institutions successfully. Following the deliberations of an ad hoc committee and consultations with local foundations and patrons of the arts, the theater was transferred to a new corporate entity with a board of its own. The Shakespeare Theatre at the Folger, as the new organization was called, was to receive some financial support from the library for two years, after which time it was expected to be self-supporting. Although the separation of the theater was bitterly contested by many, including Hardison, today it is generally seen as having been the correct decision (especially in light of the financial and artistic success that the theater has achieved).

How has the Folger fared during the nine years of Gundersheimer's tenure? After a few years of deficits, the picture has generally improved. Today, the Folger's finances are arguably the most stable of the independent research libraries in this study. It has run surpluses in five of the last six years, even if we include acquisitions as expenditures. With the exception of the theater, the range of programs initiated under Hardison has been kept intact. The coming pages examine income, expenditures, the endowment, and broader issues such as governance, all in an attempt to understand how the Folger was brought to equilibrium.

Stabilization: Expenditures

The average annual rate of growth in the Folger's expenditures over the period 1985–1993 was 4 percent. In constant dollars, this translates into an average annual growth rate of 0.5 percent, meaning that the Folger has not really grown. This is a useful illustration of the notion that "bigger is better" is not always the best yardstick against which to measure a nonprofit's performance. A more appropriate question is, Is the Folger (or any institution) fulfilling its mission within the bounds of its financial abilities?

In the field of program services, most of the individual line items have grown at the same rate as expenditures as a whole. Two program areas grew more rapidly: public programs, whose expansion in the past three years has been driven in part by restricted funds, and acquisitions, which has finally regained some of the purchasing power that was lost during the 1970s (see Figure 4.5).

FIGURE 4.5. ACQUISITIONS FUNDING, FOLGER SHAKESPEARE LIBRARY, 1973–1993.

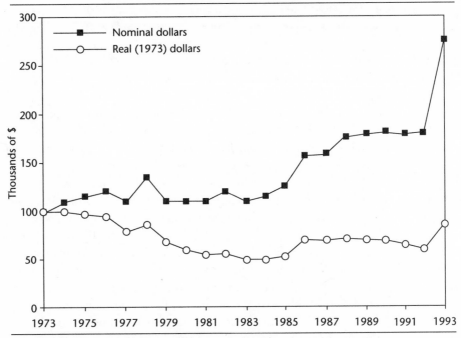

Source: Data from Tables B.4–1 and B.4–2 in Appendix B.

Among support services, expenditures for fundraising and development have grown more rapidly than expenditures as a whole. Over the period 1985–1993, development expenditures grew at an average annual rate of 8.7 percent. This phenomenon has been observed as well at other libraries and is reflective of an attitude that views development as a central part of an organization's activities, not an ancillary activity to be pursued surreptitiously.

Stabilization: Income

The library's income profile has undergone more substantial shifts. Overall, income has grown at an average annual rate of 6.2 percent, exceeding the expenditure growth rate by roughly two full percentage points. In the post-1979 period, Figure 4.1 shows that income did not really begin to grow in earnest until 1988. Since then, it has grown at an average annual rate of 7.5 percent.

The Folger's income comes from three sources: investment income, which until the late 1960s was almost the exclusive source of income; gifts and grants; and earned income, which includes payment for academic and public programs, as well as earnings from the museum shop. Figure 4.3 depicts changes in the level of funding obtained from two broad types of income.

Investment income, the single most important source of income, has grown at an average annual rate of 7.5 percent. In 1986 and 1987, though, investment income actually fell as the spending rate was cut. By 1988, the endowment corpus had grown enough to produce an increase in investment income, even though the spending rate did not increase. This was due in no small measure to the high returns realized in 1985 and 1986.

Gifts and contributions, the second-largest source of income, has grown overall at only 2.9 percent per annum. Overall, gifts and grants generally declined through 1989, and most of the increase visible in Figure 4.3 came in just two years: 1990 and 1992. The increase in 1990 consisted mostly of restricted grants and the Folger's annual grant from the Capital Arts Fund. In 1992, the Folger's Jubilee Year, most of the growth came from private giving.

Earned income, the final piece of the Folger's income profile, has increased as well, at an average annual growth rate of 10.4 percent. Although it seems as if earned income has grown the most of the three income sources, it is worth remembering that the earned-income totals are gross figures. A more appropriate measure would be growth in the level of net income from earned-income ventures. Such figures, however, are difficult to determine. Some earned-income categories, such as academic programs, represent attempts to subsidize part of the cost of operations. Others, like the museum shop, are more properly seen as ventures that should be profitable. The museum shop is a useful example of the difference between gross and net figures and the importance of comparing the two. Although gross income from the museum shop has increased steadily (at a rate of 9.9 percent per annum between 1985 and 1993), net income has stayed constant or declined, averaging $32,000 annually during the 1985–1993 period.

Stabilization: Endowment

The Folger's long-term financial equilibrium cannot be assessed without analyzing the endowment, which provides roughly half of the Folger's income. The Folger's financial statements are particularly informative with regard to the endowment, which facilitates the development of a clear and accurate picture of events over the past ten to fifteen years. Analysis of the endowment focuses on three measures of endowment performance: the total return, the spending rate, and gifts to endowment.

The Folger's average total return over the period 1982–1992 was 14.8 percent.[18] This compares favorably with the Morgan's 14.5 percent and the Newberry's 12.5 percent but is lower than the Huntington's 15.7 percent and the American Antiquarian Society's 15.9 percent. In other words, the Folger's returns were normal. Without a closer look at the different levels of risk adopted by the institutions, there is no way to tell whether any one institution has been more successful than others at investment management.

The Folger's spending rate, shown in Figure 4.4, has fallen significantly since the last years of O. B. Hardison's tenure. The average spending rate for the period

1979–1985 was 8.5 percent; from 1986 to 1993, the average was 5.1 percent. The cuts in the spending rate that began in 1986 were institutionalized in 1987 with the adoption of a spending rule. According to the rule, the Folger attempts to distribute no more than 5.5 percent of the projected value of the endowment at year end. The Folger was fortunate in that the first year of lower spending rates, 1986, coincided with the single highest total return in the 1980s. The combination of the two increased the value of a unit of endowment by 30 percent.[19]

Of course, cuts in the spending rate, unless offset by endowment growth, will have the deleterious effect of starving the operating budget. Aside from reinvesting returns, the size of the endowment can be increased through gifts. As seen in Figure 4.6, gifts to endowment have increased substantially since 1986 (with the exception of 1991) and averaged $662,000 per year over the period 1985–1993. In percentage terms, gifts since 1985 have averaged only 1.3 percent of the market value of the endowment. Although this percentage is rather low, as it is at most heavily endowed institutions, it has increased in recent years. As long as the spending rate stays low, gifts continue to come in, and the investment markets perform well, the Folger's endowment will continue to grow.

Redefining a Mission

In addition to the three interlocking financial areas just discussed—income, expenditures, and the endowment—the Folger has devoted effort in recent years to improving the less quantifiable contributors to institutional success: clarity of mission, planning, and governance. The library's mission, reaffirmed by the trustees in 1989, is a useful place to start. The mission of the Folger Library is as follows:

FIGURE 4.6.   GIFTS TO ENDOWMENT, FOLGER SHAKESPEARE LIBRARY, 1979–1993.

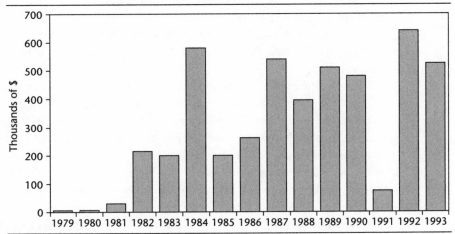

Source: Data from Table B.4–2 in Appendix B.

- To preserve and enhance its collection and to render the collection accessible to scholars for advanced research
- To advance understanding and appreciation of the Library and its collections through interpretive programs for the public.[20]

This mission statement, which clearly accords primacy to the traditional elements of the Folger, reflects the founder's desire that the Folger be "first and foremost a library." At the same time, public programs are also clearly an integral part of the Folger's activities.

In 1988, the Folger created a long-range plan. The process of creating such a plan is often as rewarding as the plan itself. This was particularly true in the Folger's case. Because independent research libraries are such peculiar institutions, without clear archetypes or models, they are often viewed in different lights by different trustees (or committee members). In the case at hand, where the governing body is comprised partly of individuals whose primary role relates to a different institution altogether, it is even more important to develop a shared understanding of what the Folger is and does.

The main thrust of the long-range plan should not be surprising, in light of the preceding discussion. The Folger's top priority is to improve the financial foundation that undergirds its activities. Without a reliable funding source, future growth in the scale of those activities is not foreseen. One exception, as discussed elsewhere, is funding for acquisitions, which had stagnated for many years.

The 1988 long-range plan concluded that the current governance arrangement "works well and does not require any important alteration."[21] The Folger committee, although officially just one committee of the Amherst board, functions as a board of its own, with subcommittees as appropriate. There are several advantages to the Folger's relationship with Amherst, especially institutional expertise in administrative matters such as budgeting, endowment management, and development. The Folger pays Amherst about $20,000 a year for these services. On the downside, the Folger must pay Amherst $226,000 per annum from the returns on the Folger fund. Also, despite the inclusion of public members, most trustees are on the board because of their commitment to Amherst College, not to the Folger Library. For the present, at least, it appears unlikely that the situation will change.

In sum, the Folger appears well positioned to face the challenges of the future. A balanced budget, strong leadership, and a prestigious set of programs all augur well. Absent unforeseen developments, such as a massive drop in the securities markets, it is likely that the Folger will remain financially stable. The steps that have been taken under Gundersheimer's directorship—focusing on the endowment, cutting spending, developing new fundraising vehicles, and keeping costs down—can be understood as useful prescriptions for other institutions in similar predicaments. Whether or not other institutions can swallow this sometimes painful medicine remains to be seen, but the Folger is certainly well along the road to recovery.

Notes

1. King (1959, p. 9).
2. Kane (1976, p. 8).
3. Kane (1976, p. 8). It is worth noting that Folger was "once-bitten" by the sting of publicity, when a disclosure by Rosenbach that Folger had paid $100,000 for a book led John D. Rockefeller to question Folger's soundness of mind.
4. Kane (1976, p. 8).
5. Kane (1976, p. 9).
6. King (1959, p. 32).
7. 1966 annual report and personal memorandum from M. A. McCorison, May 19, 1994.
8. Letter from C. W. Cole and E. Seligman to L. B. Wright, November 24, 1947.
9. Kane (1976, p. 15).
10. 1965 annual report.
11. 1970 annual report.
12. 1977 annual report.
13. 1977 annual report.
14. The Folger's audited statements have a separate line for grant activities, rather than incorporating such projects in the program area for which the funds are targeted. This probably reflects the historical development of the Folger's income structure, with grants being relative latecomers.
15. The series in Figure 4.2 labeled "with theater" is the surplus or deficit reported on the Folger's financial statements. The second, labeled "without theater," differs from the "with theater" series in that the theater's income and expenditures are excluded; acquisitions are included as an expense; and since 1990, when they are first listed separately, quasi-endowment gifts are excluded (the "with theater" series includes them as current income).

    The reasoning behind the creation of the "without theater" series was as follows: first, the theater is excluded to facilitate comparisons with other periods at the Folger; second, acquisitions are legitimately expenditures, not transfers; and third, based on discussions with the Folger's staff, it seemed more appropriate to treat the "quasi-endowment gifts" as capital gifts.
16. 1983 annual report.
17. Even the balanced budget of 1983 is somewhat suspect. The theater received a "stabilization grant" from the Ford Foundation in 1978, one of the stipulations of which was that the theater's books had to be balanced by 1983. The internal 1983 budget-to-actual statements reveal an unbudgeted "Folger Library Support" line for approximately $40,000, which may have helped to produce a balanced budget.
18. This is the period for which we have comparable figures for all five institutions.
19. Dividing an endowment into units helps differentiate between gifts and transfers, which create more units, and returns, which increase the value of each unit.
20. Folger Committee (1992, p. 2).
21. Folger Committee (1992, p. 20).

CHAPTER FIVE

THE AMERICAN ANTIQUARIAN SOCIETY

In 1812, Isaiah Thomas, printer, collector, and amateur historian, submitted a petition to the Massachusetts General Court calling for the creation of an organization, to be known as the American Antiquarian Society, that would "encourage the collection and preservation of the antiquities of our country, and of curious and valuable productions in art and nature [that] have a tendency to enlarge the sphere of human knowledge."[1]

The men who founded the American Antiquarian Society (AAS) believed firmly that the records of the United States' founding were worthy of preservation, as they were the birthright of future generations. Isaiah Thomas explained, "We cannot obtain a knowledge of those who are to come after us, nor are we certain what shall be the events of future times; as it is in our power, so it should be our duty, to bestow on posterity that which they cannot give to us, but which they may enlarge and improve and transmit to those who shall succeed them. It is but paying a debt we owe to our forefathers."[2]

It should be apparent that the AAS differs from the other libraries in our set. The AAS was the third historical society to be founded in the United States, the first with a national focus. Its founding in 1812 preceded by twenty-five, thirty-five, and forty-five years, respectively, the births of J. Pierpont Morgan, Henry E. Huntington, and Henry Clay Folger. Those men, and the libraries they created, were outgrowths of a later era in which America was rapidly becoming the world's premier industrial power and producing previously unimaginable wealth in the process. Men such as Henry Huntington and Pierpont Morgan built their libraries, to a large extent, by obtaining from Europe the treasures that its nobility had held for hundreds of years. The Gutenberg Bibles, first folios, and other manuscripts and first editions that found their way to these shores attested to the shift in wealth and power from the Old World to the New. The aspirations of the Huntington's Policies Statement also reflect this awareness: "Less than a century ago de Tocqueville, in his *Democracy in America*, described the American people as that portion of the British nation whose duty it is to clear the forest of the New World, leaving the intellectual development of the race to be accomplished in Great Britain. . . . The establishment in California of a research institution like the Huntington Library shows how far America has encroached upon the duties of the Old World."[3]

The American Antiquarian Society's roots lie in that earlier time and place that de Tocqueville described. The AAS did not aspire to supplant or even compete with the great libraries and societies of England and the Continent. In its historical roots, the AAS's closest American relatives are the other historical and learned societies that arose later along the East Coast. The AAS's focus was broader, however, than its American counterparts. It defined its field of collecting as the entire United States—initially as the entire hemisphere.

The AAS's collections are outstanding and are focused on American printed materials from 1640 through 1876. There are approximately 675,000 items in the collections, not including roughly three million newspaper issues, maps, manuscripts, graphic art images, and other materials. Particular strengths of the collections include American newspapers, pamphlets, and almanacs. The Mather family papers, railroad and canal archives, and children's books are also at the AAS.

Since the 1970s, the society has increased its programmatic offerings in keeping with an increased commitment to active support of scholarship. There are fellowships for teachers and academics, seminars for graduate students, and lectures and conferences. There are also long-term projects, a good example of which is the society's Program in the History of the Book in America. The AAS also plays a leading role in the development of on-line catalogs for rare and specialized materials. More recently, the society has explored new options in increasing public involvement in its activities. These efforts range from simple—improving the signage in front of the library building—to complex—bringing the society "on-line" on the Internet. The common theme in all of these ventures is that the society's holdings should be made accessible—and relevant—to all Americans, not just scholars.

Financially, the AAS today is the smallest institution in our set. Its endowment is significantly smaller than the endowments of other institutions, as is the scale of its expenditures (see Table 1.1). This is not to say that the AAS is undercapitalized. In fact, as Table 1.1 shows, the AAS actually has the highest ratio of endowment to expenditures in our set. In many ways, though, the fact that the AAS has a lower level of expenditures is significant; differences in scale have real ramifications, especially for governance, development, and endowment policy.

The story of the society's growth and evolution is a long one. Rather than attempt to cover it exhaustively, this chapter deals first with some salient developments in the society's affairs during its first 150 years. Using this material as background, the remainder of the chapter focuses in greater detail on the past thirty years, when the society altered significantly its role in the scholarly community. In doing so, it encountered programmatic success, increased recognition, and, not surprisingly, financial difficulties. By studying the society's development, we hope to understand an institution that has essentially succeeded. Deficits and cost-cutting measures notwithstanding, the AAS grew from a somewhat staid institution with a membership that had become small and generally localized to a well-respected national institution. Significantly, this period of growth was followed by a period of refinancing and retrenchment that, though difficult, has put the society on solid financial ground. This transformation, and the consequent risks and pitfalls, is the primary subject of this chapter.

The First 150 Years (1812–1962)

When Isaiah Thomas died in 1831, he left to the society his library and his financial estate. He had already donated the 150,000 bricks that were used to build the first library building. At the time, membership in the society was limited to 140 individuals, who were (and still are) elected by their peers. The society took as its field of interest both North and South America, and it did not limit its collecting to books. Thus in its early years, the AAS became the owner of such objects as the mummified remains of an Indian woman buried in a cave in Kentucky, plaster statues of Moses and Jesus, stone ax heads, and the lead monument buried at the mouth of the Muskingum River in Ohio in 1749 to mark the claims of the French king to the territories of the Ohio Valley. The "Cabinet," as this collection of artifacts was known, was not disposed of until the beginning of the twentieth century, during the administration of Clarence S. Brigham.

A perusal of the membership rolls provides an interesting glimpse into an earlier era. In its early days, the society consisted largely of amateur gentleman-historians, many of whom were collectors as well. (At the time, of course, there were no professional historians in the modern sense of the term.) Members were elected from both North and South America, including Simon Bolívar (elected in 1829) and Pedro II, emperor of Brazil (1858). In addition to its regular meetings and the ongoing acquisition of library materials, the society published from time to time two journals, known as *Transactions* and *Proceedings of the American Antiquarian Society. Proceedings* dealt with the affairs of the society itself, including reports, new members, records of meetings, and obituaries; after 1880, it included scholarly articles as well. *Transactions*, which was published intermittently through 1911, presented research conducted by members of the AAS as well as primary documents from the collections that were useful for research.

The first Antiquarian Hall, built in 1820, was one of the earliest buildings in this country designed specifically as a library. The society's second building was built under the tenure of Samuel Foster Haven in 1854 and, with one addition, served the AAS until 1910. During these years, the society collected actively and made its collections available to all who wished to study them, but it did not conduct any formal outreach to scholars or members of the local community. It is not clear whether there was an established collecting policy or whether all gifts and donations of materials were accepted.

Financially, the AAS derived most of its support from the Isaiah Thomas bequest. In the earliest years of the society's existence, annual dues of $2 were levied on members; these were soon phased out, apparently due to a lack of interest. The Worcester community helped pay for large outlays, such as the second Antiquarian Hall, which was funded by AAS president Stephen Salisbury II. Following the "canalization" of the Blackstone River in 1828, Worcester assumed greater prominence in commerce and industry; this brought more wealth to the city and thus enlarged the society's potential donor base.

The modern era at the AAS began with the appointment of Clarence S. Brigham in 1908. Brigham served as librarian until 1930 and then as the society's first director through 1959. Before his arrival at the AAS, Brigham had been at the Rhode Island Historical Society, and at the comparatively young age of thirty, he was already well known as a scholar and librarian.

In 1910, Brigham oversaw the building of the third Antiquarian Hall, which today still serves as the AAS's home. This building, which was funded by a bequest from Stephen Salisbury III, reflected a shift in the society's mission. The society's councillors (the society's board is called the council) felt, and Brigham agreed, that the AAS should become a research library, not "a local, state or national attic."[4]

The society ceased functioning as an "attic" in 1910. The various relics, anthropological artifacts, monuments, and other ephemera that had been amassed over the years were given to museums and other institutions as appropriate, leaving the society free to focus on its strengths: books, broadsides, newspapers, and other printed objects. At the time, the society's library collections numbered just under one hundred thousand volumes. (The decision to stop being both a library and a museum was an important one, and one that spared the AAS the problems faced by other institutions with a dual nature, such as the New-York Historical Society.) The third library building was built to the specifications of a research library. The central rotunda was set up as the reading room and was lined with shelved alcoves. The five stories of bookstacks were built of steel, and the electric wiring was run in separate conduits to minimize the chances of fire. A state-of-the-art ventilation system was installed but soon burned out.

Few things are more tempting to a librarian than empty bookshelves. During his tenure as librarian, Clarence Brigham dramatically increased the AAS's holdings. One of the many fields on which Brigham focused was early (pre-1821)

American newspapers; this process culminated in 1947 with the publication of the *History and Bibliography of American Newspapers, 1690–1820*. The collection of newspapers continues to this day, and from time to time the society sends letters to smaller libraries and historical societies, offering to accept one copy of each newspaper that is not yet in the society's possession.

The publication of *History and Bibliography* is also a good example of a defining characteristic of the society's work: in a sense, the AAS is a librarian's library. Its publications tend to consist of bibliographies, catalogs, short-title listings, and other scholarly tools, rather than works analyzing particular historical events or trends. This tendency is in keeping with the society's mission, which is not simply to collect Americana but also to make it accessible. The best illustration of this commitment is the collaboration between the society and the Readex Microprint Corporation, which, over a period of some twenty-five years, reproduced all of the surviving nonserial material issued in this country between 1639 and 1820, thereby allowing libraries and scholars all over the world to have access to these works. Since the advent of fellowship programs in the 1970s, the range of topics covered by the society's publications has broadened gradually; nonetheless, the AAS's commitment to producing scholarly tools continues to this day.

The society's acquisitions under Brigham were so prodigious that by the 1920s, the collections had outgrown the shelf space in Antiquarian Hall. The first of three additions to the library building came in 1924, with the construction of a five-story bookstack that was funded primarily by contributions from a few wealthy local businessmen. The fundraising drive that took place at the time is worth noting because it reflects a need for outside funding at an earlier date than other institutions. The addition was the first in a string of events that, taken together, marked the institutionalization of the changes in the society's role that had begun in 1908. The next event in this process came in 1930, when Brigham was appointed to the newly created post of director. By creating a separate directorship, the council was responding to the increased need for professional administration and oversight that had developed over the previous twenty years. The growth of the collections, the expanded physical plant, and the increasing amount of research being conducted meant that administration could no longer be a part-time job. In general terms, the director handled the society's administrative functions, while the librarian's role was more scholarly. The degree of separation should not be overstated, however; not only did both positions allow time for some scholarly pursuits, but from 1930 until 1992, every director of the society served first as librarian, thus developing familiarity with the collections and acquiring some basic administrative experience.

Another change in the society's operations came in 1934. After the deaths of Calvin Coolidge and Waldo Lincoln, both of whom had been active leaders in obtaining financial support for the society, Brigham conducted the first broad appeal to the society's membership since dues had been eliminated in the 1830s. The newly expanded society could no longer survive on the income from its endowment and the largesse of Worcester's philanthropic elite. The society—meaning, in this instance, the membership—began to function both as an association of scholars with a commitment to American history and literature and as a body whose role it was to provide financial support. Although there had always been members of the society who gave money as needed, the idea that every member should give something on a regular basis did not take root for many years. The developing dual nature of membership—which is both elective and honorary, on the one hand, and carries heavy responsibilities, on the other—created tensions that persist to this day. Even in recent years, the annual reports have bemoaned the fact that more than a third of the society's members do not contribute at all.

With Brigham's ascension to the directorship, R.W.G. Vail became the next librarian. During his nine-year tenure, he completed volumes twenty-two through twenty-nine of Sabin's *Bibliotheca Americana*. Vail left in 1939 to become the librarian of the State of New York and eventually head of the New-York Historical Society. He was succeeded by Clifford Kenyon Shipton.

Shipton led the AAS, first as librarian and later as director, until 1967. During his twenty-seven-year tenure, he continued the process of transforming the AAS into a national institution. As librarian, it was Shipton's job to catalog, organize, and classify the enormous flow of acquisitions that had marked Brigham's tenure as librarian. He developed a new classification system, based loosely on the one used by the Library of Congress yet unique to the AAS and its particular interests. Shipton also refined further the society's mission. If Brigham had led the transformation from museum and "attic" to library, Shipton's accomplishment was accentuating the society's commitment to research. In 1955, Shipton initiated what may be his most lasting contribution to scholarship: the aforementioned Readex Microprint Project.

Shipton succeeded Brigham as director in 1959. The changing of the guard marked the end of a cycle of expansion and increased professionalization. Under Brigham, the society had left behind its roots as a small yet indiscriminate museum-*cum*-storehouse. The collections grew fivefold, but the society did not broaden its focus: it was a research institution that collected American materials prior to 1877.

The 1960s: A New Era Begins

Marcus Allen McCorison became the society's twelfth librarian in 1960, when Shipton assumed the directorship. A librarian by training, McCorison came to the society from a position as the head of the special collections department at the State University of Iowa Library. The society's finances at the time were solid and generally in line with those of the other libraries in our set. Expenditures in 1960 were roughly $106,000, and income was $122,000. The market value of the endowment was $2.2 million, and gifts totaled $25,000. Like the other libraries, the AAS had an operating surplus, although its situation differed in that it was already dependent on annual giving for a portion of its budget.

The 1960s was a transitional decade for the society. The early years represented a collective catching of breath after the expansion that occurred during Brigham's tenure. By the end of the 1960s, the seeds of future growth had been planted, and the AAS was well on its way to becoming a larger, more active institution, with all of the attendant benefits and problems.

The process of expansion began in earnest in 1967. In that year, Shipton stepped down and was named director emeritus. One of his last actions as director was to urge the council to take a new step in expanding the resources available to the society: to conduct a capital campaign. The need for a larger endowment was summed up well by McCorison in the 1967 report of the librarian: "A great collection of manuscripts and documents is lying fallow because of the inability of the Society to engage the services of a trained person to provide guidance and assistance to users. . . . There is absolutely no doubt that we require an increased annual income to prevent the Society from stagnating. Improved salaries, an enlarged staff, and more funds for books are necessities, not luxuries. In addition, within a very few years we will be faced with a building problem, not only for enlarged stack space but also for better reading and work areas."

After extensive meetings with a fundraising consultant, the goal for the campaign was set at $5 million for endowment and the building fund. The capital campaign was inaugurated in 1967, and the first professional development officer in the society's history was appointed. The council also recognized and moved to address a related problem: the declining size and increasingly New England–based nature of the society's membership. As a national organization, especially one that was about to launch a capital campaign, the need to expand the membership rolls was clear. At the society's annual meeting in 1968, the by-laws were amended, raising the membership ceiling from two hundred to three hundred. Members were urged to nominate individuals "whom you consider outstanding," and a membership committee was created to facilitate this process.

In 1971 and 1972, an addition to Antiquarian Hall was built, increasing substantially the space available for the collections and improving the climate control systems for the entire building. The shelved alcoves were removed from the rotunda, thus enlarging the reading room. Although construction was completed on time and on budget, the fundraising proved to be a difficult task. The annual report for 1971 noted that "unless new money is raised . . . specifically for construction of the building, and that in large amounts, the treasurer will be required to use the society's invested funds to pay the bills. The income from these funds is already committed to the annual operations of AAS." Eventually, though, the funds were raised. The new space relieved some of the society's more pressing space problems but not the broader financial worries.

The capital campaign, the need for an addition to the library building, and the expansion of the society's membership were all important, but they did not impinge directly on the library's day-to-day activities. Here, too, there were changes during the 1960s. The enormous growth in the higher education system was a mixed blessing for the society. Increased funding for research and burgeoning numbers of doctoral candidates meant that more people than ever were using the library's collections. Although this was clearly a positive development, it brought with it the need for more professional staff (at higher salaries) as well as other expenses.

In addition to the relatively straightforward financial problems engendered by increased use of the society's collections, the cultural changes of the 1960s posed more fundamental challenges to the way the society had traditionally functioned. How many people could be served with the limited funds available and the limited numbers of seats in the reading room? Was there a place in the era of democratization for an elective learned society that had husbanded its intellectual resources by sharing them only with advanced scholars? The AAS's library collections were not truly a private resource; generations of librarians, directors, and councillors had pronounced them a national trust, of which these people were but stewards. What was the best way to make this trust available to its designated beneficiaries, the American people?

The society's first tentative responses to these questions came in the late 1960s. The by-laws were amended to permit entry to the collections for undergraduates and graduate students who possessed the appropriate qualifications. In 1972, a modest fellowship program was begun, marking the AAS's first foray into actively encouraging and supporting scholarship. In later years, as the society obtained better funding, long-term fellowships were offered, with stipends that sometimes equaled academic salaries. Initially, though, fellowships were short-term opportunities, lasting generally between one and three months, with only modest stipends attached.

In a different sense, the society was well prepared for the changes of the 1960s and 1970s. The new inclusion of previously excluded groups in the national discourse, coupled with the importance of writing "history from below," fit perfectly with the society's holdings. The AAS is not primarily a repository of treasures in the normal sense of the word; many of its collections document daily life. Such works may not be as exciting to the public as illuminated manuscripts and incunabula, but they were exactly what the new social historians wanted. From the point of view of its collections, the society was well positioned to meet the new age.

The 1970s: Financial Shackles on Antiquarian Dreams

The growth initiated in the 1960s accelerated during the 1970s. Figure 5.1, which depicts income and expenditures for the period 1960–1978, shows that both grew more rapidly in the 1970s. Although income actually declined between 1970 and

**FIGURE 5.1.   INCOME AND EXPENDITURES,
AMERICAN ANTIQUARIAN SOCIETY, 1960–1978.**

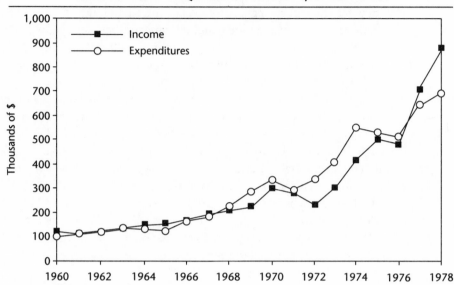

Source: Data from Table B.5–1 in Appendix B.

1972, the overall trend was upward. To be sure, a good part of this growth can be traced to inflation. Even in constant dollars, however, growth in expenditures during the period 1970–1978 averaged approximately 8 percent per year, as opposed to 6 percent per year during the 1960s.

McCorison and the council felt that the AAS should grow with the other sectors of higher education and that its collections should be made available to greater numbers of people. At the same time, tension was developing between the society's aspirations and fiscal realities. The extent of this tension, alluded to with almost depressing regularity in the annual reports, can be seen as well in Figure 5.2, which depicts the surplus or deficit for the period 1960–1978. Deficits began in 1968 and continued, on a fairly small scale, until 1971. Even before the onset of deficits, the society had felt the pinch of tight budgets. Outright deficits had been avoided in time-honored ways: by skimping on costs, deferring maintenance, and holding staff salaries down. As McCorison put it, "The staff at AAS, as at most such institutions, has for years subsidized the society. We cannot ask them to continue to do so. . . . The Society must face its responsibilities to its own staff, by *paying*."[5]

By the 1970s, though, no amount of scrimping could forestall deficits. The problem worsened during 1972–1974, when the combination of inflation, poor investment returns, increased compensation, and the cost of new programs produced deficits averaging 26 percent of expenditures. The society faced a difficult

FIGURE 5.2.   SURPLUS/DEFICIT,
AMERICAN ANTIQUARIAN SOCIETY, 1960–1978.

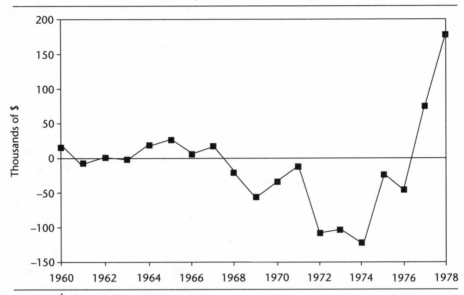

Source: Data from Table B.5–1 in Appendix B.

choice: raise significantly more money than it had in the past, or curtail its services. As the following passage from the 1975 annual report indicates, the latter option was considered extremely unpalatable: "The Council has addressed itself to the continuing problem of securing sufficient annual income to fund the society's work. There is no comfort in the thought that services can be curtailed to reduce costs, especially at a time when increasing reliance upon AAS collections indicates that the society is reaching a wider clientele. The Council concluded that services should not be reduced and that additional annual funds must be raised to meet those costs."

The 1970s were difficult years for all cultural institutions; fundraising was especially hard for organizations branded with the dreaded epithets *elitist* and *old-fashioned*. Broadening the AAS's constituency was an important goal of its leaders, which in part explains their reluctance to cut services or otherwise appear unhelpful. Of course, good intentions do not balance budgets. Only two years later, McCorison discussed again the dilemma facing the society: "The Council sees the matter thusly: the essential and continuing work of the Society requires expanded financial support through increased endowment and additional annual income. To meet the needs and expectations of modern society, AAS must sponsor additional programs which will carry the unique resources of AAS to a more diverse public. The latter efforts also will require additional funding. Over the next few years the Society must either successfully meet these demands or radically reduce even its traditional services. We are reaching the point at which very real choices will have to be made."

The following year, two new divisions were added to the library: Research and Publications, and Education. With the help of a grant from The Andrew W. Mellon Foundation, the society began planning a series of formal education programs. The first AAS seminar in American history was conducted in the fall of 1979, attended by undergraduates at five local colleges. In addition, the society began to conduct intermittent lectures and poetry readings for local residents.

AAS leaders must have been heartened by the good news they received in 1977 and 1978: the society had surpluses in both years. Figure 5.3, which depicts income by source from 1960 to 1978, shows that much of the increase can be traced to a combination of private and government giving. These increases were directly related to a National Endowment for the Humanities (NEH) challenge grant, the first that the society had received for purposes other than fellowship grants. The $285,000 challenge grant had to be matched at a 3:1 ratio, thus spurring private giving.

A related development in 1978 was the creation—or, more accurately, the resurrection—of what must be the most unusually named support group for a library, the Worcester Association of Mutual Aid in Detecting Thieves (WAMADT). This name, adopted by a volunteer police force founded in 1795 but long since expired, was appropriated by the AAS to lend flavor to the often mundane activity of

FIGURE 5.3.   INCOME BY SOURCE, AMERICAN ANTIQUARIAN SOCIETY, 1960–1978.

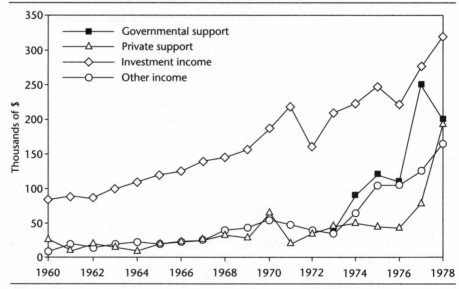

Source: Audited financial statements, American Antiquarian Society, 1960–1978.

giving away money. The creation of WAMADT allowed its members, known as "thief detectors," to support the society without altering fundamentally the elective and honorary character of the society itself.

Returning to Figure 5.3, we can see that investment income also increased in 1977 and 1978, despite the adverse stock market returns that the society experienced in both years. Figure 5.4, which shows the spending rate for the AAS's endowment, explains this phenomenon. The society's spending rate, which, despite worrisome deficits, did not generally exceed 5 percent in the early 1970s, began to climb after 1975. One of the factors responsible for this increase was a shift in the portfolio's asset allocation. After a precipitous drop in market value during 1974, the society's assets were invested more heavily in bonds. Because at the time the society's policy was to spend interest and dividends, the shift from stocks to bonds produced more spendable income.

To sum up, by the end of the decade, the society appeared successfully to have completed a period of growth. The choice that was presented during the 1970s can be summed up as follows: "sink or swim; treading water is not an option." By expanding its staff and broadening the scope of its operations, the

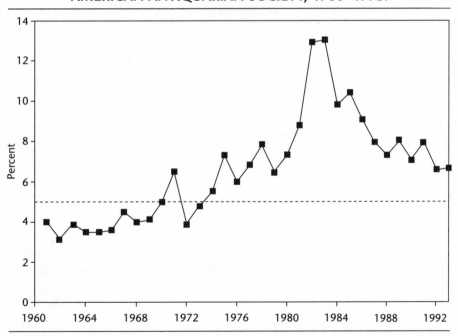

FIGURE 5.4. SPENDING RATE, AMERICAN ANTIQUARIAN SOCIETY, 1960–1993.

Source: Data from Tables B.5–1 and B.5–2 in Appendix B.

Note: Dotted line represents a spending rate of 5 percent, which is commonly regarded as prudent.

AAS had chosen to swim. Most of this growth was funded with gifts and grants from private and governmental sources. A comparison of growth rates is informative in this regard. During the period 1970–1978, current gifts and grants from all sources increased at an average annual rate of 38 percent. Investment income, which was adversely affected by the market conditions of the 1970s, grew only at 6 percent. In inflation-adjusted dollars, gifts and grants increased at an average annual rate of 29 percent, while investment income actually declined at 1 percent per annum. The introduction of well-received new programs, as well as the successful pursuit of grant funds from the NEH and private donors, appeared to ratify the validity of the society's choice.

The 1980s: Strengthening the Foundations

Between 1970 and 1980, the budget almost tripled, the staff more than doubled, and more than 150 new members were added to the society's rolls. It is to the enduring credit of McCorison and the council's leadership that the need to undergird this newly enlarged structure was recognized. Essentially, the AAS faced up to the challenge of recapitalizing itself. In 1970, the ratio of endowment to expenditures was approximately 15:1. By 1980, growth in the society's annual expenditures had brought this ratio to roughly 6:1. To bring stability to the society's finances, the endowment had to be augmented. The alternative was reliance on "soft money," the dangers of which became apparent in 1981. As McCorison wrote:

> Two other events . . . have occurred since last October and intrude into all the thinking and planning that have gone on. One of these is related to the new national prominence of "supply side" economics and suggests massive cuts of at least fifty percent in the funding for the National Endowment for the Humanities and other federal agencies supportive of libraries. . . . The other event was a tax referendum in Massachusetts called Proposition 2½. . . . This misdirected protest has created for cities like Worcester a desperate revenue crisis. Some voices locally and throughout the state are suggesting currently untaxed property of nonprofit institutions as a source of much-needed tax revenues.

The AAS's past growth had been funded primarily by government money and private donations. With new political winds blowing, the continued availability of those funds seemed less than certain. In addition to the dangers of soft money, other expenses loomed. The newly enlarged and professionalized staff was underpaid, the costs of books and journals were rising more rapidly than inflation, and the society had begun the process of computerizing its collections.

It is not entirely accurate to align the periods of growth and retrenchment with the changing decades. The years during which the society grew rapidly began with McCorison's assumption of the directorship in 1967 and lasted until 1983. For the period from 1973 to 1983, the average annual rate of growth in expenditures was 15 percent; from 1983 to 1993, it was 5 percent. As noted earlier, it is fallacious to assume that all growth is good and that its absence is bad. Events in the late 1980s would prove the wisdom of the course charted by the society.

Another reason that the society's growth slowed had to do with a constraint that could not be remedied easily: physical space. The tremendous increase in the society's activities, especially in the size of the staff, had exhausted the space in Antiquarian Hall. Even the addition of the Goddard-Daniels House, a bequest to the society that added space for meetings and lodgings for visiting scholars, did not provide a long-term solution to the problem. In addition to the lack of space, the society confronted another, more threatening space problem: the collections were increasingly open to damage from fire or water. When Antiquarian Hall was built in 1910, the builders had employed state-of-the-art technology. But seventy-five years of wear had left the society exposed. Although these dangers were not as severe as at the Newberry or at the Morgan (which at one point had stored rare manuscripts next to a kitchen facility), it was clear that there was not much room for additional growth.

In 1982, recognizing the fact that the library was somewhat overextended, McCorison and the council announced the launch of a new capital campaign, dubbed the Isaiah Thomas Fund. The most broadly based campaign in the society's history, it had a goal of approximately $8.7 million in new endowment, to be divided among acquisitions, conservation, personnel, and education. The campaign was geared toward the society's 175th anniversary in 1987, by which time it was hoped that the new endowment would put the institution's finances on a solid footing, immune from the vagaries of government funding.

In the midst of all the planning and campaigning, the daily business of running the library continued apace. Figure 5.5a shows income and expenditures for the period 1979–1993, and Figure 5.5b shows the surplus or deficit for the same period. As Figure 5.5b indicates, the delicate balance between income and expenditures that had been attained in the late 1970s unraveled in the early 1980s. These deficits, which appear to have been rather small at first, were kept in check by recourse to a high endowment spending rate. The second series in Figure 5.5b demonstrates this point by showing what the deficit would have been had the society abided by a more conservative spending rate. This series, which replaces the society's actual investment income with the amount that would have been produced by spending 5 percent of the endowment's value, shows a much more serious imbalance in the society's finances after 1981.

In 1983, the society launched the last of its major new programmatic initiatives, the Program in the History of the Book in American Culture. This topic, for which the AAS is especially qualified by virtue of its collections, takes a multidisciplinary approach to the subject, combining seminars, workshops, lectures, and publications. With the exception of this initiative, most of the growth in the

FIGURE 5.5A.   INCOME AND EXPENDITURES, AMERICAN ANTIQUARIAN SOCIETY, 1979–1993.

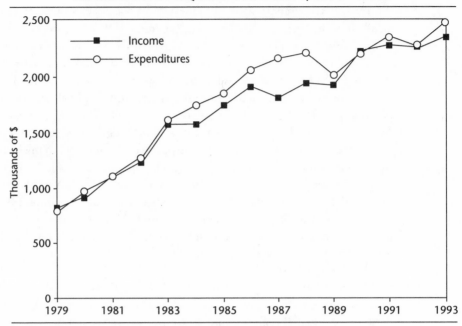

Source: Data from Table B.5–1 in Appendix B and author's tabulations.

FIGURE 5.5B.   SURPLUS/DEFICIT, AMERICAN ANTIQUARIAN SOCIETY, 1979–1993.

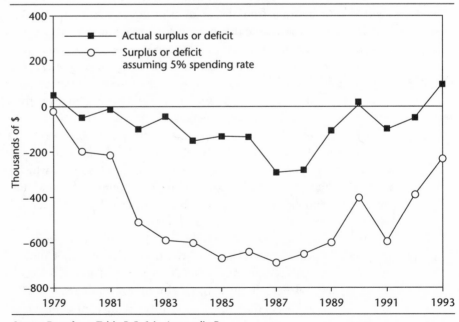

Source: Data from Table B.5–1 in Appendix B.

society's expenditures during the 1980s and into the 1990s came under the rubric of library operations.

Figure 5.6, which provides a breakdown of expenditures by function, demonstrates this point clearly. In 1983, the society committed to research and publications approximately the same share of expenditures as it did to library operations: about 35 percent. By 1993, library operations were responsible for almost 50 percent of expenditures, whereas research and publications was down to 16 percent.

Although the society's expansion had been stabilized, and in spite of the increased investment income that was produced by the financial markets of the 1980s, deficits persisted. Several factors were responsible for these deficits. On the income side, the energies of the development staff were focused on the Isaiah Thomas Fund campaign, which may have had an adverse effect on annual giving. On the expenditure side, despite stringent budgeting efforts, several portions of the cost structure continued to rise. The addition to Antiquarian Hall had outlived its intended useful life of ten years, and maintenance costs were rising. Computerization was a significant ongoing expense, as was the cost of research materials, which rose inexorably. The most significant contributory factor, however, was overspending on acquisitions. Between 1984 and 1988, acquisitions exceeded the budgeted limit by an average of 85 percent. McCorison, like

FIGURE 5.6. EXPENDITURES BY FUNCTION, AMERICAN ANTIQUARIAN SOCIETY, 1980–1993.

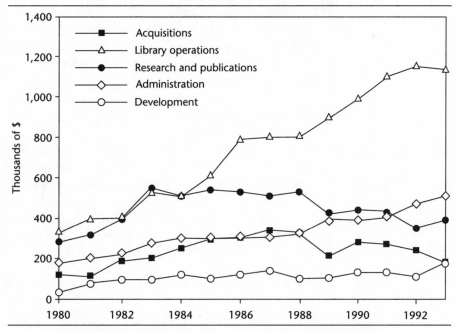

Source: Audited financial statements, American Antiquarian Society, 1980–1993.

many of his predecessors, seemed unable to resist buying a good book. Admirable as this quality may be in a librarian or collector, it is less appropriate to a financial manager, and the society's operating balance was hurt by these actions. During the period from 1984 to 1986, deficits averaged 7.4 percent of expenditures. Although this was clearly cause for concern, two factors kept the alarm from sounding too loudly. First, it was felt that the successful resolution of the Isaiah Thomas Fund campaign would help close the gap. Second, the capital appreciation that characterized the 1980s meant that the value of the endowment continued to rise, despite the deficits.

The society's 175th anniversary, in 1987, brought mixed tidings. The good news was that the Isaiah Thomas Fund had surpassed its goals. The bad news was that the operating deficit had worsened. The deficits of 1987 and 1988 were the two largest that the society had ever incurred, owing primarily to shortfalls in income and overspending on acquisitions. The society's financial problems were intensified in fiscal 1988, when the market value of the endowment fell significantly as a result of the October 1987 stock market crash, thus cutting the amount of income produced.[6] In the 1988 report of the council, McCorison alluded to the problems confronting the society: "Buoyed by a grand celebration upon completing one hundred and seventy-five years of service to historical scholarship and to the nation, the American Antiquarian Society has weathered its 176th year, a year marked by decided accomplishments in the pursuit of our essential goals and, yet, one fraught with fiscal worries."

One of the main problems confronting the society was the increasing competition for funds from its traditional supporters. The proliferation of humanities centers at universities, as well as a general shift in philanthropic priorities away from culture and higher education and toward human services, did not bode well for the future. Also, the increasingly fractious politics at the NEH made life difficult for the society's development staff. As always, McCorison expressed these worries succinctly: "The uncertainty of intentions of private and individual philanthropies, coupled to the disarray of federal and state cultural agencies from which we have traditionally drawn support, casts a shadow over our prospects of continuing to obtain adequate funding in the future for the society's work."

As uncertain as the future may have seemed, the society was able to seek solace in its large endowment. Thanks in large part to the ambitious goals of the Isaiah Thomas Fund, the society was far less susceptible in 1988 to drops in outside funding than it was in the early 1980s. To a degree, this phenomenon was a result of the market conditions in the 1980s, a rising tide that lifted all boats. The relative rapidity with which the AAS was recapitalized, however, reflects positively on the benefits of the Isaiah Thomas Fund campaign. Despite this fact, the continued success of the American Antiquarian Society was still clearly dependent on outside funding; potential changes in that funding necessitated a reexamination of the society's activities.

One of the issues that was studied at length was the nature of the society itself and its potential utility in the future. The efforts undertaken in the 1970s to increase the size and geographic diversity of the society's membership had succeeded, at least from a numerical standpoint. The elective nature of the society itself, coupled with the fact that so many of its members were "starving academics," meant that it was less useful as a fundraising body than any of the support groups at the other libraries. Despite the exceptional generosity of some members, up to 40 percent of the membership did not give at all. Although it was obviously helpful, the Worcester Association of Mutual Aid in Detecting Thieves remained primarily a local organization. The AAS's size, location, and lack of "glamorous" treasures meant that it lacked some of the connections exploited by other institutions, especially the Morgan and the Huntington.

In 1990, the council took several steps to broaden the society's fundraising base. The WAMADT was absorbed into the Alliance for the Antiquarian Society, a tripartite organization with three different support levels: Friends ($50 per year), WAMADT ($200 per year), and the Isaiah Thomas Society ($1,000 and over). A renewed appeal was made to all members to contribute; the annual report noted somewhat menacingly that for those who did not, "the result must be a reduction of services." Thus fiscal realities were addressed while retaining the central elements that make the society unique. Figure 5.7, income by source for the period 1979–1993, shows the sustained jump in private giving since 1990 that is undoubtedly related to these changes.

The 1990s: Transition

As a new decade began, the trends on which McCorison had commented in his last annual report continued. Like Joseph's handiwork in Egypt, the merits of raising endowment for core functions during the 1980s were not recognized until lean years arrived. As 1992's report for the year noted: "Recently, two major national foundations that significantly supported humanistic enterprises in the past have announced changes in their programs, thereby excluding independent research libraries as eligible institutions. In conversations with local foundations we have learned that they, too, under pressure to replace human services that have been cruelly reduced by state and federal agencies, will devote more of their resources toward the funding of social concerns. We must acknowledge, also, that the "Massachusetts Miracle" appears to have dissolved before our very eyes." The downward-sloping "government grant" line in Figure 5.7 is further evidence of this point; the days of magnanimous government funding for the arts and humanities appeared to be, for the moment at least, over. (Space considerations further limit the AAS's ability to take on new NEH projects.)

The 1990 annual report also announced McCorison's intention to resign as of the end of 1992 after thirty years at the society, twenty-three of them as director. The announcement signaled the end of an era. During 1991 and 1992, the council engaged in intensive discussions about the future of the society's finances, programs, and leadership.

**FIGURE 5.7. INCOME BY SOURCE,
AMERICAN ANTIQUARIAN SOCIETY, 1979–1993.**

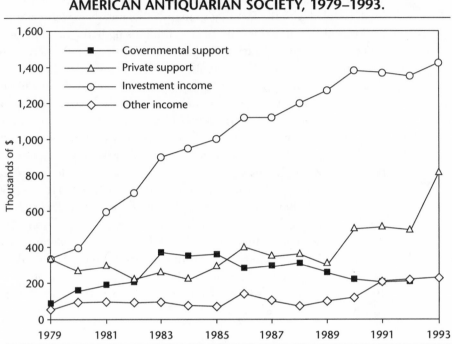

Source: Audited financial statements, American Antiquarian Society, 1979–1993.

Once again, the council found itself facing the proposition "sink or swim; treading water is not an option." To maintain funding for core operations, it was necessary to commit the society to renewed efforts to increase access for more diverse constituencies; this commitment, in turn, would have to bring in enough money for both the new programs and the old. In light of the society's history over the past thirty years, it is interesting to note that the council's analysis of the situation bears a striking resemblance to its perspective in the late 1960s:

> The Council generally continues to support the aggressive growth of the collections and the means of exploiting them for scholarly purposes. However, Councillors believe that the Society must make its resources more meaningful to a larger constituency if AAS is to attract the financial support it needs to move into the twenty-first century. The balancing of financial, intellectual, and emotional energies to continue our unique and excellent traditional services while mounting the "popular" initiatives will provide a severe test of the Society's ability to adapt to changing times and expectations.

Returning to the practice that it had followed from 1930 until 1967, the council decided that the roles of librarian and president could be filled best by two separate people. Nancy Hall Burkett, a member of the AAS staff since 1973, became the society's thirteenth librarian in 1991. For the president's position, the council chose Ellen S. Dunlap, director of the Rosenbach Museum and Library in Philadelphia. Dunlap took office toward the end of 1992.

In many ways, some symbolic and others substantive, these appointments represented a real transition for the society. First of all, Burkett and Dunlap are the first women to hold their positions. Second, Dunlap is the first president to come directly to that position from outside the society. Each of the three directors that preceded her served first as librarian, thus learning about the society and absorbing its culture. Third, Dunlap is the first president of the society to have prior administrative experience. Her appointment is a reflection of the general trend at these institutions toward greater professionalization at managerial levels.

Although it is still too early to assess the directions the society is taking under its new leadership, it appears to be continuing down fruitful paths. Dunlap has expressed her desire to continue the society's efforts in computerized cataloging, to increase access to the collections, and to broaden the set of individuals and institutions that support the society. In addition, major projects lie in the future, including an addition to or renovation of Antiquarian Hall and the long-term replacement of flat or declining government and foundation funds.

In retrospect, it appears that Marcus McCorison succeeded at two different tasks: first, he led the society through a period of growth, coinciding with the broader cultural tides of the 1960s and the 1970s. Second, unlike others who faltered, he was able to follow that period of growth with one of retrenchment and financial stabilization. (Of course, his willful overspending of the acquisitions budget was considerably less helpful, at least from a financial perspective.) At the other libraries in this book, these tasks have fallen to the new generation of chief executives who took office in the mid to late 1980s. The society will face many challenges in coming years; as a result of McCorison's prescient focus on endowment in the early 1980s, his successor will do so with a financial house that is largely in order.

Notes

1. Burkett and Hench (1992, p. 19).
2. Burkett and Hench (1992, p. 20).
3. Huntington and others (1925).
4. This and all further uncredited quotes and statistics in the chapter are taken from the society's annual reports, 1967–1991.
5. Emphasis in the original.
6. Because the society's fiscal year ends August 31, the events of October 1987 affected fiscal 1988.

PART TWO

THE DYNAMICS OF CHANGE

CHAPTER SIX

GROWTH IN EXPENDITURES AND PROGRAMS

The histories of the individual libraries are important in their own right. They are important, too, as the source of data that take on new meaning when we view them comparatively—our objective in Part Two of the study.

As is evident from the histories of the five libraries presented in Part One, total expenditures grew rapidly over the course of the past thirty-five years. Understanding the forces behind this growth is important because it was dramatic escalations in expenditures that put pressure on the libraries' endowments and led to recurring deficits and the associated dilemmas. Why did expenditures grow so rapidly? Were conscious choices made to expand, or did expenditures rise rapidly simply because of external waves that, in effect, washed over all of these libraries? Are there systemic characteristics of nonprofit entities that encourage growth? How well managed was the growth that occurred?

In the first section of this chapter, we compare trends in expenditures across the five libraries, identifying common patterns (and exceptions to the patterns), for the entire period under study and in subperiods. In the remaining sections of the chapter, we examine both the underlying forces pushing up expenditures at many nonprofits and considerations more specific to the independent research libraries.

The Statistical Record

Table 6.1 shows the average annual growth rates for expenditures at the five libraries for the whole period from the early 1960s through 1993. The figures are presented in both nominal and real dollars (calculated by using the implicit GDP

TABLE 6.1.   AVERAGE ANNUAL PERCENTAGE INCREASE
IN TOTAL EXPENDITURES, BY LIBRARY, 1960–1993.

	Nominal	Real
American Antiquarian Society	11.8	5.9
Folger Shakespeare Library	9.0	2.9
Huntington Library	8.1	2.4
Newberry Library	10.8	4.8
Pierpont Morgan Library	9.8	3.7
Average	9.9	3.9
Gross domestic product (GDP)	8.7	2.7

Source: Tabulations based on data in Appendix B.

Note: Folger data lacking for 1960–1963, 1966–1968, and 1971; Morgan data begin in 1963.

price deflator).[1] The average for all five libraries was 9.9 percent per year in nominal dollars and 3.9 percent per year in real dollars.

The detail in the table demonstrates the ubiquity of a phenomenon that was documented at length in the earlier part of this study: during the past thirty-five years, measured by total expenditures, each of the libraries in our set has grown markedly and, in all cases except one, appreciably more rapidly than the economy as a whole. The average annual growth in real GDP between 1960 and 1993 was 2.7 percent. The average for our five libraries was more than one-third greater: nearly 4 percent per year, ranging from a high of 5.9 percent for the AAS (over twice the growth rate for GDP) to 2.4 percent for the Huntington (the only library that grew at a slightly slower rate than the economy as a whole).

This is a remarkable record of sustained growth by any standard, over an extended period of time. But it is far from unusual in the nonprofit sector. A recent study of trends in expenditures among 32 arts and culture organizations from 1972 to 1992 found that expenditures increased at an average rate of 10.6 percent per year in nominal dollars and 4.5 percent in real dollars. The five historical societies in that sample (which are probably more similar to research libraries than most other nonprofits are) had average annual increases of 9.3 percent and 3.3 percent, in nominal and real terms, respectively—growth rates only slightly lower than those for the five libraries in this study.[2]

More refined patterns are revealed by the annual data assembled in Figures 6.1a and 6.1b, which, to facilitate comparisons, show total real expenditures at all five libraries indexed to 100 in 1964. (The base year was set at 1964, rather than 1960, because it is the first year that data are available for as many as four of the five libraries.) To understand major developments, it is helpful to examine three subperiods, which are demarcated by the vertical broken lines. Average annual growth rates in expenditures for each library, in each subperiod, are summarized in Table 6.2. We shall discuss Figures 6.1a and 6.1b and Table 6.2 together.

FIGURE 6.1A.   EXPENDITURES IN REAL DOLLARS, FOLGER, HUNTINGTON, AND MORGAN LIBRARIES, 1960–1993.

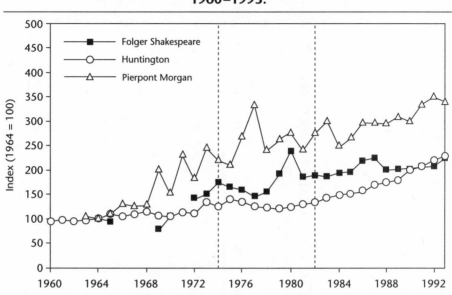

Source: Tabulations based on data in Appendix B.

FIGURE 6.1B.   EXPENDITURES IN REAL DOLLARS, AMERICAN ANTIQUARIAN SOCIETY AND NEWBERRY LIBRARY, 1960–1993.

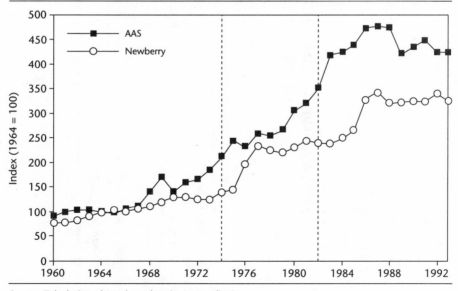

Source: Tabulations based on data in Appendix B.

TABLE 6.2. AVERAGE ANNUAL PERCENTAGE INCREASE IN TOTAL EXPENDITURES, BY LIBRARY AND SUBPERIOD, 1960–1993 (INDEX = 100).

	Nominal			Real		
	1960–1974	1974–1982	1982–1993	1960–1974	1974–1982	1982–1993
American Antiquarian Society	10.2	14.5	4.6	6.1	5.9	0.9
Folger Shakespeare Library	10.7	10.6	4.8	5.7	2.3	1.1
Huntington Library	6.0	8.0	8.8	2.1	-0.1	4.9
Newberry Library	8.1	15.5	6.9	4.1	6.8	3.1
Pierpont Morgan Library	13.3	10.1	6.2	8.3	1.8	2.4
Average	9.7	11.7	6.3	5.2	3.3	2.5
Gross domestic product (GDP)	8.2	10.7	6.5	3.4	2.4	2.7

Source: Tabulations based on data in Appendix B.

Note: Folger data lacking for 1960–1963, 1966–1968, and 1971; Morgan data begin in 1963.

During the first subperiod (1960–1974), only the Huntington grew less rapidly than the economy as a whole. Overall, this set of libraries experienced steady—and rapid—growth in expenditures. Their collective growth rate averaged 5.2 percent per year in real terms, as compared with 3.4 percent for the economy as a whole (more than a 50 percent differential).

In the second subperiod (1974–1982), there was a drop in the real growth rate for four of the five libraries—for three of them a dramatic drop. These three, the Folger, Huntington, and Morgan (shown in Figure 6.1a), dropped from an average of 5.3 percent real growth in the first period to only 1.3 percent in the second. In terms of conditions in the general economy, the nine years from 1974 to 1982 were far from favorable. The subperiod was marked by high inflation (averaging 8 percent per year), a rather stagnant economy, and poor performance in financial markets. This combination of conditions created difficulties for almost every type of organization, especially for ones heavily dependent on endowments and investment income. During the 1970s, these libraries, like other organizations, had to struggle to keep pace with skyrocketing energy costs; they also had to take at least some account of rapid escalations in the consumer price index in paying their staff. As a result, the rate of increase in *nominal* expenditures was far greater in this subperiod than in the previous one (nearly 12 percent overall), even though the real growth rate was, in general, substantially reduced.

One of the truly remarkable facts is that for two of the libraries, the AAS and the Newberry, real growth continued unabated. To be sure, the picture for the Newberry is mixed, with extremely rapid growth through 1977 combined with flat growth for the balance of the subperiod. The AAS, however, is a true exception: its growth continued at a rapid rate throughout all of the 1970s and up until 1983. As we will see in the next chapter, both the early, very large spurt of growth at the Newberry and the more sustained growth at AAS were attributable in no small part to special factors—prominent among which were grants by the National Endowment for the Humanities. This infusion of funds had a particularly large relative impact at the AAS, which is the smallest of the five libraries in terms of budget.

Growth in expenditures at all of these libraries hit a plateau at one point or another in the 1970s, the exact timing depending on circumstances specific to each, as shortfalls in revenues compelled austerity measures. By the late 1970s to mid 1980s, growth resumed, although generally at a more modest rate than earlier.

In the most recent period (1982—1993), growth rates continued to decline, or remained low, for most of the libraries. For the first time, the five-library average fell below average growth in GDP. Even the Newberry, which continued to grow rapidly through the early 1980s, reached a second plateau beginning in 1988. The AAS in particular reversed its earlier trend and experienced practically no real growth during the 1980s. The exception in this period was the Huntington. Following a period of declining real expenditures in the 1970s (the only library in Table 6.2 to show negative real growth), it rebounded with an average annual growth rate of nearly 5 percent, which has since shown no sign of abating. The situation of the

Huntington notwithstanding, the general picture at the end of the period covered by this statistical analysis is one of slower growth and greater stability.

Baumol's Disease

Broadly speaking, there are only two possible explanations for an increase in expenditures. The most obvious one is that the organization has expanded its activities. For example, a library may begin new programs and services that require additional staff and larger facilities. However, even if the output of an organization remains constant, the cost of producing that output is likely to rise. This section explains why this is almost always the case at research libraries—and, for that matter, in much of the nonprofit sector. Then, the next section discusses the kinds of programmatic expansions that have taken place at all five of the libraries included in this study.

There are powerful forces that drive unit costs upward in any labor-intensive entity. Most nonprofit organizations, including research libraries, provide services that are, by their very nature, highly labor-intensive. This is why cost increases are so ubiquitous. The culprit is known as *Baumol's disease*.[3] Central to an understanding of Baumol's disease is recognition of the fact that productivity grows at a faster rate in sectors of the economy whose output does not depend heavily on labor as an essential input (such as automobile manufacturing), as compared to others in which labor inputs dominate (for example, dance performances or teaching).

Baumol and his coauthors term the former outputs "progressive" and the latter "stagnant." They explain the key relationships by citing two activities,

> one highly progressive, say, the manufacture of watches, and one extremely stagnant, say, harpsichord performance. We have data indicating that before the introduction of the revolutionary quartz watch, labor productivity in watchmaking had risen almost exactly a hundredfold since the time that Domenico Scarlatti was composing his harpsichord works (circa 1700). But, of course, neither the labor time nor the amount of equipment required to play one of those pieces has fallen one iota since the day they were written.
>
> With the aid of these two examples it is easy to show the logic of the first of our conclusions—that the persistently more stagnant of two activities must also rise persistently in cost and price. The reason is that the more progressive activity constantly uses less and less input per unit of its output. The stagnant output does not, or at best does so to a far lesser degree. If, then, both activities must pay the same wage rate and the same prices for other inputs, it follows that the relative cost and price of the progressive output must fall, or put the other way, that those of the stagnant output must rise. If, in the year 1700, one watch required as much labor as 100 harpsichord performances, the watch would have been correspondingly more expensive than a performance. But by,

say, 1960, when watch productivity had risen a hundredfold, the cost of a watch and a concert would have been about the same. This means that in these 260 years the price of concert tickets must have risen about a hundred times as fast as the price of a watch, if both their costs were to be covered.[4]

Research libraries clearly fall into Baumol's stagnant category because of their labor-intensive nature. At their core, research libraries are responsible for organizing, preserving, and making available their holdings. Libraries that also have an active in-house research staff can claim the "production" of scholarship as another function. Each of these activities is labor-intensive. Cataloging, especially of rare books, is a slow and time-consuming process; every page must be checked for annotation, the book's provenance must be established, and all distinguishing marks must be noted. Conservation, too, requires painstaking hands-on effort. "Paging"—the act of getting books down off the shelves and delivering them to researchers—can obviously be done only one book at a time. And it goes without saying that the conduct of scholarship itself, as well as providing assistance to other scholars, is labor-intensive. (This is precisely the lesson that Max Farrand taught Henry Huntington.) Most of these activities require the work of skilled professionals, whose salary levels must be kept at least roughly comparable with the pay of compatriots in other sectors.

Moreover, every single book that is added to the collection means more work. There are few economies of scale: twice as many books means twice as many catalog cards, twice as much shelf space, and more time involved in finding books for scholars. It is a great mistake to think of books merely as conventional "assets"; they also carry with them substantial "liabilities" in that they must be cared for— permanently.

The quantitative impact of Baumol's disease depends on the extent to which organizations such as research libraries raise their salaries in line with trends elsewhere in the economy. Unfortunately, we lack sufficient data to make precise comparisons. We suspect, however, that the full impact of Baumol's disease was reduced at these research libraries by restraints on salary increases. Because there is mobility between sectors of the economy, holding down salaries can only slow the onslaught of Baumol's disease; it cannot prevent it. That is, there is a limit on the size of the "penalty" that staff members in libraries can be expected to pay for the privilege of working at these organizations; ultimately, failure to keep pace with general salary trends will both harm morale and impede efforts to replace departing staff.[5] Also, as we will note later, the explosive increase in higher education during the 1960s led to a general increase in the demand for librarians, which increased pressures to raise salaries at these libraries quite directly.

In considering the likely impact of Baumol's disease, one must also remember that the muted impact of salary increases has been offset to some degree by other factors. During the past few decades, serial prices and acquisition costs (especially rare book prices and the costs of reference materials) have risen at a faster rate than prices in general.[6] This is another instance of a cost increase that it is difficult, if not impossible, for libraries to offset by productivity improvements. Although it is often argued that computerization should offer opportunities to raise productivity and reduce costs in libraries, experience to date indicates that this powerful technology has served mainly to allow libraries to do more things more effectively—but at a higher cost.[7]

How much of the overall increase in expenditures at the five libraries has been due to Baumol's disease and how much to expansionary tendencies? To answer this question confidently, we would need to measure increases in the output produced by the libraries so that we could track increases in unit costs. Unfortunately, this is a near-impossible task. The audited statements from which most of our financial data are taken contain only aggregated totals. Even if one were to return to the archives in search of finer-grained data, the fact is that each possible measure of output—reader-days, books bought, books paged, questions answered— is imperfect because it captures only part of what an independent research library does. Furthermore, such measures are flawed because they lack standardization; for example, all reader-days are not equal.[8]

Still, rough conjectures are possible. A starting point is the proposition that labor-intensive organizations will experience increases in unit costs that are greater than the overall rate of inflation (which is a kind of weighted average of increases in costs in progressive and stagnant industries, to use Baumol's terminology). In higher education, it has been estimated that over long periods, costs tend to rise roughly two percentage points faster than the general price level.[9] In the case of the research libraries, the corresponding rate of increase may have been slightly lower because of the restraints on salary increases noted earlier; it seems reasonable, as a very rough estimate, to surmise that Baumol's disease may have increased the rate of growth in expenditures at research libraries by something like one percentage point above the general inflationary trend.

The essential point is that even in a no-growth situation, in which there is absolutely no expansion in a library's function, the cost of its activities will inevitably increase—and at a rate that is at least somewhat above the general inflationary trend. The significance of this phenomenon, even in a well-run organization, is not commonly appreciated. Independent research libraries seeking only to maintain the programmatic status quo must increase their income on an annual basis in keeping with their "internal inflation rate," which is often higher than the economywide rate of inflation. In short, they are consigned to live on a rather fast treadmill.

Programmatic Expansion

In understanding growth in expenditures, input prices are a major part of the story—but only part of it. For the three decades covered by the data in Table 6.1, we estimate that a combination of general inflation and Baumol's disease led to average annual increases in nominal expenditures of perhaps 7 percent per year. Because total expenditures rose 10 percent per year, on average, the implication is that programmatic expansion raised costs at an average annual rate of about 3 percent.

This empirical estimate, although imprecise, is entirely consistent with known developments. It is an indisputable fact that substantial programmatic expansion took place at all five of the libraries in the past three decades. During this period, the independent research libraries transformed themselves from essentially private, clubby institutions with small, exclusive clienteles to more open institutions, actively involved in a broad range of scholarly programs and in public outreach. This section examines five different forces underlying that transformation: a growing demand for scholarly materials stimulated by an extraordinary expansion in higher education in all fields, including the humanities; an increase in scholarly activity within the libraries themselves; the increasing pressures for democratization (including broader access to collections and outreach) that characterized the 1970s; additional spending for support staff, including development offices; and the need to renovate and add space that followed from all of the other developments. We will not, however, attempt to estimate the fractions of the increases in programmatic activities due to each of these variables. We will consider, at the end of the chapter, more general questions: Did the directors and trustees of these libraries have a real choice to make? Or were the underlying forces so strong that the only option was to expand?

Increased Demand for Scholarly Materials

The unprecedented expansion of higher education in the 1960s affected all forms of scholarly activity and all educational institutions. Developments in the humanities are of particular relevance to this study. Enrollments in humanities courses and departments swelled, as did the number of faculty and the number of degrees conferred, both bachelor's and doctorates.[10] Growth in the humanities had two consequences for the independent research libraries. First, because demand for use of the libraries' collections comes primarily from scholars and academics (and historically was limited to them), growth in humanities departments had a direct effect on demand for library services.

There was also an increased demand by many institutions for librarians, which put extra pressure on salaries for professionals in all library-related fields. As higher education expanded, demand for library services increased at existing campuses; simultaneously, the creation of new schools, including community colleges and satellite campuses, meant new libraries. The rapid escalation in demand for library professionals translated into new positions and rising salaries. According to one study, the total personnel at fifty-eight university research libraries grew at an average annual rate of 5.3 percent between 1950–51 and 1968–69; over that same period, salaries and wages increased at an average annual rate of 9.7 percent.[11] At colleges and universities, rapid increases in tuition revenues, combined with other sources of income, made it possible to hire more people and to pay higher salaries. The independent research libraries felt the increased demand too, but they had no access to tuition revenues, to a large body of successful alumni, or to sponsored research funds. They were ill prepared to deal with the demands created by this new environment.

Increased Scholarly Activity

Programmatic expansion also took the form of increased scholarly programming within these libraries. In tracing the development of active support for scholarship by the independent research libraries, it is useful to posit a spectrum of activities, with short-term, one-time individual fellowships at one end and permanent centers for organized research, idea sharing, and dissemination at the other. Over time, the libraries in our set have moved along this spectrum, becoming more deeply involved in scholarship itself rather than simply enabling it by providing books and reference materials.

A common first step was the development of a fellowship program. Such programs brought individuals to the libraries to do research and helped them defray the related costs. The Huntington was the first to have such a program, which built on the work of the permanent research staff. When Louis B. Wright left to assume the directorship of the Folger, he instituted a fellowship program there as well. The Newberry began to award fellowships in the 1940s, under the leadership of Stanley Pargellis. At the American Antiquarian Society, Marcus McCorison created a modest fellowship program around 1970. Because such programs preserved the normal library paradigm of individual scholars sitting at carrels working on their own projects, they were an easy first step away from the more passive repository model.

Other activities—publications, lectures, and conferences—reflected a broader commitment to furthering scholarship by a wide range of people. These activities went beyond research to the dissemination of the fruits of scholarship, whether in written or oral form. Publications were considered from the beginning to be an important part of the Huntington's mission and were viewed similarly at the AAS. Conferences were held at the Newberry beginning in the 1950s. The Folger sponsored a series of occasional lectures that all staff could attend, regardless of position.

A still more fundamental step toward institutionalization of active support for scholarship consisted of the establishment of new centers (or institutes or programs, depending on the library). Many were created in collaboration with surrounding entities, such as smaller colleges that did not have access to state-of-the-art research facilities of their own. The Newberry's cooperation with the Associated Colleges of the Midwest, the AAS's work with five colleges in the Worcester area, and the Folger's Institute for Renaissance Studies are all examples of this approach. Other notable examples of long-term, quasi-permanent institutionalized programs are the Newberry's centers and the AAS's Program in the History of the Book in America. The sequence of these developments in research libraries forms an interesting contrast with the sequence in universities. Universities developed in this country primarily as places for teaching—they built research collections later to facilitate learning and scholarship. The independent research libraries, by contrast, started out as research collections and then came to emulate some of the other functions of universities.

The independent research libraries increased their commitment to scholarship in yet another way—by broadening access to their collections. In large part, this was a result of the broad interest in "democratization" during the 1960s and 1970s, which we discuss in detail in the next section. Here we should comment on a related development: the increased use of documentary reproduction, first photographically, later using microfilm, and most recently via computers.

These technological advances have contributed enormously to wider use of the collections but also to increased pressure on budgets. In earlier times, constraints on who could conduct research in a given discipline were tighter. Advanced students of English history, for instance, generally had the options of going to the Huntington, to the Folger, or to England. With the advent of duplicative technologies, copies could be made of entire collections, which could then be disseminated widely among college and university libraries. Thus, to take one example, the various "papers" projects—of presidents, the nation's founders, and others—contributed to the broad dissemination of materials that were previously inaccessible to all but a select few. The availability of such materials has changed the face of scholarship, for today graduate students at almost any leading university can work in their own libraries with a wide range of primary source materials, especially in well-developed fields such as English and American history and literature. Thus the new technologies provided a means whereby these specialized libraries could serve a much broader constituency. But these new opportunities were not cost-free.

In an interesting twist, the ready technical ability to copy primary source materials has diminished the institutions' importance as "sole repositories" at the same time that it has furthered their basic missions. To illustrate, the Readex Microprint Series reproduced the AAS's entire collection of American imprints from 1640 to 1815. On the one hand, this meant that fewer scholars needed to go to the AAS; on the other hand, these materials are now available to scholars everywhere, thus furthering the society's broader interest in the preservation and dissemination of American history.

Computers have played a similar role. Every one of these five libraries has spent considerable amounts of money on computerization of aspects of their collections. Most of the work done thus far has consisted of cataloging materials and establishing on-line linkages. Such steps have increased knowledge of the various libraries' holdings, which has in turn brought more users. In the future, the capacity to create and transmit digital images may have far more profound effects on access to library collections—but there are substantial economic issues to be confronted. It will not be easy to obtain the resources needed to take advantage of what is possible technically or to find the most appropriate ways of sharing costs and setting prices.

Pressures for Democratization: The Urgent Dogtrot

Innovative and substantial as it was, the shift to more active modes of scholarship was consonant with the missions of the independent research libraries as traditionally understood. The pressure for democratization—and the attendant public expansion that took place during the 1970s—was more of a departure from the past. It was stimulated in large part by broader societal forces that demanded new access to governmental, cultural, and educational institutions. Given their histories, the independent research libraries were particularly susceptible to accusations of being elitist, closed institutions. It was extremely difficult for them to resist pressures for more openness—nor did the leaders of these institutions necessarily have any desire to do so. At the same time, facing other needs and other pressures on expenditures, these libraries were forced to seek new sources of funding to pay for "outreach." Many programmatic steps were taken in an effort to seem more attractive to individual donors, foundations, corporations, and government agencies.

The evolution—which is what it was—in the attitudes of these libraries toward the broader public has been described well by one of the architects of the changes that occurred: O. B. Hardison, director of the Folger Library from 1969 to 1984. Of the Morgan, the Huntington, and the Folger in their early years, Hardison wrote: "For much of their histories, they were as close to being ivory towers as any institutions in the United States—so close that they were often accused of just this crime not only by the public, but by many scholars who felt excluded from them." Hardison went on to outline the initial shift into "the arena" that occurred in the 1950s and 1960s, noting the introduction of seminars, public lectures, and symposia. He then addressed the search for funding that a commitment to meeting this demand entailed, coining in the process the phrase incorporated in the title of this section: "Toward the end of the sixties, what had been a genteel stroll toward the arena turned into an urgent dogtrot. Economic pressures were mounting rapidly. They consisted of inflation, stagnant endowment income, increased demands for service, new technologies, and increased usage."[12]

It is important to note once again distinctions among the libraries in our set. Each library responded in different ways to the pressures for outreach, reflecting its particular capabilities. The Folger, the Huntington, and the Morgan relied on traditional ways of appealing to broad audiences: welcoming visitors to museum exhibits, gardens, and theater productions. The Newberry and the AAS lacked these mechanisms and therefore had to find new ways of creating a public face.

The Morgan's primary mode of outreach was and is its museum. Since the 1970s, the Morgan has offered more exhibits, tours, and interpretative lectures. However, because the museum has been from the start an integral part of the institution, the perceived purposes of the Morgan Library have remained essentially the same. Whether the newly expanded Morgan will differ is unanswerable at present, but Charles Pierce has intimated that it very well may: "The Garden Court also makes an important public statement through the language of architecture, and therefore achieves something more. A metaphor for the guiding principle behind the expansion program, the sunlit, glass atrium communicates our desire to open and make more accessible this institution, its magnificent holdings, and the pleasure and learning they promote."[13]

The Huntington was similarly fortunate when it sought to expand its public activities because both its art galleries and its gardens had drawn hundreds of thousands of visitors ever since the institution opened to the public. Even though its Policies Statement placed research at the head of the Huntington's diverse agenda, the public saw things differently; the musty world of the research library was invisible to most visitors. Apparently, at least some of the trustees felt the same way. Louis B. Wright recalled that one trustee "professed complete disdain for the research program, saw no reason to pay scholars to do research, [and] scoffed at the notion of buying 'a lot of trash' (meaning photostats, reference books, and pamphlet literature). He wanted to use the funds to buy more pictures for the art gallery."[14]

Under James Thorpe, the Huntington changed the way it interacted with its visitors, making a visit less like a tour of a wealthy man's estate and more of an edifying, or at least informative, experience. In 1971, public programs were begun, including performances of music or scenes from plays, dramatic readings, and gallery or garden talks. There were guided tours, printed booklets for self-guided tours, and educational programs for schoolchildren. The scale of this expansion in activities is remarkable in light of the fact that the Huntington's expenditures grew slowly in real terms during the 1970s. In his memoirs, Thorpe recalled that "all these increases in services were accomplished with only about a ten percent increase in the paid staff. The secret was the great increase in the volunteer staff during these years, when their numbers doubled, to more than four hundred. They did the things that we could not otherwise have possibly done, from pruning roses to repairing rare books."[15]

Public outreach efforts sometimes represented a departure from an institution's traditional activities and led to controversy. The best (and best-documented) example is the use of the Folger's theater for productions. Although nothing might seem more logical than the idea of an institution devoted to Shakespeare mounting plays, the long-standing perception of the Folger's leadership prior to the 1970s was that the theater was there as an exhibit and that it would be both impracticable and financially draining to put on productions. The function of the theater has engendered conflict and strong feelings on the part of at least the last three Folger directors: Louis B. Wright, O. B. Hardison, and Werner Gundersheimer. Their varied views, and the consequent fate of the small (250-seat) theater, have followed something of a dialectical process that is illustrative of changing times and missions.

Wright's thesis, which he stated repeatedly in his reports to the Amherst trustees, is summarized here in his own words: "Thoughtless visitors were constantly remarking: 'What a lovely little theater! Why don't you have Shakespearean plays here?' Folger had never dreamed of encroaching on library time, library energy, or library expense by using the little period room as a living theater. . . . Actually, as anyone knows, the effort to produce plays and run a library within the same small physical structure would mean a devastating encroachment on the library's facilities and the staff's energies and time—not to mention the drain on the budget."[16] Wright was a product of his times. Independent research libraries were seen as the preserve of the advanced scholar, and any distraction from a central research agenda was just that: a distraction.

O. B. Hardison felt differently, and the Folger Theater Group was in many respects the centerpiece of the Folger's outreach efforts during his tenure. Part of this centrality was due to the public relations value of a theater, but the outreach program was more than just a way of garnering publicity. Hardison believed that productions represented a legitimate interpretation of the founders' wishes. The following passage in *The Widening Circle*, a book prepared during his administration, makes this point: "A Shakespeare memorial without live drama? Not according to Henry Clay and Emily Jordan Folger, who provided their Library with an Elizabethan theater and the dressing rooms, lighting equipment, and backstage space necessary to mount productions."[17]

It is particularly interesting to note that both of these perspectives were framed as legitimate representations of the founders' wishes. Although there was pressure on the institution to change and to increase its public outreach, no one wished to be seen as betraying an established mission by moving too far afield. Both Wright and Hardison managed to argue their cases without seeming to threaten other purposes.

The subsequent history of the theater confirmed Wright's fiscal concerns. This is not to say that the theater was unimportant, just that it could not be supported within the financial framework of the library. The solution reached in the first year of Werner Gundersheimer's administration—reconstituting the theater group as an independent entity—was controversial at the time, but it has proved both Wright and Hardison correct. Although the theater could not function effectively within the financial structure of the library, it has since achieved both artistic and financial success operating on its own, as the library has.

The American Antiquarian Society, which has the longest tradition of emphasizing scholarship, did not really engage in public outreach programs per se.

The Huntington had gardens, the Morgan had a museum, and the Folger had a theater. The AAS had no such venue to exploit, and there is still no category in its audited statements labeled "public activities." The Newberry developed along similar lines; its programs for the public are of a scholarly kind and consist primarily of educational courses and lectures.

Growth in Support Services

Another form of expansion that took place during these years can hardly be called public, and yet it was a direct consequence of the expansion of public activities. As the independent research libraries grew, they required increasingly elaborate support services. In earlier years, the director and the trustees handled the administrative aspects of the library, with time usually left over for research. The proliferation of new programs and the need to raise money meant that it was no longer possible for a single individual to handle all the administrative details. Larger scale and greater complexity led to increases in staff, as well as to more sophisticated management systems.

The existence of fundraising departments is a fairly recent development and a good illustration of this component of increased expenditures. The Newberry was the first to move into annual fundraising, following the purchase of the Louis Silver collection in 1964. In 1966, the Huntington followed suit, suggesting in its annual report that gifts would be appreciated. All of these efforts were somewhat ad hoc, however, and did not involve professional development staff. The first library to hire a professional development officer was the AAS, in 1968. Whether it was first because it was relatively less well-off or because it recognized coming problems earlier is not clear. The Huntington hired its first development officer around 1970, and the Newberry did not hire one until 1975, when it embarked on its massive Campaign for the Newberry Library. The Morgan's 1960 capital campaign had a "secretary," but a full-time development officer was not hired until much later. The Folger set up its Development Office in 1972.

These steps represented the institutionalization of a new reality, the need to rely on external funding year in and year out. Even though most of the development officers were hired initially for capital campaigns, their work soon came to include annual fundraising as well. In recent years, the development offices at the various libraries have been expanded even further, based on the time-honored (yet oft-abused) axiom "It takes money to make money." These staffing increases have often followed the arrival of new directors, who arrived knowing that fundraising was an important part of their job.

There is clearly an institutional learning curve when it comes to fundraising. Some libraries, particularly the Huntington and the Newberry, had difficulty finding a professional development officer who met their expectations. Such difficulties may be related to the missions and activities of these libraries, which cannot be marketed easily and are not always interesting to the layperson. Also, the scholarly environment and genteel approach to financial matters that traditionally characterized the independent research libraries did not always fit well with the "money culture" that development officers represented.

The more recent increases in fundraising expenditures are reflective of another shift in institutional orientations. Raising money was seen initially as a regrettable concession to the unfortunate realities of the times and in some ways below the dignity of such august institutions. Development efforts have now been accepted as essential on an ongoing basis, and the more skillful development offices have become an integral part of their organizations.

The increased complexity of management and control systems has also led to growth in support services. As outside funding grew in significance, the need increased for accountability and stewardship reporting. Also, increased financial pressures and the need to curb deficits led to tighter fiscal controls. One consequence has been increased reliance on computerization, which has improved budgeting and the monitoring of expenditures.

For all of the reasons given, expenditures on support services increased significantly under the new leaders who arrived during the late 1980s and early 1990s. They were expected to manage their enterprises with precision and to be held accountable. In addition, the libraries themselves were now much more complex than they had been in earlier years. Several of them had simply outgrown their administrative control mechanisms—as well as the ad hoc approach to fundraising that had sufficed in earlier days. On essentially all administrative fronts, there was more to be done.

Space Needs

A more substantial set of financial pressures affected all of these libraries: those associated with space. At the most basic level—admittedly a gross understatement—a library is a warehouse. A research library is one step more advanced: it is a warehouse with a reading room attached. Over time, the number of books stored in the warehouse increases, and the amount of space must increase accordingly. Similarly, changing (more ambitious) programmatic objectives, involving a broader range of activities and greater access to collections, require additional space—and in some instances, new kinds of space that will appeal to a visiting public. Although physical modifications and expansion imply additional capital outlays—to pay for added space or the renovation of existing premises—the financial ramifications go well beyond the costs of construction. The implications for operating costs are all too real. First, if debt financing is involved, the interest charges are evident and immediate. And if the institution borrows from its own endowment, there are the opportunity costs involved in forgoing some amount of investment income. The longer-term costs of operating and maintaining the space are generally most significant of all.

Like the endowments, which, as we discuss in Chapter Eight, could not keep place with the libraries' rapidly evolving needs, the physical plants at the various independent research libraries were designed to handle neither the incredible growth in the collections nor the programmatic expansion that followed. The AAS's original building was as much of a museum as it was a library. Even its third building, built in 1910, was outgrown during Clarence Brigham's tenure as librarian. The Huntington, Morgan, and Folger were built to hold personal collections that were relatively static; even when room was left for new materials, it was exhausted quickly by the early librarians.

The Newberry's architectural history is especially interesting in that it had the advantage of having been built for the public as well as for scholars. William Poole, the Newberry's first librarian, was a leader in the effort to move library design away from traditionalism and toward functionalism. The older type of design, in which there were great circular halls with books around the sides, had its roots in the monasteries and abbeys of Europe. Poole criticized it as follows: "Why library architecture should have been yoked to ecclesiastical architecture, and the two have been made to walk down the ages *pari passu,* is not obvious, unless it be that librarians in the past needed this stimulus to their religious emotions. The present state of piety in the profession renders the union no longer necessary, and it is time that a bill was filed for divorce."[18] Ironically, Poole's own alternative—a series of subject-related rooms with all of the relevant books on the adjacent shelves—did not work much better. Increased awareness of preservation concerns and security needs, along with other factors, made Poole's model obsolete. It was only in the 1980s that the Newberry adopted the bookstack and reading room model that is standard today.

The growth in scholarly use, the development or expansion of public programs, and the ever-growing numbers of books and research materials that marked the 1960s and 1970s transformed the libraries into much larger institutions. At various points in the 1970s and 1980s, each of the libraries in our set engaged in expansion or renovation of the physical plant. Most of the expansions were designed in part to add space that had never before been needed: rooms for meetings, conferences, and symposia, additional offices for larger support staffs, and so forth. The time, planning, and especially money that went into those expansions marked the institutionalization of the libraries' evolution from private to public institutions. Fellowship programs can be curtailed and public performances canceled; a building, however, represents a more permanent commitment.

Was Expansion Inevitable?

Some of the factors driving up expenditures, like Baumol's disease, could not have been avoided under any circumstances. Nor could these libraries have hoped to be spared the economic crises of the late 1970s and early 1980s. But could the pressures for programmatic expansion have been resisted? Could the directors of the libraries, many of whom were strong, charismatic leaders, have simply said no and maintained the programmatic status quo? Could they have thereby avoided some of the resulting financial problems?

One relevant piece of context is that the cost increases of the 1960s and the 1970s, combined with sharp increases in the demand for traditional services, were more than the libraries' endowments could support in any event. Because the libraries in our set had never drawn substantial funds from any other source, they faced an obvious choice. One option was to attempt to maintain the traditional size and scale of the library's operations and to continue to rely almost exclusively on endowment income, even if that meant leaving some of the new demand for services unfilled. The opposite choice was to try to meet the increased demand and to seek additional funding as necessary.

In light of the libraries' histories and missions, the first option—holding the level of services steady (or, more likely, cutting back, given the pressures on costs)—was extremely unpalatable. By the 1960s, these libraries had come to view their role in the scholarly community not just as passive repositories but as active participants in the search for and dissemination of knowledge. This role was embraced most fully by the Huntington and the AAS, which were given this charge by their founders. The Newberry as well had emphasized from its earliest days the importance of educational activities. Even the Folger, which until 1948 was essentially a repository, had by the 1960s become an active research library. The Morgan's case differs because until quite recently, it was more a museum than a library.

If any of these institutions had failed to expand their services (never mind cut back), they would surely have been criticized severely. Independent research libraries have long been perceived as exclusive, if not elitist entities. Throughout most of their histories, they were supported more or less exclusively through their endowments; they often limited use of their collections to the "right" individuals, including those holding Ph.D.'s; and they drew their trustees and supporters from society's upper echelons. At the same time, their collections are widely understood to be of central importance in many fields of scholarly endeavor. Because their holdings are so important, "exclusive" policies were bound to lead to criticism and even hostility. In 1969, the independent research libraries had to fight efforts to classify them as private foundations, with the stricter tax requirements that would have followed. If services had been curtailed, it is likely that a hue and cry would have been raised by scholars and other users of the collections because in many cases, important and otherwise inaccessible materials would have been removed from the scholarly universe known to many potential users.

Although endowed institutions do not have to respond to external opinions in the same way that organizations that are dependent on gifts and admissions do, both scholarly and public opinion still matter. Trustees generally do not like to be perceived as impeding progress. Few trustees would have felt comfortable presiding over an institution that was stagnating or declining. It is also highly unlikely that the staff at the various libraries, which consisted mostly of scholars and library professionals, would have accepted a conscious institutional decision to retreat from what they perceived as the scholarly frontier.

Of course, the existence of such clear-cut choices may not have been as apparent at the time as it is in hindsight; a third choice might have been simply to muddle through, trying to limit growth so as to maintain a more or less constant level of operations within the constraints of the existing funding structure. However, the inexorable manner in which costs rise and the extent to which society's expectations have changed (and continue to change) made it then—and make it now—very difficult to pursue such a strategy.

The Huntington is perhaps the best example of an institution that tried to muddle through, doing more while retaining its original funding pattern. Although none of the Huntington's staff would have said that they were doing less (in fact, the opposite is true), the fact is that during the 1960s and 1970s, growth in expenditures at the Huntington was less rapid than at any other library in our set. Ultimately, however, even the Huntington chose the path of expansion; twenty-five years of attempting to maintain traditional funding patterns exhausted the reserves and brought the institution to the point where the choice between growth and decline was inescapable.

In the end, all five libraries chose growth. As a result, each faced the need to achieve a fundamental restructuring of its funding pattern—to accomplish a veritable transformation that has not proved easy for any of the libraries. For some, it has been as much a leap of faith as anything else. And it is to the implications for funding that we turn in the next chapter.

Notes

1. It should be recognized explicitly that "real" increases exaggerate the extent of increases in programmatic activity because of the tendency for unit costs in labor-intensive fields to rise more rapidly than the general price level. (See the discussion in the second section of this chapter.) This problem notwithstanding, we generally use real growth rates in the text; however, there are periods (for example, the 1974–1982 subperiod) when real growth rates can be understood only by looking simultaneously at the nominal figures.

   It should also be noted that the fiscal years for the libraries differ somewhat, and as a result, specific year-to-year comparisons are imperfect.

2. Bowen, Nygren, Turner, and Duffy (1994, chap. 10 and tab. G.10–2). If it had been possible to begin the analysis of the data for the group of historical societies in the early 1960s (rather than in 1972), it is likely that the corresponding rates of increase would have been even closer together. Real growth was especially rapid in the 1960s for the independent libraries and, we would surmise, for many other nonprofits as well, including historical societies.

3. The hypothesis was originally developed by Baumol and Bowen (1966) in their study of the performing arts. It has also been called *Bowen's law* when applied in higher education; see Clark Kerr's foreword to Bowen (1968).

4. Baumol, Blackman, and Wolff (1989, pp. 124–125).
5. See on page 104 Marcus McCorison's poignant comments on the problems created by doing too little for staff.
6. Between 1963 and 1990, the price of periodicals increased at an average annual rate of 11.3 percent, compared to an average rate of 6.1 percent for the GDP deflator (Cummings and others, 1992, chap. 6).
7. See Cummings and others (1992, pt. 2).
8. These difficulties of quantification are as serious a problem for major universities as for independent research libraries. The Mellon Foundation is sponsoring a major new study by Professor Charles Clotfelter of Duke University that is intended (among other things) to disentangle rising unit costs from increases in output at selected universities and colleges.
9. Bowen (1968, p. 10).
10. Bowen and Rudenstine (1992, pp. 24–28, 81–85) and Turner and Bowen (1990).
11. Baumol and Marcus (1973, p. 7, tab. 1.3).
12. Hardison (1979, p. 38).
13. Pierce (1993, p. 3).
14. Wright (1976, p. 94).
15. Thorpe, (1994, p. 8).
16. Wright (1976, p. 141).
17. Kane (1976, p. 61).
18. Williamson (1963, p. 154).

CHAPTER SEVEN

THE EMERGENCE OF NEW FUNDING PATTERNS

The organizational transformations that took place over the past thirty-five years have been reflected in significant shifts in the revenue profiles of the independent research libraries. The purposes of this chapter are to describe the evolution that has occurred, the reasons for it, and its implications. We shall continue to note differences among the libraries, but the commonalities are what dominate when we examine the pronounced shifts that have occurred in the relative importance of different sources of revenue.

The most dramatic change, evident in the histories of all five libraries, is a decided movement away from near-complete reliance on endowment income. These libraries have been transformed from *income spenders* into *fund seekers*, in that they must now search constantly, sometimes under insistent pressure, for means by which to balance their budgets.

The choice of words in the preceding paragraph and in this chapter's title is deliberate. It is intended to highlight the distinction between income and funding. Income connotes gain, or revenue, whereas funding presupposes a liability that must be paid for. When they were founded, and indeed until the 1960s, the libraries in our set had a great deal of income in relation to their needs: the returns on the endowment were there to be spent, and at the end of the year, there was usually some money left over. Since that time, they have become institutions that spend considerably more money than is generated by the returns on their endowments, and each year, they must gather together the resources needed to fund their obligations. This shift from income spending to fund seeking has led to a host of changes in organizational life, ranging from governance to financial control systems and from programmatic initiatives to the principles and policies involved in managing endowments.

Basic Funding Patterns: Continued Reliance on Contributed Income

Before describing changes in funding patterns, we need to underscore a central characteristic of independent research libraries both "then" and "now." These institutions have always been, and will always be, dependent on income that is *contributed* in one form or another (either as endowment income, reflecting past donations, or as current giving). In this respect, they are near one end of a continuum within the nonprofit sector. Many other types of charitable nonprofits, especially "service providers," rely much more heavily on earned income. Over 70 percent of the total revenue of the typical college, for instance, comes from tuition payments made by students and their families; organizations like hospitals and daycare centers are heavily dependent on fee income; and the typical performing arts organization earns roughly half of its income at the box office, with theaters often earning an appreciably higher share of their total revenues.[1]

For the five independent libraries in this study, earned income has averaged between 10 and 15 percent of total income. The pattern is evident in Figure 7.1, which is based on "snapshots" for 1981–1983 and 1991–1993.[2] The range is from a low of roughly 5 percent (the AAS and the Newberry in 1981–1983) to a high of around 20 percent (the Folger in both subperiods and the Huntington in 1991–1993). In the last section of this chapter, we examine the types of earned income in more detail. Our point here is that even in recent years, when considerable efforts were being made to generate more earned income, the share of revenues from this source has remained low.

The pattern for these five libraries is quite typical of the larger universe of organizations of a similar type. For example, the earned-income share in 1988 was about 8 percent for the median historical society, while median earned income was 13 percent for art museums (higher for larger museums) and 20 percent for "other" (nonscience) museums.[3] Among our libraries, the AAS and the Newberry are most like historical societies, and their earned-income shares correspond quite closely to the median for that group of institutions; the Folger, the Morgan, and the Huntington, by contrast, have some of the attributes of museums, and it is not surprising, therefore, that their income shares are at least slightly higher—more like those for the museums.

Why do independent research libraries derive such a small share of their revenues from earned income? The reason is rooted in the basic characteristics of the "output" that they produce. An understanding of the economic implications of these characteristics helps explain why the libraries started out as endowed institutions and why the need for continued patronage exists today.

FIGURE 7.1. EARNED INCOME AS A PERCENTAGE OF TOTAL INCOME, BY LIBRARY, 1981–1983 AND 1991–1993.

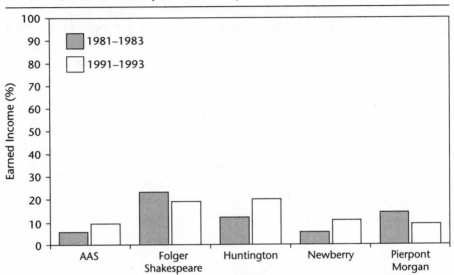

Source: Tabulations based on data in Appendix B.

Independent research libraries have two primary functions: they preserve their collections for the benefit of present and future generations, and they make these collections accessible to scholars who in turn seek to disseminate widely the results of the research carried out within these libraries. Neither of the "ultimate constituencies" comes to the library's doors, and the costs of building and operating the libraries cannot be charged to them. Nor can scholars, who do use the library directly, be expected to pay the high costs involved in creating and maintaining such a library.

Put another way, the outputs of independent research libraries have the attributes of what economists call *public goods.* Henry Hansmann has provided a clear definition in layman's terms: "A public good . . . has two special attributes: first, it costs no more to provide the good to many persons than it does to provide it to one, because one person's enjoyment of the good does not interfere with the ability of others to enjoy it at the same time; second, once the good has been provided to one person there is no easy way to prevent others from consuming it as well. Air pollution control, defense against nuclear attack, and radio broadcasts are common examples of public goods."[4]

Research libraries fit both of these criteria. Their fixed-cost base is exceedingly high, and increases in the number of users have relatively modest (though not negligible) effects on total costs. Because of the nature of research, scholars' findings are disseminated as widely as possible; no one is excluded from them. Moreover, one of the principal outputs of these libraries—the preservation of a cultural inheritance for future generations—obviously cannot be divided into units and sold in pieces to individuals alive today.

Because they provide a public good, research libraries cannot live by fees alone; some constituency must be found to subsidize their activities. The founders believed in the importance of learning and of books, and thanks to their generosity, each library originally had, in the founder, a single powerful constituency. As we have seen, developments during the 1960s and 1970s increased by an order of magnitude the cost of funding the libraries' activities. The endowments were outgrown, and the libraries had to find new sources of revenue. Dramatic increases in earned income could not—and cannot—be anticipated by these institutions. The only recourse was to other donors, private and public, who had to be relied on to provide both additional endowment and a steady stream of current giving.

The primary characteristics of this evolution will occupy us throughout this chapter. We begin by examining the decline in the relative importance of endowment income—first by summarizing the statistical record and then by providing a more general commentary on the underlying forces at work.

Trends in Investment Income

As recently as 1963, investment income for these five libraries averaged 100 percent of total expenditures. This figure, while dramatic, is also somewhat misleading in that it is influenced heavily by the situation at that time at the Newberry, where investment income was still approximately 120 percent of total expenditures (having been about 135 percent of total expenditures in 1960)—percentages that signify the extent to which resources then exceeded current needs.[5] The Newberry trustees of today, who face more serious financial problems than the trustees of any of the other libraries in this study, must look back on these ratios with something approaching disbelief. Putting the unusual situation at the Newberry to one side, however, the comparable percentage for each of the other libraries was at or above 80 percent in the early 1960s.

An exceptionally clear picture of the subsequent downward slide in investment income, as a percentage of expenditures, is shown in Figure 7.2a. The five-library average fell steadily during the 1960s and through most of the 1970s. A floor was reached in 1977 at just over 40 percent—less than half the corresponding level just 15 years earlier.

Variations among the individual libraries are revealed by Figure 7.2b (which uses three-year moving averages to smooth out year-to-year aberrations). We see at once how extraordinarily precipitous was the slide in the investment income percentage at the Newberry—from the astronomical heights of 100-plus percent in 1960 to about 35 percent of expenditures in recent years. More generally, the events of the late 1960s and 1970s are reflected in sharp downward movements

FIGURE 7.2A.   INVESTMENT INCOME AS A PERCENTAGE OF TOTAL EXPENDITURES, THREE-YEAR MOVING AVERAGE FOR ALL FIVE LIBRARIES, 1960–1993.

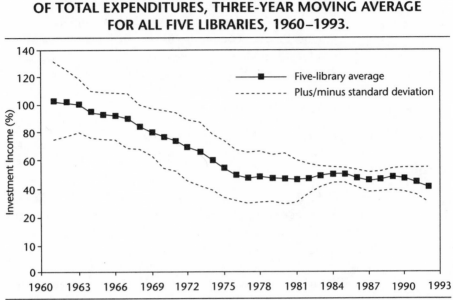

Source: Tabulations based on data in Appendix B.

FIGURE 7.2B.   INVESTMENT INCOME AS A PERCENTAGE OF TOTAL EXPENDITURES, THREE-YEAR MOVING AVERAGE FOR EACH LIBRARY, 1960–1993.

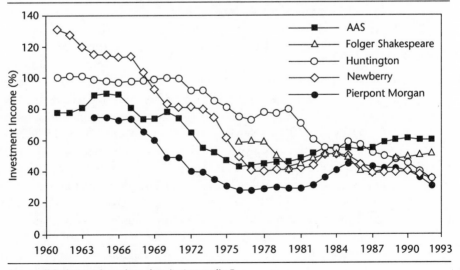

Source: Tabulations based on data in Appendix B.

in the investment income percentage at all of the libraries. The timing at the Huntington is a mild exception to the general pattern in that investment income as a percentage of total expenditures held steady longer there than at any of the other libraries; but in 1971, the Huntington too began to experience what turned out to be a long and steady decline in its investment income share. Clearly, deep currents were at work, with generically similar effects on all of the independent research libraries.

How the Endowments Were Outgrown

Original Intent

The men who founded the five libraries in this study had specific beliefs as to what their libraries should do. These beliefs were perpetuated in written form as trusts and indentures; they were also carried forward in the initial choice of trustees, often friends or relatives of the founder, whose ideas set the tone for the future. It was certainly the founders' understanding that their endowments would support the libraries' operations in perpetuity. The language that was used to describe the founding of the other libraries—"to bestow on posterity" (AAS), "a gift to the nation" (Folger), "give something to the public" (Huntington), "render them permanently available for the instruction and pleasure of the American people" (Morgan), "a free public library" (Newberry)—demonstrates this point.

Unanticipated Growth in Collections

In one sense, the very success of the libraries, and especially their rates of growth, foiled the philanthropic intentions of the founders. Three of these men— Huntington, Folger, and Morgan—were voracious book collectors who paid record prices for rare books on a fairly regular basis. Because they were collecting for themselves, money was rarely an object. Even so, the librarians and directors who came later frequently outdid the founders. If the founders' acquisitive urges can be attributed to a combination of bibliomania and wealth, the librarians' buying habits can be traced to a mix that is even more potent: bibliomania and someone else's wealth. The Newberry's Stanley Pargellis almost tripled the size of the collections in his twenty-year tenure.[6] At the AAS, Clarence Brigham "multiplied the collections five-fold."[7] The Folger's initial expansion into the vast territory of non-Shakespearean materials was initiated under Joseph Q. Adams, the first librarian. The Harmsworth collection, which was acquired *en bloc* during the 1930s, was at the time one of the largest collections remaining in private hands.

Such enormous growth in library collections was possible in the early years of this century, when many of the great private libraries of England and the Continent were sold, the great American fortunes were formed, and rare books were less expensive. It was still possible as recently as the 1940s and 1950s; although materials had become scarcer, collectors combed war-ravaged Europe in search of remaining treasures. Furthermore, it is misleading to assume that only rare books and manuscripts were acquired. Most acquisitions were inexpensive, ranging from early local American newspapers to the archival records of the Pullman Corporation. Collecting was in the past even more of an integral part of library operations than it is today (when acquisitions generally make up only about 10 percent of expenditures). Acquisitions were a cherished part of the librarian's or the director's responsibilities; often, trustees were involved as well. The comfortable funding situation of the early years encouraged active collecting policies and enabled librarians to amass collections of extraordinary value to scholars today.

At the same time, the unanticipated growth in the size of these collections—on a scale unforeseen by the founders[8]—led inescapably to the later shift in funding patterns documented in this chapter. Because the collections were so much larger than the founders had foreseen, the endowments, which were expected to provide funding in perpetuity, proved inadequate. It was large-scale acquisitions, more than anything else, that ultimately led away from full-endowment funding. Two sets of consequences reinforced each other.

First, there were the long-term implications for costs. Increasing a library collection fivefold is eventually an expensive proposition, even if all the books are cheap. By proceeding with ambitious acquisitions programs, the early librarians laid the groundwork for many of the cost pressures discussed in detail in Chapter Six (related to space needs, staffing, maintenance of the collections, and even greater interest in access, which was stimulated by the depth and quality of the collections).

Second, there were subtle effects on future income flows. The money that was spent on acquisitions came out of the endowment, or out of accumulated surpluses, which is essentially the same thing. Every dollar spent was one less dollar to reinvest and hence one less dollar to accumulate returns over time. Denied the magic of compounding, each of the dollars spent on acquisitions never became five or ten or twenty dollars of endowment in later years.

"Prudent" Investment Philosophies

The traditional understanding of prudent investment management played a part in this history. First of all, bonds were the generally approved form of "prudent investment" until well after World War II. Moreover, until the 1970s, investment income consisted solely of the interest and dividend payments that the corpus produced, and bonds generally produced a higher current yield; hence when more income was needed, the trustees invested the portfolio even more heavily in bonds. Because bond-heavy portfolios are less likely to appreciate in value, these decisions limited the endowments' growth potential. Thus even as the collections and the associated costs grew, the endowments remained relatively fixed in dollar value (we provide a more detailed discussion of endowment management in Chapter Eight).

The consequences of this mismatch were not apparent for many years. Even if the expenditure growth rate was greater than the income growth rate, for many years the *amount* of income from the endowment remained significantly higher than expenditures. There was still a hefty cushion between the two, leaving enough for operating costs, acquisitions, and reserves. Not until the 1960s did cost increases and growth in the demand for library services exhaust this surplus. We should recall that the average rate of increase in expenditures between 1960 and 1993 was 10 percent per year—and nearly 12 percent between 1974 and 1982 (see Tables 6.1 and 6.2). There is no way that the corpus of any one of these endowments could have been expected to grow this rapidly while simultaneously contributing a current yield of 5 or 6 percent to the operating budget each year. In this fundamental arithmetical sense, the economic conditions and other pressures of the 1960s and 1970s made it inevitable that the libraries would outgrow their original endowments.

The process of outgrowing the endowments was accelerated by another set of developments discussed in much more detail in Chapter Eight. The real purchasing power of the endowments declined, relative to what might have been achieved, as a result of new policies regarding the spending of capital gains. In the course of the 1970s, it became acceptable to spend at least some part of realized capital gains. Directors and trustees facing budget shortfalls often elected to spend large amounts of capital gains, raising spending rates well above what would today be considered prudent levels. The effects on the endowments were predictable and adverse. Meanwhile, the underlying economic problems of the libraries—created by circumstances in which expenditures were rising much more rapidly than sustainable sources of income—were both hidden and postponed.

Current Giving: Gifts and Grants

As already explained, contributed income of one kind or another must continue to be the dominant source of support for independent libraries producing public goods. Accordingly, growth in current giving had to be the flip side of the downward trend in the share of total revenues provided by investment income. As one declined (relative to total expenditures and total income), the other had to increase; today, gifts and grants account for approximately 40 percent of total expenditures.[9]

Broad Trends

Active fundraising is a surprisingly recent phenomenon at three of the five libraries under study here. Only the AAS and the Morgan were actively engaged in raising money back in the 1960s. At the Newberry, the Folger, and the Huntington, the emergence of gift and grant income dates from the early 1970s, when pressing needs left the trustees no option but to pursue this source of revenues. (Some gifts were of course received earlier by all three of these libraries, but their relatively modest scale is reflected in the fact that they do not appear separately in the accounting statements for earlier years; rather, they were lumped together with various forms of "other income.")

Three "area graphs" (Figures 7.3, 7.4, and 7.5)[10] illustrate broad trends since the 1960s for the AAS, the Morgan, and the Huntington, respectively. The AAS has the longest fundraising history of any of these libraries; it has received a rather steady, if modest, inflow of gifts and grants for many years. Never as wealthy as its younger sister institutions, it was ahead of its time when it mounted its first capital campaign in 1924. Figure 7.3 shows the regular, if not large, inflow of gifts and grants to the AAS during the 1960s, with some acceleration at the end of the decade. Then, starting in 1973, its gifts-and-grants share began to increase quite dramatically. The volatility of this curve from the 1970s forward is due primarily to the timing of campaigns and of large National Endowment for the Humanities (NEH) grants. (The other noticeable feature of this figure—the jump in real investment income in the early 1980s—was due almost entirely to a steep rise in spending rates and the performance of financial markets, as will be explained in Chapter Eight.)

The Morgan (Figure 7.4) illustrates even stronger growth in fundraising in the mid 1960s. As the figure makes clear, gifts and grants at the Morgan have been

FIGURE 7.3. INCOME BY SOURCE, AMERICAN ANTIQUARIAN SOCIETY, 1960–1993.

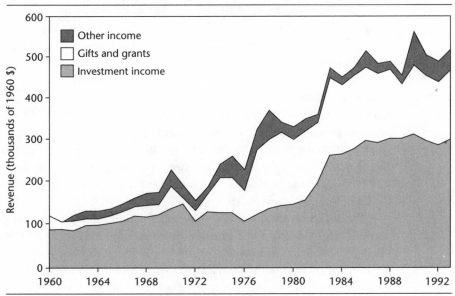

Source: Data from Tables B.5–1 and B.5–2 in Appendix B.

FIGURE 7.4.   INCOME BY SOURCE, PIERPONT MORGAN LIBRARY, 1960–1993.

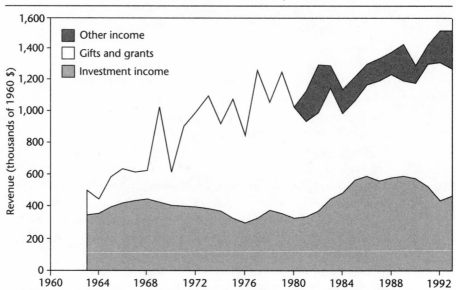

Source: Data from Tables B.5–1 and B.5–2 in Appendix B.

important revenue sources ever since the late 1960s—even more important than investment income in most years. Like the AAS, the Morgan was active in fundraising before the other three libraries. A Fellows (support group) program was established in 1960, and most of the gifts and grants received in that period—as well as much of the gift revenue received later—was restricted to spending on acquisitions. Strong support from gifts and grants for the operating budget has come much more recently.

The Newberry (Figure 7.5) represents a third case: there was almost no revenue called "gifts and grants" prior to 1975. Then, in one dramatic spurt, reported gifts and grants suddenly exceeded investment income. The NEH was primarily responsible for this drastic change in funding patterns, as we will see later in this chapter. Both the Folger and the Huntington exhibit patterns similar to the one at the Newberry, though slightly less extreme and slightly different in their timing. (We do not present separate area graphs for these last two libraries; the raw data for them may be found in Appendix B.)

These area graphs are especially useful in reinforcing a general point made earlier in the discussion of trends in investment income. At all of these libraries, the steady fall in the investment income *share* of total revenues occurred alongside a rather flat plateau in the total *amount* of real income contributed by the endowment. Even when measured in real (inflation-adjusted) terms, investment income rarely declined in absolute amount; it simply failed to increase at anything like the rate exhibited by total real expenditures, driven as they were by the combination

FIGURE 7.5. INCOME BY SOURCE, NEWBERRY LIBRARY, 1960–1993.

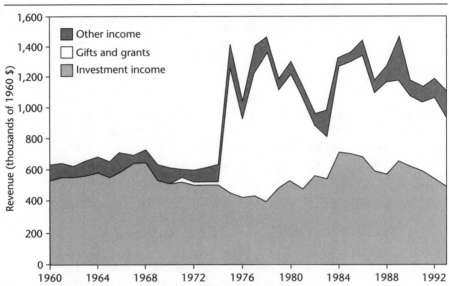

Source: Data from Tables B.5–1 and B.5–2 in Appendix B.

of rising costs and programmatic expansion described earlier. The higher levels of expenditure were funded almost entirely by dramatic increases in gifts and grants—which in three of the cases we are studying rose from almost nothing to quite high levels in the space of just a few years. The AAS is the only one of the five libraries in which increased real income from endowment has contributed significantly to the rise in total expenditures, and even in its case, large increases in gifts and grants came first.

Government Funding: The Special Role of the NEH

Broadly speaking, there have been two main sources of governmental support for these institutions: appropriations from city or state governments, or their arts councils, and federal grants from the National Endowment for the Humanities. At the state and local level, the Folger has received substantial grants from the Washington Arts Council, and the AAS has received considerable support from the Massachusetts Council on the Arts and Humanities. State and city funding have been of lesser importance to the other three libraries, and the Morgan even made a conscious decision, in the interest of fundraising efficiency, not to seek support from New York City.

At the federal level, the National Endowment for the Humanities, which was founded in 1965, played a leading role in fostering the growth that took place during the 1970s. As the first federal agency to make substantial grants to the independent research libraries, the NEH represented a valuable new source of funds at a time when privately provided endowments were increasingly unable to meet the demands placed on them. The NEH was (and still is) important for symbolic reasons: the existence of a government agency devoted to the humanities makes a powerful statement about society's priorities.[11]

But the existence of the NEH has had consequences that were much more than merely symbolic. Through the NEH, federal funds were made available for programs and efforts that meshed well with the interests of many librarians and directors in "democratizing" their institutions by expanding access and introducing additional services aimed at new constituencies. These programs ranged from traditional preservation projects to lectures, publications, and fellowships of many kinds (including support for graduate students and high school teachers). NEH grants were awarded on the basis of a competitive application process, and no institution was ever compelled to apply; still, the internal and external pressures to participate in these new programs were very great indeed. In many cases, the prospect of NEH funding was essentially an offer that could not be refused.

Much of the growth in expenditures at the independent research libraries during the 1970s followed increases in the NEH's budget. The extent of NEH support is evident from Figure 7.6, which shows three-year moving averages of NEH

FIGURE 7.6.   FUNDING FROM THE NATIONAL ENDOWMENT FOR THE HUMANITIES, THREE-YEAR MOVING AVERAGE BY LIBRARY, 1970–1993.

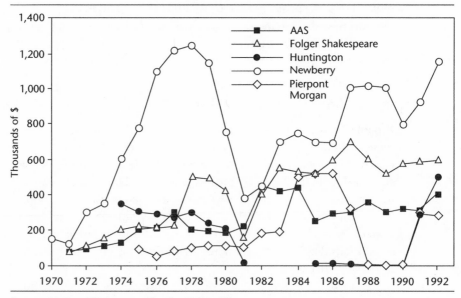

Sources: National Endowment for the Humanities.

grants to the five libraries. Three libraries—the Newberry, the AAS, and the Folger—obtained significant sums throughout the 1970s. (Note, however, that the Morgan received NEH funding in the mid 1980s and the Huntington in the past few years.)

The experiences of these libraries with the NEH illustrate well the interplay between the expenditure and income sides of the budgets of institutions such as these. On the one hand, the libraries themselves were often eager to expand their activities in the directions favored by NEH funding guidelines; to this degree, the NEH was mainly a convenient source of revenue that could be used to meet internally defined needs. On the other hand, it is no less true that the known availability of NEH funding for certain kinds of "outreach" activities stimulated more programmatic expansion than would have occurred in the absence of the NEH; in this sense, expenditures rose to match a new source of funding.

Of course, with increasing sums comes (at least the possibility of) increasing dependency; Table 7.1 shows the ratio of NEH grants to total gifts and grants in three successive periods: 1970–1977, 1978–1985, and 1986–1993. The vast majority of all gifts and grants at the Newberry and the AAS during the early period were from the NEH (with ratios of 0.77 and 0.70, respectively). It is no exaggeration to say that the major programmatic expansion at these two libraries was tied almost exclusively to NEH support.

NEH support has continued to be highly consequential for the AAS, the Newberry, and the Folger—representing, in the 1986–1993 subperiod, 45 percent of all gifts and grants at both the AAS and the Newberry and 36 percent at the Folger. There was, however, a rather sharp drop-off in funding from this source in the early 1980s, when NEH grants became more difficult to obtain. A new administration sought to serve a different constituency. Similarly, there was a different conception of government's role in supporting the humanities. Despite some resurgence of funding in recent years, the high percentages characteristic of the 1970s have not been seen again—and no one expects that they will be. Some of the libraries in our set (especially the Newberry) have struggled

TABLE 7.1. RATIO OF GRANTS FROM THE NATIONAL ENDOWMENT FOR THE HUMANITIES TO TOTAL GIFTS AND GRANTS, BY LIBRARY AND SUBPERIOD, 1970–1993.

	1970–1977	1978–1985	1986–1993
American Antiquarian Society	0.70	0.60	0.45
Folger Shakespeare Library	N.A.	0.39	0.36
Huntington Library	0.17	0.06	0.04
Newberry Library	0.01	0.08	0.03
Pierpont Morgan Library	0.77	0.43	0.45

Sources: Appendix B; National Endowment for the Humanities.

Note: N.A. means not available.

mightily to sustain programs started with NEH funding. Whether these efforts will prove successful remains to be seen.

Private Donors

The large private foundations are in many ways closer cousins to the NEH than either corporate sponsors or individual donors are. It is our general impression that the number of major foundations interested in the independent research libraries has declined between the 1970s and the present day, but we have not tried to quantify this proposition. (Detailed patterns of support by private donors are both harder to characterize and largely unknown due to inadequacies of data.) Foundations, and their trustees, can be as much the product of their times as government funders (sometimes more so), and so it should not be surprising if the same societal forces affect both sets of funders.[12]

Smaller foundations may be more consistent donors and more reliable partners for the independent research libraries. These foundations are sometimes administered by or otherwise affiliated with trustees or other supporters of the library in question. For example, the Virginia Steele Scott Foundation gave the Huntington its American Art Collection and a substantial endowment. Similarly, the Ahmanson Foundation in California has continued to be very generous to the Huntington.

Gifts from corporations, which have figured prominently at institutions such as the New York Public Library, have not been substantial. Firms connected to board members or leading supporters have made contributions, one example of which is the Times-Mirror Endowed Chair at the Huntington Library. The Huntington's chairman, Robert Erburu, is chairman and CEO of Times-Mirror. The Morgan has also reaped the benefits of corporate connections, especially corporations with the Morgan name.

As a general rule, though, the relatively low profile activities of the independent research libraries have not led to substantial corporate giving. Visibility and reputational enhancement are often considerations in corporate giving, and it is not clear that the independent research libraries offer either. Also, some institutions are worse off than others. Washington, D.C., for instance, is not home to many corporate headquarters; for that matter, neither is Worcester, Massachusetts. So even though corporate funding may be an option, to date it has not figured prominently in its own right.

Gifts from individuals comprise most of the balance of contributed income. The range of donors is very broad: there are visitors who give $5 at the door, and there are trustees who give millions of dollars. Furthermore, there are individuals and support groups at every level in between. One direct consequence of the need to raise larger sums of money annually to support operating budgets has been the establishment of far more elaborate fundraising structures and the creation of organized support groups of every conceivable kind (including the "thief detectors" at the AAS). Lectures, private tours, and other events are offered to engage the interests of potential donors.

Trustee giving in particular has undergone a veritable sea change over the past thirty years. Today, trustees are expected to make meaningful financial contributions to the libraries they serve. Current gifts, capital gifts, and bequests are expected to reflect the trustee's commitment to the institution. Such expectations are not always realized; nonetheless, a significant financial commitment is seen increasingly as an indispensable part of trusteeship. Charles Haffner's $6 million gift to the Newberry and the prominent role played by trustees in the Morgan's recent capital campaign are two good examples.

Continuing to increase donations is no easy task, as data for the period 1981–1993 indicate (see Figure 7.7). In recent years, the clear standout among these libraries is the Huntington, whose annual fundraising has increased from $1.2 million in 1981 to $6.6 million in 1993. This growth may be related to the relative absence of growth in the 1960s and 1970s, when the administration and the board concentrated on restraining expenditures. Also, the Huntington has invested heavily in a larger, more professional development staff, and the current director, Robert Skotheim, has worked hard and successfully at this key task. Annual fundraising at the Morgan increased nearly as rapidly between 1990 and 1992, right after the expansion of the physical plant was completed. The Folger's contributed income also increased markedly in the early 1990s, in part as a result of the Jubilee

FIGURE 7.7. GIFTS, GRANTS, AND ADMISSIONS, BY LIBRARY, 1981–1993.

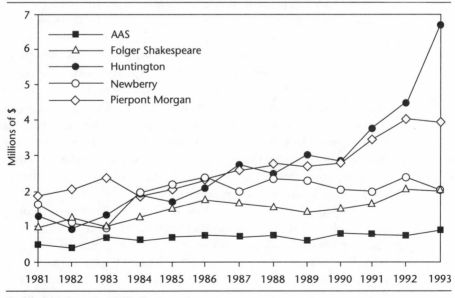

Source: Data from Appendix B.

campaign. The Newberry is an interesting case, particularly if we separate current giving into restricted and unrestricted funds. Since 1986, unrestricted gifts and grants have increased at an average annual rate of 12.7 percent; at the same time, restricted income has decreased at an average annual rate of 11.3 percent. The rapid growth in unrestricted giving at the Newberry has been especially important because unrestricted investment income dropped over the same period. Overall, however, the trend in gift-and-grant income at the Newberry has been essentially flat.

Earned Income

Having established in the first part of this chapter the basic proposition that earned income can never be expected to do the "heavy lifting" for independent research libraries, we now return to the question of the more limited role of this source of revenue—and of the dangers of exaggerating its importance. *Earned income* is a very broad term and covers a wide range of activities at the libraries in our set. The Huntington, the Newberry, the Morgan, and the Folger all have bookshops and retail operations, although none is in a position to compete with major retailers. There are portions of the libraries' regular activities for which fees are charged; publications and lectures are two of the most obvious examples. "Contributions" in lieu of admission charges can also be considered, at least in part, a form of earned income. The common element in all these endeavors is that the consumer of the goods or services in question pays a price.

Broadly speaking, income-earning ventures can be divided into two categories. The first includes projects such as bookshops and mail-order catalogs, which are meant to be primarily revenue-earning activities and net providers of funds to the operating budget. For such programs, "success" is attained if income exceeds the related costs. The second category of earned income, which includes such things as fees for academic or public programs, are really attempts to limit losses. Unlike ventures whose primary purpose is raising money, there is no expectation that income from such fees will exceed all costs of the related program. Activities of this kind are part of the libraries' operations and will occur regardless. Fees limit the need to subsidize these programs, but such sources of earned income need not be subjected to the same scrutiny as "pure" moneymaking enterprises. If a program is closely linked to the institution's mission, judgments based solely on profitability are not as applicable.

Although the line between these two types of revenue-earning activities can be difficult to draw,[13] it is important nonetheless to have the distinction in mind—and to pay close attention to the financial results obtained from any venture intended, in whole or in part, to "make money." We have reliable information for only two libraries in which even a crude estimate of net returns can be computed. One is the Huntington, which reports earned income as revenue and the "cost of sales" as an expense. A comparison of these two figures for the period 1990–

1993 shows that 63 cents was spent for every dollar in earned income. The other example is the Folger, whose supplementary statements treat the museum shop separately. For the same period, the Folger spent 87 cents for each dollar of earned income.

The promise of earned income—that retail stores, catalog sales, or restaurant revenues can become highly profitable—must be analyzed rigorously. It can prove misleading.[14] The Folger's experience is relevant in this context. Figure 7.8 compares costs and revenues for the Folger's museum shop and its mail-order catalog during the years 1978–1993. These data provide a good illustration of the difference between gross and net valuations. Earned income alone would have shown very rapid growth (41 percent per annum); net income, however, would have shown deepening losses. In 1985, the Folger eliminated its mail-order catalog, leaving the profitable museum shop. Even though its profit margin has narrowed somewhat in recent years, the shop is still a net contributor of funds.

This example underscores again the importance of accurate accounting. Income-generating activities, especially those that are peripheral to an organization's functions, should be reported net of the related costs. Treating earned income as revenue and the related costs as expenditures can inflate the overall size of the budget even in a year when activities undertaken solely to earn income were not profitable. Needless to say, paying inordinate attention to earned-income ventures, even those that are potentially profitable, can also entail another kind of cost: diversion of attention from the institution's mission.

FIGURE 7.8. EARNED INCOME, FOLGER SHAKESPEARE LIBRARY, 1978–1993.

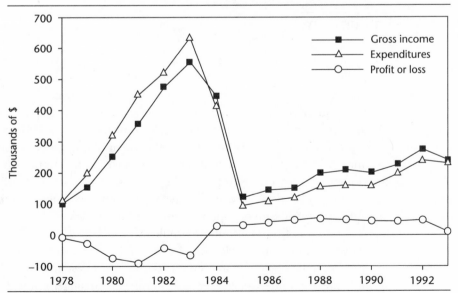

Source: Audited financial statements of the Folger Shakespeare Library, 1978–1993.

In sum, apparent opportunities to earn income have to be considered carefully, with both the real objectives to be served and the net results kept firmly in mind. Entrepreneurial instincts are surely not to be disparaged, but they need to be conditioned by both a clear sense of the institution's mission and a cold-eyed view of the implications for the bottom line.

At least brief mention should be made of one other source of earned income that is highly significant for many other types of nonprofit entities: admission charges. Unlike bookstore and catalog operations, admission does not entail any significant increase in operating costs and hence, at least in theory, is attractive because any revenues are equivalent to contributed income. Technically speaking, none of these five libraries currently charges admission, though two (the Morgan and the Huntington) encourage contributions in lieu of admission. Not surprisingly, these are the two institutions that are museums as well as libraries and can mount exhibits in suitable fashion and number to attract visitors willing to pay (or "contribute").

Even at the Morgan, admissions are responsible for only between 3 and 4 percent of operating income. At the Huntington, the corresponding percentage has been higher. Contributions by visitors were 11.5 percent and 13.9 percent of income in 1991 and 1992, respectively. Because hundreds of thousands of people visit the Huntington each year, the potential revenues from an admission charge are even greater. If the California attorney general approves the Huntington's application to alter the provision of the indenture that prohibits an admission charge (as mentioned in Chapter One), the Huntington could substantially increase its earned income. It seems unlikely, however, that any of the other libraries in this set could elicit significant revenue from this source.

A New Equilibrium?

The years covered by this study have seen a radical transformation of the funding profiles of these five independent research libraries. Having started out as income spenders, with assured flows of endowment income available to meet essentially all needs, they have now become institutions that receive, characteristically, well under half of their income from returns on the endowment. Gifts and grants typically contribute about 40 percent of total income, and earned income (and "other income") make up the balance. Although these five libraries have pursued quite different paths, they have undergone essentially the same transformation, and all now seem to be approaching what appears to be a new and quite different kind of equilibrium. The funding profiles of the mid 1990s are very different from the funding profiles of 1960.

These new funding profiles are of course related explicitly to broadened sets of programmatic objectives and enlarged, more inclusive missions. As a consequence, directors and trustees of these libraries can no longer think of themselves simply as the stewards of a founder's resources, charged with spending the available income as wisely as they can. Now they must also exercise responsibility for active management of much more complex enterprises. Of course, they must raise large sums of money regularly—and aggressively. But their tasks are not nearly as simple as that. For example, a much higher fraction of revenues these days is likely to be restricted in one form or another, and that is a complication of great import. Plans must be made on the basis of an assessment of the incremental costs and revenues associated with each proposed activity.

At the most fundamental level, directors and trustees have to relate to—and cope with—the demands (and interests) of a much more varied set of constituencies. The founders of these great libraries would be surprised indeed by the ways in which their institutions have been transformed by a combination of growth in collections, unrelenting economic pressures, and changed societal aspirations.

Notes

1. See Bowen, Nygren, Turner, and Duffy (1994), especially Chapter Eight, for an extended discussion of differences among nonprofits in revenue profiles and considerable data of the type cited in the text.
2. We calculated three-year averages for each library over these two intervals to avoid having the figures unduly biased by outliers. Data for earlier years are less reliable since in many cases it is hard to distinguish "earned income" from "other income." The figures are low for some of the libraries because they exclude "requested contributions" collected from visitors, which are at least as much earned income as they are contributions. The figures are also high in that they generally represent gross receipts, not net receipts. (See the last section of the chapter for a discussion of this point.)
3. Bowen, Nygren, Turner, and Duffy (1994, p. 131, fig. 8.2).
4. Hansmann (1987, p. 29).
5. We express investment income as a percentage of total expenditures rather than as a percentage of total income for two reasons: first, to show, as the example of the Newberry in 1963 does, that there were times when investment income was so large that it permitted a substantial building of reserves, and second, to reflect a problem with the data—for the early years, in particular, it is not always possible to distinguish capital gifts from current gifts, and when all gifts are lumped together, the total-income figures are inflated in confusing ways and do not serve as appropriate reference points.
6. Towner (1993, p. 141).
7. Burkett and Hench (1992, p. 24).
8. The Newberry's case is an interesting variation on this theme. It is impossible to say that this library's collections outgrew the founder's expectations because Walter Loomis Newberry had none; if he did, he never expressed them. Furthermore, he did not leave a specific amount for the establishment of a library, mandating only that "half of his estate" should be used for that purpose. Nonetheless, the same pattern can be seen in the history of the Newberry. The Louis H. Silver collection, whose acquisition in 1964 cost the equivalent of 15 percent of the Newberry's endowment, forced the library into active fundraising. As Bill Towner explained: "Buying it certainly changed the nature of my position, probably permanently, for the $2,687,000 had to be recovered, especially since it came on the heels of a $1,250,000 million renovation of the building. . . . We are probably now committed to periodic fund-raising programs for the first time in the Newberry's history" (Towner, 1993, p. 178).

9. One matter of definition, pertaining to the treatment of admission "contributions," needs to be explained at the outset of this discussion. Unless otherwise indicated, all "contributions" related to *admissions* to exhibitions, galleries, or gardens are subsumed under the heading of "gifts." None of the libraries in our set has a mandatory admission fee, and those that do collect contributions in lieu of charges treat such revenue as current giving. Although we have accepted this accounting convention, we believe that there is at least as strong a case for treating such revenue as earned income. In any event, in only two of the five libraries (the Morgan and the Huntington) are admission "contributions" large enough to matter; see the later discussion of trends in earned income.

   Another problem with the figures for "gifts and grants" is that they do not always distinguish consistently between current gifts and capital gifts. This is a particularly serious problem in the earlier years.

10. These graphs, expressed in 1960 dollars, permit us to examine simultaneously both relative rates of increase in the various revenue sources and the shares of total real revenues coming from each source in each year (the areas under the respective curves). Because of changes in accounting conventions, the data for individual years are more reliable after 1980.

11. For an inside look at the NEH and at the intersection of politics and the humanities, see Berman (1984).

12. See the comments on pages 112 and 113 by Marcus McCorison, director of the AAS, lamenting the changing priorities of private foundations and the state arts council.

13. Hence a gift shop whose merchandise reflects the collections and programs of the library and its peers performs an educational function that should not be overlooked in valuing the contribution it makes to the institution.

14. A reader of the Metropolitan Museum of Art's annual report for 1992, for instance, might note total income of $172 million, of which $93 million was earned income from auxiliary activities. Upon closer examination, the reader would note that costs for the same set of activities were $94 million, meaning that in 1992, there was really an "earned-income deficit." See Bowen, Nygren, Turner, and Duffy (1994, p. 237).

CHAPTER EIGHT

CHANGING POLICIES AND PRACTICES IN ENDOWMENT MANAGEMENT

The endowment of an institution such as an independent research library is almost always its most valuable financial asset. As such, it deserves to be treated with great respect and to be managed with as much thoughtfulness and skill as can be brought to the task. Actually, there is no single task; the wise management of a large endowment requires attention to all of the following:

- Setting investment objectives appropriate to the mission and circumstances of the institution (consciously and deliberately balancing risk and potential return)
- Investing the funds so as to achieve the maximum total return obtainable given the predetermined risk and return objectives
- Determining how best to apportion the total return on the endowment between the needs of the present and the claims of the future—for example, setting an appropriate spending rate or determining an appropriate policy for determining what part of the total return can properly be "harvested" today and what part should be reinvested
- Seeking to augment the size of the endowment by securing new capital gifts

In this chapter, we will discuss how the five libraries in our study have discharged these tasks over the past thirty-five years (with much more detail available for the 1981–1993 period). Substantial changes in thinking and in the laws governing the management of endowments have occurred during these years. The policies and practices followed by these libraries, as well as by other nonprofits, can be understood only in this historical context—which we summarize in the first section of the chapter. The goals and concepts we have used to define the issues confronted by the people responsible for managing endowments are described in the second section of the chapter; they reflect a simplified version of modern portfolio theory and what has come to be called the *total return approach*. The remainder of the chapter presents data that allow us to discuss what has in fact happened to the endowments of these institutions over the past thirty-five years.[1]

The Historical Evolution of Policies Governing Endowments

The traditional view of endowment management, referred to in shorthand as the *dividends-and-interest model*, had a major impact on the management of almost all endowments until quite recently. Even today, some charitable nonprofits (though none of the five independent research libraries included in this study) still follow this approach. Most endowed nonprofits, however, have adopted newer concepts that place less emphasis on the form in which returns are earned (dividends and interest as opposed to capital gains) and give trustees more flexibility both in investing endowment funds and in utilizing the returns.

Origins

The use of endowments as a form of charitable donation dates back to the twelfth century.[2] In their earliest form, endowments commonly consisted of land; income from the land came in the form of rents. As the value of the land appreciated, increased rent provided enough income both to compensate for inflation and to allow for expanded activities. As Richard M. Ennis and J. Peter Williamson pointed out in their 1976 study of endowment funds, "This land-based origin of endowment funds is important, for it explains to a substantial degree the traditional spending practices that have been characteristic of endowment funds up to at least the second half of the twentieth century."[3] Ennis and Williamson are referring to the traditional division of an endowment into principal and income. If an endowment consists of a plot of land, there is a clear distinction between appreciation—which could be realized only by selling off part of the land—and income, which is derived in the form of rents. This distinction was retained long after land ceased to be the most popularly held asset.

In the early years of this country's history, endowments were invested largely in land holdings or in bonds. In 1830, for instance, 98.6 percent of Harvard's endowment was invested in mortgages and other real estate investments; 76 percent of Princeton's endowment was invested in local banking enterprises in Trenton and New York City.[4] At the time, investment options were minimal: there were few common stocks, and bonds were limited mostly to government-issued debt.

By the turn of the twentieth century, various economic and legal forces had shifted the definition of prudence to focus largely on the minimization of risk to principal, defined as the book value of the fund in question. Many states had lists or categories of appropriate investments, and most of these were limited to fixed-income securities. Equities were not viewed as proper investments because they carried higher risk; also, reporting requirements for companies were far less stringent than they are today, which was one of the factors that made investing in equities more speculative. In 1904, fully 58.7 percent of Harvard's endowment was invested in bonds (with another 33 percent in real estate), as was 94.4 percent of Princeton's endowment.[5] By shifting their focus to bonds, which lose value in an inflationary period, endowed institutions and their trustees had given up the protection from inflation that land ownership had traditionally provided. However, the traditional (land-based) definition of principal and income was applied to bonds and eventually codified in law.

Inflation did not become the persistent scourge that it is today until after World War II, and for that reason, its potential effects on the real value of an endowment fund were not seen as a crucial concern until relatively recently. In fact, as Bevis Longstreth has pointed out, "It is important to remember that before World War I, periods of deflation were as common as those of inflation. During the long deflationary period from 1864 to 1900, when much American corporate and trust law was developed and a public market for industrial securities commenced, the value of the dollar in purchasing power almost doubled. Bonds offered a good return for income beneficiaries and a marked increase in the real value of the principal. It is no surprise that over this period they . . . came to be viewed as inherently safe."[6]

The late nineteenth century was also the period in which the Newberry was founded and in which Huntington, Morgan, and Folger began to make their fortunes; undoubtedly, the experiences of these years shaped the outlooks of the people involved. Inflation remained a distant concern through the early years of this century, despite the increase in prices associated with World War I. The 1929 stock market crash and the depression that followed accentuated the importance attached to protecting principal, a goal that the conventional wisdom of the day held could be met best by holding high-quality bonds. One commentator on the financial problems of higher education has been quoted as saying in 1960 that "fifty years ago most trustees would have argued that it was immoral to purchase common stocks with endowment funds."[7]

The Post–World War II Years

Not until the decades following World War II did inflation, coupled with high rates of return in the stock market, call into question the established understanding of prudence. Investment in common stocks had become more acceptable prior to the end of the war, but budgetary constraints and the need for high current income limited the extent to which a more aggressive investment strategy could be adopted. The stocks that promised the greatest growth, and hence the greatest benefit to principal, tended to be those with low dividend payouts.

Because the 1960s was also a period of both expansion and rising costs (see Chapter Six), the need for additional endowment income was great. Only comparatively wealthy institutions believed that they could afford to sacrifice current yield in order to gain appreciation. Most other institutions lacked this flexibility, with serious consequences for growth in the corpus of the endowment. According to one study, between 1959 and 1968 the cumulative total return for fifteen educational institutions was 134 percent, with an average annual return of 8.7 percent. This result compares unfavorably with the returns on twenty-one balanced mutual funds, whose cumulative return was 143 percent and whose average annual return was 9.2 percent. It compares dismally with the record of ten large growth funds, whose cumulative return was 295 percent and whose average annual return was 14.6 percent.[8]

Adoption of the Total Return Concept

In the late 1960s, economists and investment professionals began to argue that the traditional understanding of endowment management was outdated. Modern portfolio theory, which treats interest, dividends, and capital gains as different forms of a single "total return," started to gain ground as an investing rationale.[9] An important corollary was that capital appreciation was not sacrosanct and that the legal requirement to preserve principal should be understood as referring to the fund's real purchasing power, not to an arbitrary book value. Prudence, therefore, was a matter of the total amount of spending from the endowment, not the particular form which that spending took.

Several institutions, notably Yale University in 1965 and 1966, began to shift toward an endowment management approach that focused on total return and an explicit adoption of a "spending rate" for budgetary purposes.[10] By permitting the expenditure of a prudent portion of capital gains (to be combined with dividends and interest to reach the level of spending permitted by the spending rate), Yale was free to invest for growth without worrying about the short-term effects on the operating budget. Unfortunately, Yale moved aggressively into equities at what proved to be an unpropitious time. But this accident of timing should not be allowed to affect judgments concerning the wisdom of the essential change in endowment philosophy—which has been adopted by almost all universities today.

As many institutions pondered what they should do, the most contentious issue in considering whether to move to a total return spending-rate model was often legal, not financial. The financial and portfolio management arguments in favor of the total return approach were rarely disputed. Many trustees felt, however, that the laws governing charitable corporations did not allow for the expenditure of principal, a restriction that precluded spending any capital gains. A major step toward changing this widely held opinion came with the publication of two important studies sponsored by the Ford Foundation: *The Law and the Lore of Endowment Funds* and *Managing Educational Endowments*.[11]

The Law and the Lore dealt with the perceived legal issues and noted that although trust law might treat capital gains as principal, the analogy to charitable corporations was inapposite. Trust law's distinction between income and principal grew out of the competing claims of a life beneficiary and a remainderman (the individual who is to obtain the principal of the trust on the death of the life beneficiary). Treating capital gains as income would help the income beneficiary but hurt the remainderman. Because one's gain was the other's loss, the law had to distinguish unambiguously between competing interests. In the case of an endowment supporting a nonprofit, however, there is no such sharp distinction. Bright and Cary argued that corporate law was a better legal model; in corporate law, realized capital gains are treated as part of income.[12] They also surveyed the relevant case law and found no support for the view that the expenditure of capital gains was categorically forbidden. If donors had stated explicitly that the principal of their donations was to be kept intact, that restriction had to be followed (and Bright and Cary were willing to interpret this restriction to preclude any spending of appreciation, realized or unrealized). Otherwise, a prudent portion of capital gains could be expended in support of current operations. On the strength of this report, institutions began changing their policies.

Managing Educational Endowments was published a few months after *The Law and the Lore,* and it dealt with some of the practical issues involved in moving to a total return spending-rate model. In particular, it laid out a set of strategies that could be pursued by institutions willing to change their approach and outlined a way to measure results (the unit method, now commonly used). The authors called for a reexamination of all the gifts and bequests that comprised the endowment, with an eye toward identifying those that were legally restricted to an interest-and-dividends approach, and loosening the constraints on those that were not. Taken together, these two studies laid the groundwork for the changes in law and in practice that followed.

In 1974, the Ford Foundation published *The Developing Law of Endowment Funds: "The Law and the Lore" Revisited.*[13] This work, also by Bright and Cary, surveyed the field of endowment management and tracked the growing acceptance and application of the total return model. There were some encouraging developments. Many prestigious endowed institutions—the University of Chicago, Dartmouth, Princeton, the Smithsonian—had adopted a total return framework, accompanied by some version of a spending rule. Furthermore, the change in perspectives had filtered down: a 1971 Louis Harris poll of 660 nonprofits with endowments in excess of $5 million in market value found that 58 percent approved the total return concept and its corollary, the permitted expenditure of an appropriate share of capital gains.

Another significant step toward acceptance of this new approach was the drafting of the Uniform Management of Institutional Funds Act (UMIFA). UMIFA was approved by the National Conference of Commissioners on Uniform State Laws in 1972; today, it is law in twenty-eight states and in the District of Columbia. The act states: "In the administration of the powers to appropriate appreciation, to make and retain investments, and to delegate investment management of institutional funds, members of a governing board shall exercise ordinary business care and prudence under the facts and circumstances prevailing at the time of the action or decision. In so doing they shall consider long and short term needs of the institution in carrying out its educational, religious, charitable, or other eleemosynary purposes, its present and anticipated financial requirements, expected total return on its investments, price level trends, and general economic conditions."

The passage of UMIFA brought the law into line with modern portfolio theory and allowed many institutions to modify their investment policies and practices. Although most of the five libraries in this study continued for a time to use the old model, the legal door was open. Not long thereafter, the total return approach was endorsed, in one form or another, by all five of them.

Goals and Concepts

What are the substantive goals of endowment management? The current consensus is that the baseline goal is to provide, at the minimum, a stream of income whose purchasing power remains unchanged over time. The reasoning behind this formulation has been characterized as a commitment to intergenerational equity: future scholars (or librarians, students, or visitors) should not be given short shrift relative to today's scholars. This notion has a particular resonance for the libraries in our set. The collections are part of the world's cultural inheritance, and they are no more the property of this generation than they were the property of the founders' generation. The independent research libraries are the guardians of this trust, and their endowments serve to guarantee the perpetual maintenance and accessibility of the collections. Endowments and collections are well matched: one is an asset, the other is a (financial) liability; both are regarded as permanent.

It is worth noting, before going forward, that the conventional view of the goals of endowment management is not shared universally. Henry Hansmann, for one, has argued that the intergenerational argument is flawed and that the use of other criteria would lead universities—and by extension, perhaps, other heavily endowed institutions such as independent research libraries—to manage their endowments differently.[14]

These are valid points, and it is beyond the scope of this book to challenge them or engage them in a meaningful way. Instead, we have stayed with the conventional model and its set of underlying assumptions. For our purposes, it is sufficient merely to note that there are those who disagree.

Analyzing the performance of endowments is a complicated task. Inflows and outflows—spending, gifts, transfers, withdrawals—alter the value of the fund regularly and in interrelated ways. Dividing the endowment into units simplifies the analysis greatly. Some transactions change the number of units: gifts, transfers, and withdrawals, for instance. Others affect the price, or value, of a single unit. The total return earned each year and the spending rate are the two main variables. The total return increases the value of each unit through market appreciation, dividends, and interest; spending part of the total return reduces it. The reinvestment rate, which is the total return net of spending, is the amount by which each unit's year-end value (after the unit has made its annual contribution to the operating budget via the spending rate) increases over the course of one period, usually a year.[15]

Against this backdrop, the responsibilities for managing the endowment can be divided into three components: investing, spending, and augmenting.

Investing includes defining investment goals—choosing the appropriate balance between risk and return. Investment results obtained after the fact do not determine the appropriateness of the investment strategy. Rather, the question is whether the objectives chosen are prudent and err neither on the speculative side (by investing in overly risky assets) nor on the more conservative side (by, at the extreme, keeping the entire endowment in cash). The next question for those charged with investing funds is whether the endowment managers—the individuals or firms assigned responsibility for selecting particular investments—have attained returns comparable to those achieved by other portfolios with similar risk and return characteristics.

Spending involves deciding what portion of the total return per unit of endowment is to be used for current expenditures, irrespective of the form of the returns. The reinvestment rate is the obverse (total return minus spending rate equals reinvestment rate). In the long run, the spending rate for an endowment should not exceed the difference between the total return and the projected internal inflation rate. Otherwise, the objective of maintaining the purchasing power of each unit of endowment cannot be achieved.

Augmenting, the third facet of endowment management, refers to the process of securing gifts of new endowment. Although achieving a satisfactory reinvestment rate may allow existing units of endowment to serve specific purposes into the future, new endowment will still be needed to support new activities, as well as growth in existing activities. If a nonprofit is growing and wishes to maintain or enlarge the share of its budget covered by investment income, it must seek new endowment. And for reasons that have been given, such growth is almost inevitable. The natural tendency of nonprofits is to grow; if endowments are to continue as a meaningful source of funding, they must grow as well.

With these ideas in mind, we now turn to the data. How successfully have the five libraries managed their endowments over the past three decades?

Measures of Performance

Maintaining Purchasing Power

The grossest baseline measure of success or failure is growth in, or at the very least maintenance of, the purchasing power of the endowment over time. Changes in the real value of the endowment reflect all aspects of endowment management—the total return, the spending rate, and new gifts (or withdrawals)—and thus serve as a useful summary measure. Later in the chapter, for the years for which adequate data exist, we will parse out responsibility for results among the various facets of endowment management.

As explained in Chapter Six (note 1), the ideal way to measure changes in the real value of the endowment would be to use a specially constructed price index, the components of which track trends in the costs of the main inputs of independent research libraries. In the absence of the necessary data, the main option is to use the general price level. Because the libraries have costs that rise more rapidly than prices in general, this is a minimum standard.

Figures 8.1a and 8.1b show the nominal and real values of the endowment at each of these libraries for the period 1960–1993. Figures 8.2a and 8.2b index the real values (1960 = 100) so that we can compare results across the libraries. Finally, we summarize the average annual growth rates for the entire period (Table 8.1) and then for the same three subperiods used earlier (Table 8.2).

We draw four main conclusions from these data:

1.   Certain broad trends have affected the endowments of all of these institutions (see especially the roughly similar patterns evident from the nominal values presented in Figure 8.1a). This is not surprising, because (a) the endowments are invested in basically the same financial markets, although to varying degrees; (b) the broad societal changes in attitudes toward investing and spending capital gains affected all of the libraries more or less simultaneously; and (c) the demands for higher spending occurred at roughly the same time at all of the institutions, thus affecting spending and reinvestment rates.

2.   We are reminded again of the incredible differences in investment opportunities between the earlier decades (especially the 1970s) and the 1980s and early 1990s. The "takeoff" in values during the most recent subperiod (1982–1993) is simply extraordinary; if the 1980s had been anything like the 1970s, this study might have been included one or more institutional obituaries.

3.   Inflation had a debilitating effect on these endowments. Over the entire period of this study (1960–1993), inflation averaged 4 percent per annum, which means that in every year that the reinvestment rate did not exceed that figure, a portfolio lost real value. A simple comparison of the nominal and real market values provided in Figures 8.1a and 8.1b makes the point convincingly, as do Figures 8.2a and 8.2b, which present the real values on an indexed basis.

At the Huntington and the Morgan, the real value of the portfolios was appreciably lower at the end of the first subperiod (1974) than it had been at the start; the Newberry and the AAS did not fare all that well either. During the second subperiod (the latter half of the 1970s and the first years of the 1980s), the slide in real values was even more dramatic for all of the libraries except the AAS; the five libraries as a group had an average annual return of −6.1 percent.

FIGURE 8.1A.   MARKET VALUE OF ENDOWMENT IN NOMINAL DOLLARS, BY LIBRARY, 1960–1993.

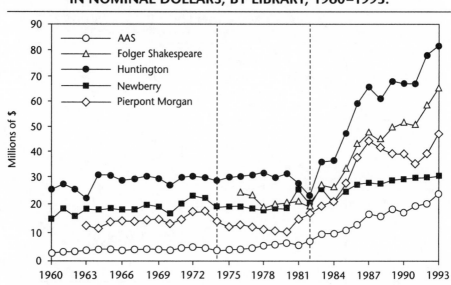

Source: Data from Appendix B.

FIGURE 8.1B.   MARKET VALUE OF ENDOWMENT IN REAL (1960) DOLLARS, BY LIBRARY, 1960–1993.

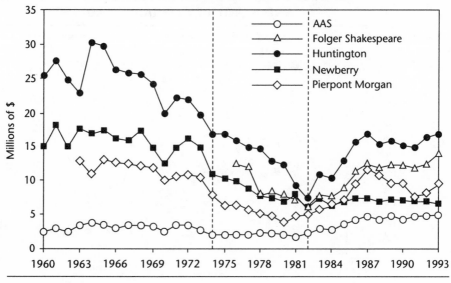

Source: Data from Appendix B.

**FIGURE 8.2A.   INDEXED MARKET VALUE OF ENDOWMENT
IN REAL DOLLARS, FOLGER, HUNTINGTON,
AND MORGAN LIBRARIES, 1960–1993.**

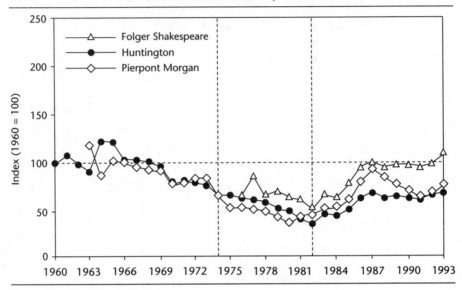

Source: Data from Appendix B.

**FIGURE 8.2B.   INDEXED MARKET VALUE OF ENDOWMENT
IN REAL DOLLARS, AMERICAN ANTIQUARIAN SOCIETY
AND NEWBERRY LIBRARY, 1960–1993.**

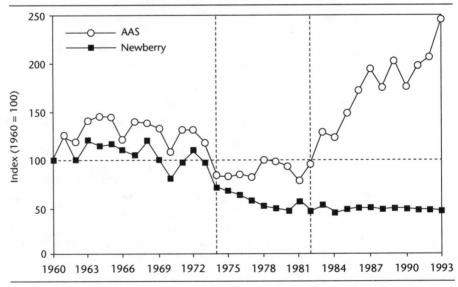

Source: Data from Appendix B.

TABLE 8.1. AVERAGE ANNUAL PERCENTAGE CHANGE IN MARKET VALUE OF ENDOWMENT, BY LIBRARY, 1960–1993.

	Nominal	Real
American Antiquarian Society	7.14	1.42
Folger Shakespeare Library	N.A.	N.A.
Huntington Library	3.09	−2.41
Newberry Library	1.92	−3.52
Pierpont Morgan Library[a]	<u>4.54</u>	<u>−1.28</u>
Average	4.17	−1.45
Gross domestic product (GDP)	8.63	2.83
Inflation	5.64	

Source: Tabulations based on data in Appendix B.

Note: N.A. means not available.

[a]Morgan data begin in 1963.

Only in the 1980s—which by historical standards provided anomalously high returns—did real values begin to recover. Even so, by 1993, only two of these libraries—the AAS and the Folger—had endowments with real values equal to or higher than the real values of their portfolios in earlier years. For the entire period, the portfolios of these five libraries declined on average nearly 1 percent per year in real terms (see Table 8.1).[16]

4. The similarities having been mentioned, one cannot help noticing the substantial differences in results among the endowments. The range of differences is much larger than one might have expected, given the common forces and tendencies at work. Although both the state of the financial markets and the general rate of inflation are systemic factors, beyond the control of any individual library, investment policies, spending (and reinvestment) rates, and success in raising new endowment are not. The star performer, without question, has been the AAS. It had the best overall results in each of the three subperiods and, naturally, for the entire period (see Tables 8.1 and 8.2). The difference between the AAS and the Newberry revealed by the indexed graph (Figure 8.2b) is striking. At the other end of the scale, we see that despite the rising tides for investors of the 1980s and early 1990s, the Newberry's endowment has shown no growth in real value at all.

Without more detailed information, it is impossible to disentangle the reasons for the disparate results obtained by the various endowments during the 1960s and 1970s. Why did the AAS's endowment grow in the 1960s at 5 percent per annum (nominal), while the Huntington, the Newberry, and the Morgan averaged only 2.4 percent growth? Why did the real value of the Morgan's endowment decline during the 1970s at an average annual rate of −4.7 percent, while the Huntington's declined at only −0.8 percent? Although we (and others with even

TABLE 8.2.   AVERAGE ANNUAL PERCENTAGE CHANGE IN MARKET VALUE OF ENDOWMENT,
BY LIBRARY AND SUBPERIOD, 1960–1993.

	Nominal			Real		
	1960–1974	1974–1982	1982–1993	1960–1974	1974–1982	1982–1993
American Antiquarian Society	3.26	8.68	10.89	-0.62	0.48	6.94
Folger Shakespeare Library[a]	N.A.	-1.89	9.50	N.A.	-9.55	5.59
Huntington Library	1.16	-1.50	9.55	-2.64	-8.92	5.65
Newberry Library	2.04	1.74	3.47	-1.79	-5.93	-0.22
Pierpont Morgan Library[b]	1.79	0.68	8.01	-2.72	-6.91	4.16
Average	2.06	1.54	8.28	-1.94	-6.17	4.42
Gross domestic product (GDP)	7.84	10.71	6.53	3.79	2.37	2.74
Inflation	3.91	8.15	3.69			

Source: Tabulations based on data in Appendix B.

Note: N.A. means not available.

[a]Folger data begin in 1976.

[b]Morgan data begin in 1963.

more detailed knowledge of these institutions) can speculate about the answers to such questions, the only period for which adequate data are available to provide reasonably precise answers is 1981–1993.

Total Returns and Asset Allocations (1981–1993)[17]

Analyzing the reasons for differences in returns between one institution and another is complicated, in part because the raw data do not address the intentions and plans of the parties. One factor that must be taken into account is the level of risk that trustees are willing to bear. Higher total returns do not necessarily imply superior performance; they may reflect only willingness to assume more risk in search of those returns. It is the relationship between the two that matters, and this relationship, for these libraries, is depicted in Figure 8.3.[18]

In general, we would expect total return to rise with the level of risk (which is measured by the volatility, or variance, in the annual returns), and this is what we find when we draw the "predicted" line showing the least-squares regression relationship between total return and risk for these five libraries and for a benchmark representing the "Cambridge mean."[19] The position of each institution relative to this line is one measure of relative success or failure as an investor, with a position above the line connoting success (a higher return than one would have predicted, given the level of risk assumed) and a position below the line

FIGURE 8.3. AVERAGE RETURNS FOR GIVEN LEVELS OF RISK (VARIANCE), BY LIBRARY, 1982–1993.

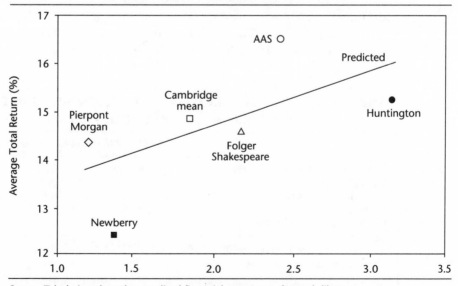

Source: Tabulations based on audited financial statements for each library.

Note: See note 19 for an explanation of the Cambridge mean.

connoting disappointing results (a lower return than one would have predicted, given the level of risk).

Using this standard, we see that the Morgan and especially the AAS achieved good results, the Folger's results are essentially on the line, the Huntington had an above-average total return but also accepted the most risk of any of these institutions (while earning a lower total return than the AAS), and the Newberry had results that were clearly disappointing (a very low total return that can be explained only in part by the low level of risk assumed). We conclude that superior investment performance was one important factor contributing to the success of the AAS in increasing the real value of its endowment, and we are also compelled to conclude that poor investment performance contributed to the decline in the real value of the endowment at the Newberry. (The position of the Cambridge mean slightly above the predicted line implies that overall, these five libraries did not do quite as well as the Cambridge universe of institutions; however, the difference is not great.)

The two main asset classes in which most endowments are invested are stocks and bonds. Because stocks have traditionally provided a higher level of return, as well as higher risk, the degree to which the endowments of the various libraries were invested in equities is another indicator of their riskiness (see Table 8.3). The interlibrary differences in asset allocation in the 1960s and 1970s are revealing. Of the five libraries, only the AAS is known to have had a clear majority of its funds invested in equities. The decision to invest in stocks during the bull market of the 1960s undoubtedly helped produce the high returns, and the associated growth in endowment, at the AAS during that decade. (The same comment probably can be made about the Folger, but we lack sufficient data to be sure.)

The Huntington's endowment has been managed differently, partly because the original indenture limited spending to interest and dividends. The low level of equities in the portfolio should be understood in light of that constraint; the consequences for the real value of the Huntington's endowment can be read from

TABLE 8.3. AVERAGE PERCENTAGE OF ENDOWMENT IN EQUITIES, BY LIBRARY AND SUBPERIOD, 1965–1993.

	1965–1980[a]	1981–1986	1987–1993
American Antiquarian Society	66.8	50.7	61.9
Folger Shakespeare Library	N.A.	58.8	60.4
Huntington Library	27.5	45.0	49.4
Newberry Library	N.A.	N.A.	14.9
Pierpont Morgan Library	47.8	52.0	48.1

Source: Tabulations based on audited financial statements for each library.

Note: N.A. means not available.

[a]Data were averaged over the following years: AAS, 1967, 1970, 1975, 1980; Huntington, 1975, 1980; Morgan, 1965, 1970, 1975, 1980.

Table 8.2—the real value of the endowment declined at an average rate of 2.6 percent per year in the 1960–1974 period and 8.9 percent per year between 1974 and 1982. In the 1980s, the Huntington's investment approach changed, and in more recent decades, about 50 percent of its endowment has been invested in equities. Funds that have been added, notably the proceeds of the two endowment-related capital campaigns and appreciation on those funds, are not subject to the dividends-and-interest clause of Henry Huntington's indenture; these funds, which at present comprise half the endowment, are invested on a total return basis.

Perhaps the most striking number in Table 8.3 is the low level of equities in the Newberry's portfolio during the most recent period. In marked contrast to the other four endowments, whose commitment to equities has hovered in the 50 to 60 percent range, only about 15 percent of the Newberry's endowment was placed in equities. Furthermore, this figure is for the endowment as a whole; the average for the unrestricted part of the Newberry's endowment is even lower, with an average of only 2.9 percent in equities since 1988. One reason for this apparently skewed distribution is the recurring need of the Newberry for large expenditures to fund persistent deficits (described in Chapter Nine). Investment in equities is most effective as a long-term strategy, and it is hard to pursue such a strategy when frequent withdrawals must be made. Another contributory factor has been the Newberry's shift back to a dividends-and-interest spending model. In the early 1980s, the portfolio was moved entirely into bonds in order to guarantee specified levels of income.

The Newberry is the only library in our set that reverted from a total return to a dividends-and-interest approach. In 1969, when the total return model was just gaining popularity, the Newberry began to invest for total return and spend a fixed portion of the endowment.[20] In 1972, this approach was formalized, and the spending rate was set at 5 percent of a twelve-quarter moving average of the value of the endowment; at the time, the policy was limited to endowment funds unrestricted as to both income and purpose. Following the enactment of UMIFA in Illinois in 1974, the Newberry's total return policy was broadened to include all funds except those with an explicit prohibition against the spending of capital gains. This policy was followed for the better part of ten years, with the spending rate raised to 6 percent in fiscal year 1980. In 1982, the Newberry's fiscal problems led its board to return to the practice of including all dividends and interest in budgeted income; however, the total return approach was retained, with roughly 50 percent of the endowment invested in equities.[21]

In late 1983, the board voted to move the entire endowment into bonds in order to increase the investment yield and safeguard against the loss of principal. Harold Byron Smith, chairman of the board at the time, has explained that this move was seen at the time as a conservative one.[22] In light of the significant cash needs associated with renovations and the ongoing operating deficit (see Chapters Three and Nine), the likelihood of capital withdrawals was high: the board did not want to risk a drop in stock values at a time when sales of securities were likely. Also, the shift into bonds was supposed to be temporary and was to be reversed after five years. As the data in the rightmost column of Table 8.3 demonstrate, this has not happened. The Newberry has paid a heavy price (in forgone returns) for this set of investment decisions—prompted as they were by severe financial stresses that date back to decisions made in the 1970s and even earlier.

Spending and Reinvestment Rates

Based on the theory of endowment management outlined in this chapter, the highest permissible spending rate should be the difference between the expected total return and the required reinvestment rate, both estimated on a long-term basis. In practice, most heavily endowed institutions have been too dependent on investment income to follow this approach rigorously. Bills must be paid, and without a formal spending rule, the temptation is strong to increase—temporarily, it is almost always hoped—the level of spending from endowment to meet pressing needs. Even with a spending rule, the presence of unrestricted endowment funds means that unless the expenditure of capital gains is legally restricted (or there is some other explicit prohibition protecting the principal against incursions), those funds may well be depleted to cover deficits. This practice, when it occurs, is tantamount to an increase in what might be called the *effective* spending rate. Both the formal spending rate (as established by the spending rule) and the effective spending rate (as measured after the fact), must be monitored closely. For purposes of this discussion, we define the term *spending rate* in its conventional sense—the amount of the return on the endowment that was spent in the year in question (whether it consisted of dividends, interest received, or capital gains), divided by the market value of the endowment at the start of the year.

Spending rates from the early 1960s forward are shown for all five of the libraries in this study in Figures 8.4a and 8.4b. A line has been superimposed on the figures indicating, for reference purposes, the 5 percent spending rate that is often regarded as prudent.[23]

The first conclusion to be drawn from this quite extraordinary set of data is that the similarities over time are nothing short of astonishing. Each of the libraries in our set has a clearly demarcated "crossover point" at which the spending rate moved above the 5 percent level. All five libraries began to spend more than 5 percent of the market values of their endowments at some point in the mid to late 1970s. As we saw earlier, demands on the endowment had reached "full capacity," and the temptation to meet the financial exigencies of the times by resorting to higher spending rates proved irresistible. Spending rates continued to rise, hitting their high points in the early 1980s: at the Morgan in 1981; at the AAS, the Huntington, and the Folger in 1983; and at the Newberry in 1985.

Since then, the spending rate has dropped at each of these libraries, in part as a result of transitions in leadership and clearer recognition of the deleterious

FIGURE 8.4A. SPENDING RATE, FOLGER, HUNTINGTON, AND MORGAN LIBRARIES, 1960–1993.

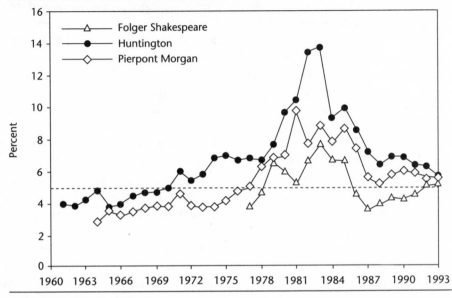

Source: Data from Appendix B.

FIGURE 8.4B. SPENDING RATE, AMERICAN ANTIQUARIAN SOCIETY AND NEWBERRY LIBRARY, 1960–1993.

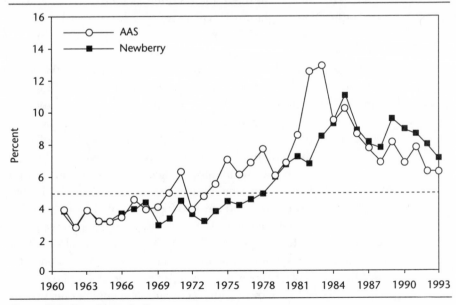

Source: Data from Appendix B.

effects of persistent overspending. For many of the newly elected directors, the need to control the level of the spending rate was not an abstract proposition: they knew that they were inheriting undercapitalized institutions and that the spending patterns of the 1980s could not be allowed to continue. Spending rates have come down more at some libraries than at others, but all five (with the possible exception of the Newberry) seem to be converging on the 5 to 6 percent range—and therefore to be reaching much more sustainable levels. The stock market crash in October 1987 was also a sobering experience for many institutions; it was a vivid reminder that stocks could fall in value as well as rise and that no one should count on realized capital gains to be available year in and year out.

The Folger deserves special comment. Its spending rate has been appreciably lower than the average for any of the other libraries (as we demonstrate in Figure 8.5); its peak rate was lower than the peak rate at the other libraries, and it returned to what would generally be regarded as a reasonable rate sooner than the others (the Morgan is a close second). One possible explanation is that the Folger is governed by the trustees of Amherst College, who have been responsible for investing the Folger's endowment. In general, colleges and universities with large endowments have had more experience with the total return approach than other nonprofits, and the more conservative stance on spending rates that is characteristic of the world of higher education may have "rubbed off" on the Folger.

Another way to assess the level of spending rates is by looking at them alongside total returns—thereby simultaneously considering reinvestment rates. How have the five libraries allocated their total returns between present and future claimants? What portion has been reinvested and what portion spent? Figure 8.5 provides the answers to these questions for each of these libraries for the period 1982–1993. The height of the bars represents the average total return (always on a per-unit basis), while the division between the black and white segments illustrates the split between spending and reinvestment.

This figure allows us to address simultaneously three of the main components of the endowment management equation: investing, spending, and reinvesting. Putting these components together illustrates their interrelationships, as is evidenced best by a comparison of the AAS and the Newberry. Along with the Huntington, these two institutions had the highest spending rates of the five libraries, averaging 8.8 percent and 8.7 percent, respectively. Clearly, these spending rates are well outside what would usually be regarded as the prudent, sustainable range. Yet because of the exceptional returns that characterized the 1980s, it was possible in some settings to spend close to 9 percent of the market value of the corpus and still reinvest enough of the total return to maintain the purchasing power of each unit of the endowment. The AAS is the perfect illustration of this possibility: its average spending rate of 8.8 percent occurred in concert with an average total return of 16.5 percent, leaving an average of 7.7 percent to be reinvested. The Newberry, by contrast, with a comparable spending rate, was able to reinvest only an average of 3.8 percent per annum because of the appreciably lower total return on its portfolio.

FIGURE 8.5. TOTAL RETURN, SPENDING RATE, AND REINVESTMENT RATE, BY LIBRARY, 1982–1993.

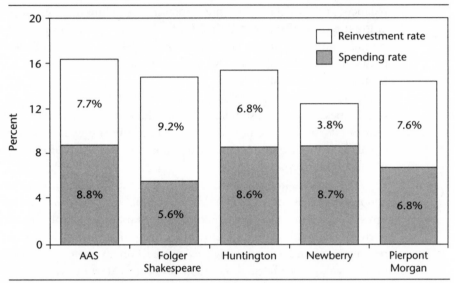

Source: Tabulations based on audited financial statements for each library.

Note: Total return is the total height of each bar (the sum of the spending rate and the reinvestment rate).

Augmenting: Gifts to Endowment

Gifts are the final piece of the endowment puzzle. They add to the number of units in the endowment and thus increase the share of total expenditures that can be covered by endowment income. Opportunities to raise new endowment are by no means equivalent for all nonprofit organizations, and they surely differ among the libraries in this study. Moreover, different libraries may have attached (for good reasons) different priorities to this type of fundraising. In any event, it is clear that some have been more successful than others in their pursuit of new units of endowment. The Morgan's record of accomplishment in this arena appears outstanding: in three separate years (including two quite recent years, 1989 and 1992), capital gifts were equal to or exceeded 15 percent of the endowment's value. This is an encouraging sign for the future, as is the successful completion of the Morgan's expansion campaign.

The AAS, the Huntington, and the Newberry occupy the middle ground. The Isaiah Thomas campaign at the AAS brought in considerable new endowment, especially in the society's 175th anniversary year of 1987. The Newberry raised between 6 percent and 7 percent of the market value of its endowment in every year between 1986 and 1990 except one (when there was a leadership transition in 1987). The Huntington's capital fundraising has been more sporadic, with successful years spread throughout the time period.

The Folger appears to have adopted a different strategy. The initial focus in the mid to late 1980s, after Werner Gundersheimer's election as director, was on balancing the budget by bringing expenditures in line with revenues and broadening the base of current giving. Only since the 1992 Jubilee campaign does capital fundraising appear to have become a priority. In light of the Folger's surpluses in 1992 and 1993 (see Chapters Four and Nine), this strategy seems to have been applied successfully.

What is an appropriate benchmark for capital gifts? There are at least three possibilities. A minimal standard can be adduced from the total return model: if reinvested earnings are not adequate to keep the endowment growing at a rate equal to the organization's internal inflation rate, new units of endowment will be needed to fill the gap.[24]

A second, higher standard would be that capital gifts (as a percentage of the endowment) plus reinvested funds should equal the real growth in total expenditures. Meeting this standard would keep constant the share of operating revenues derived from endowment income and ensure that new activities are not overly reliant on soft money. Applying this standard on a year-to-year basis is no doubt impractical, in part because new activities rarely start out with funding from endowment. More often, a new program will be initiated with some combination of contributed income (including perhaps a targeted grant) and reserves. If the program is successful—programmatically as well as in its ability to attract funds— efforts may then be made to endow it. The research and education centers at the Newberry are good examples of this model of development. Despite its limited utility for annual comparisons, this standard can be quite instructive when applied over time.

The third standard is more pragmatic. It consists simply of comparing results at different institutions in roughly the same circumstances. Despite the small number of libraries in this set, such comparisons add another dimension to the discussion.

The so-called minimal standard was met by all five of the libraries during the 1980s, but for a reason that has little to do with successes in capital fundraising. Because of the abnormally high investment returns that characterized the 1980s, each of the five libraries reinvested a sufficient share of the total return to offset inflation, and thus capital gifts were not "needed" for that purpose.

The second standard compares the sum of the reinvestment rate and the capital gifts rate with average annual growth in expenditures. Here, too, all five libraries achieved success. Figure 8.6 shows that three of them—the AAS, the Folger, and the Morgan—were able to build the endowment sufficiently through reinvestment alone to do more than keep pace with rising expenditures. (The x indicates the average annual rate of increase in expenditures, and the dark segments of the bars, showing the average reinvestment rates, are higher than the x in each of these cases.) For these three libraries, capital gifts (the light segments of the bars) could be regarded as a "bonus" from this standpoint. The other two libraries—

FIGURE 8.6. GROWTH IN ENDOWMENT VERSUS GROWTH IN EXPENDITURES, BY LIBRARY, 1982–1993.

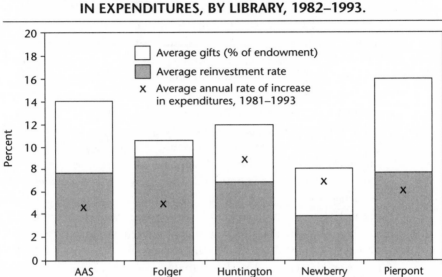

Source: Tabulations based on audited financial statements for each library.

the Huntington and the Newberry—had to rely on gifts along with reinvestments to meet the standard (the x for each falls above the dark segment but inside the light segment).

The third standard is bound to be met by some of the libraries and missed by others because, by definition, not all can outperform the five-library average. The average annual rate of capital giving for this group of libraries during the period 1982–1993 was 4.7 percent. Three of the libraries beat that average: the Morgan, the AAS, and the Huntington (barely). The Newberry came close, with an average capital gifts rate of 4.1 percent. Only the Folger's performance was significantly below average in this regard—and as we mentioned earlier, this result does not seem cause for great concern because the Folger elected another financial planning strategy that seems to have worked out well.[25]

In concluding this discussion of endowment, a cautionary flag should be raised. Although our purpose in this study is most emphatically not to offer gratuitous advice—either retrospectively or prospectively—we would be remiss if we did not call attention once again to the truly extraordinary character of the returns available in the 1980s in the equity and bond markets. Between 1981 and 1990, nominal returns averaged nearly 17 percent per year for stocks and 12 percent per year for corporate bonds; during the rest of the period from 1947 to 1994, the corresponding returns were 10 percent for stocks and 4 percent for bonds. The differences in real returns were even greater. During the decade of the 1980s, real returns averaged nearly 12 percent per year for stocks and 7 percent per year for bonds; the corresponding figures for the rest of the period from 1947 to 1994 were 5 percent for stocks and −1 percent for bonds.[26]

It would take an exceptionally optimistic (or courageous) group of trustees to project total (nominal) returns at anything approaching 15 percent per year. The consensus seems to favor, for planning purposes, a prospective total return of perhaps 10 to 12 percent per year in nominal terms. Judging from the much lower spending rates now being employed by these libraries, their trustees appear to have reached a similar conclusion.

More generally, this exercise in judging capital fundraising results for the libraries against benchmarks is more useful for the concepts it introduces than for the "facts" it reveals. The results for the five libraries would have been very different had the available data permitted us to apply the same standards of performance in earlier periods. Libraries that maintained significant positions in bonds in the 1980s were very fortunate; in any other decade, they would have paid a much greater penalty (in terms of forgone returns) for that asset allocation decision. Our suspicion is that only the AAS would have even come close to meeting the second benchmark. We know that for the period as a whole, the share of total expenditures covered by endowment income has declined markedly for these libraries, in spite of high spending rates during the 1980s (refer to Figure 8.4).

Whatever the vagaries of the investment environment, the evidence assembled in this chapter provides persuasive support, we believe, for three general propositions concerning the management of endowments. First, the skill with which endowments are managed varies considerably and matters a great deal—the AAS is the best example of a library that has been helped greatly by above-average investment results. Second, it is especially important for trustees to make wise decisions concerning asset allocation—both the Huntington and the Newberry, in particular, would be much stronger financially if their endowments had been invested more heavily in equities at earlier points in their history. Third, there is much to be said for adopting long-term policies concerning spending rates, tied to realistic expectations concerning total returns and sensible judgments concerning the share of the total return that needs to be reinvested to protect the purchasing power of the endowment. And of course it is important not just to adopt such policies but to adhere to them.

Notes

1. Salamon (1992, 1993) has analyzed the investment performance of foundations over time. Because these institutions' very reason for being is the provision of investment income to others in the form of grants, the results of the study are particularly important. They also make for a useful comparison with this chapter.
2. Much of this discussion has been culled from Longstreth (1986). Note 1 in Chapter 2 of that work (p. 76) cites additional sources for further background reading.
3. Ennis and Williamson (1976, p. 6).
4. Longstreth (1986, p. 59).

5. Longstreth (1986, pp. 53, 55).
6. Longstreth (1986, p. 61).
7. Bright and Cary (1969, p. 7).
8. Ford Foundation (1969).
9. In the case of an endowment that has a fixed number of units (receives no new gifts during a year), the total return is simply the percentage increase in the market value of the endowment over this yearly interval, assuming that all dividends and interest are retained. New gifts and withdrawals of units create significant measurement problems (explained in Appendix A, which defines all of the concepts presented in this chapter and explains how we estimate their values).
10. "Spending rates" can take many forms. Most commonly, a spending rate is expressed as some percentage of the market value of the endowment, such as 5 percent, which the trustees authorize for spending in the current year. In an operational sense, a spending rate substitutes for the earlier rule that defined spendable income as the sum of dividends and interest earned during the year. (See Appendix A.)
11. Bright and Cary (1969); Ford Foundation (1969).
12. Of course, the difference between realized and unrealized gains is a small matter of calling one's broker. Bright and Cary recognized that their argument was already pushing the legal envelope, and they did not press this point. Subsequently, more sophisticated analyses—which do not depend on the turnover of a portfolio—have often prevailed.
13. Bright and Cary (1974).
14. Hansmann (1990).
15. All units are not the same in terms of the restrictions that govern them. Designated funds can be subject to restrictions that affect the investment policy, the spending rate, or both. One good example is the Founder's Endowment at the Huntington, which restricts spending to interest and dividends only.
16. Unfortunately, data for all five libraries were not available for all years. Data became available for the Morgan in 1963 and for the Folger in 1976. In indexing the values for the Morgan and the Folger, we adopted the simple assumption that they had equivalent results for the average of the other libraries up until their own data became available.
17. All total return figures presented here and in the remainder of the chapter have been calculated on a unit basis; hence they are not affected by additions to or withdrawals from the endowments (see Appendix A).
18. An analogous curve can be drawn on the basis of long-term data showing the risk and return combinations associated, on average, with varying proportions of stocks and bonds in a hypothetical portfolio. Cambridge Associates has compiled the relevant data, which demonstrate the existence of the same kind of positive relationship between risk and reward that we see in Figure 8.3. We could have made a more refined comparison between the investment results achieved by these libraries and the opportunities presented by financial markets if we had had access to more detailed information concerning the composition of the portfolios of the libraries and had been able to compute both total returns and standard deviations for each asset class held by them.
19. The "Cambridge mean" is the average total return (and the corresponding average variance in annual returns) obtained by a large population of endowments whose performance is tracked by Cambridge Associates.
20. Minutes, meeting of the board of trustees of the Newberry Library, January 4, 1979, app. F.
21. Minutes, meeting of the finance committee of the Newberry Library, September 8, 1982. Again, audited data are unavailable; therefore, although these broad decisions are known, we lack the data needed to report specific figures in Table 8.3.

22. H. B. Smith, telephone interview, November 17, 1993.

23. One set of hypothetical calculations that can be used to arrive at a presumptive 5 percent spending rate involves assuming a total return of 11 percent and an internal inflation rate of 6 percent; this combination of total return and required reinvestment rate leaves 5 percent of the market value of the endowment available for spending in the current year. The absolute value of the stream of income available for spending in the operating budget will rise over time (by approximately 6 percent per year in this example), presuming that the total return objective is achieved. To smooth spending paths and to simplify budgeting, some organizations work with spending rates calculated as annual increments over spending in the prior year—assuming that the conventional spending rate in the base year was chosen appropriately; if market values depart from projections, the base level can—and should—be adjusted. A wide array of mechanisms, including the use of averaging, can be adopted to give effect to the kinds of spending-rate policies discussed in the text.

24. An alternative formulation would be to say that if investment returns do not allow for sufficient spending after making adequate provision for reinvestment (treating reinvestment as the first priority), *current* gifts should fill that gap.

25. These average gift rates are depicted graphically by the white segments of the bars in Figure 8.6, but the rates are not indicated explicitly.

26. Data provided by Troy Murray at Cambridge Associates.

CHAPTER NINE

DEFICITS AND THEIR DYNAMICS

Two related themes have appeared repeatedly in this study: growth and attendant financial stress. In this chapter, we will examine how the combination of steadily increasing expenditures and constraints on traditional sources of income (especially investment income) has been reflected in operating deficits and surpluses—the legendary "bottom line."[1]

Our emphasis will be on the magnitude of the resulting imbalances and on the ways in which these five independent research libraries have coped with the resulting budgetary pressures.

We do not want to impose too strong a normative tone on the discussion that follows because there are times when running a deficit is an appropriate course of action—just as there are situations in which nominally "good" surpluses are actually evidence of complacency or inadequate institutional ambition. It is also true that the underlying financial problems of an institution can be far more serious than the magnitude of a reported deficit in a given year would lead one to believe. A major part of this chapter is devoted to illustrating this important point by showing the extent to which unsustainable increases in spending rates (and hence in investment income) concealed the degree of financial distress experienced by almost all of these libraries in the 1980s.

The existence of "invisible payables" is an even more generic source of difficulties beyond those made evident by reported red ink. Organizations of all kinds face the temptation to postpone needed expenditures—for example, by deferring maintenance, by not filling positions that will have to be filled soon, or by freezing salaries that may already be too low and will have to be raised at some point to maintain morale and to hold and recruit staff. Such costs, though invisible on an accounting statement, are quite real. Ultimately, they simply have to be addressed, and postponement of action may serve only to aggravate—to magnify—the underlying problem.

Thus, at the minimum, operating deficits are a clear warning signal of an apparent disequilibrium that may be even more serious than it seems to be on the surface. Simply waiting for circumstances to improve is rarely an adequate response.

Deficits and Surpluses Viewed Historically: As Conventionally Reported and as "Adjusted"

Deficits were not always a serious problem at the five independent research libraries in this set. Over large parts of their lifetimes, these libraries were fully endowed institutions with a comfortable cushion between income and expenditures. Reserves were ample, and in periods of rapidly rising costs or when given opportunities to make major acquisitions, spending from these reserves was the obvious recourse. Only in the 1970s—when the demands made on the libraries outstripped the capacities of their endowments—did significant gaps between expenditures and income become a real and recurring concern.

This is not to say, of course, that the five libraries never faced the need to raise money prior to the mid 1960s. The creation of the Fellows at the Morgan Library in 1960 is evidence that a need for additional funding was recognized then. Similarly, the AAS has depended for many years on gifts for both current and capital purposes. Prior to the 1970s, however, deficits were sporadic and not regarded as of lasting consequence. Any deficits that did arise were usually occasioned by one-time needs to make large expenditures—for example, to construct or renovate buildings or to make a particularly costly acquisition. Once the need in question was met, the institution returned to financial equilibrium. Through most of the 1960s, it was reasonable to assume that whatever problems had created financial imbalance were temporary and in some way would be redressed by the passage of time.

The financial problems of the past twenty-five years, in which the five libraries went from being income spenders to being fund seekers, have been much more deep-seated and, consequently, much more serious. By choosing to grow and to meet the new (or at least newly recognized) needs of a wider range of scholars and other clients, the libraries committed themselves to a future in which adequate funding was no longer guaranteed. The libraries became vulnerable, in a way they had not been before, to reductions in income. They became more dependent on external funders, who had priorities of their own. One result was a much more volatile set of financial results, with the bottom line capable of swinging rather abruptly from surplus to deficit—and staying there.

A useful way to calibrate the severity of deficits (or the sizes of surpluses) is to compare them with total expenditures. In the case of deficits, for instance, the resulting percentage describes the share of expenditures not covered by current income. The solid line in Figure 9.1 shows the average surplus or deficit experienced each year by these five libraries, expressed as a percentage of average total expenditures.[2]

To recapitulate briefly: in the 1960s, surpluses were the order of the day, and for the first half of the decade, they were sizeable, averaging more than 10 percent of total expenditures. Starting in 1967, a downward trend is evident. The "crossover" year was 1970. From 1971 on, deficits have been far more common than surpluses. In fact, recurring deficits can reasonably be said to have become the norm. Between 1970 and 1993, there was only one four-year period (1977–1980) in which the average operating result for these five libraries was a surplus; in contrast, there were nineteen years of deficits.

The ubiquity of these deficits—both over time and across libraries—suggests strongly that at least some of the problems causing them transcend events specific to particular institutions. The data support that conclusion. We discussed at length in Chapter Six the generic forces that have pushed expenditures up more rapidly than in the past, and we saw in Chapter Seven that the original endowments were outgrown some years ago. The data summarized in Figure 9.1 serve mainly

FIGURE 9.1. AVERAGE SURPLUS/DEFICIT AS A PERCENTAGE OF TOTAL EXPENDITURES, 1960–1993.

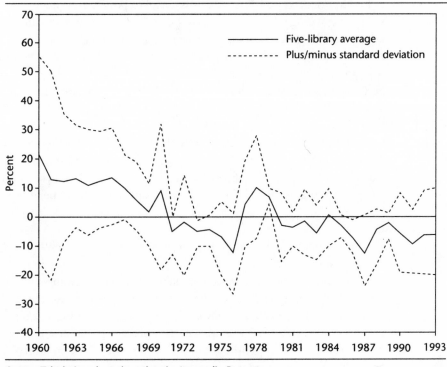

Source: Tabulations based on data in Appendix B.

to document the extent to which these divergent forces have led to a persistent imbalance between current expenditures and current income. Later in the chapter, we comment briefly on specific institutional responses to these imbalances.

First, however, we must put a gloss on the picture presented in Figure 9.1. This is necessary because the conventional measures of surpluses and deficits depicted there understate, quite dramatically, the magnitude of the real shift in financial circumstances that has taken place. When these libraries began to exhaust their financial cushions in the late 1960s and then to encounter far more serious stresses in the 1970s, a common response was to seek more support for the operating budget from the endowment. The marked upward trend in spending rates shown previously (in Figures 8.4a and 8.4b) documents the extent of this entirely understandable response. For most of the 1960s, this objective was accomplished simply by allowing spending rates to rise from previously low levels (below 4 percent in some instances) to about the 5 percent level, which many people today would regard as prudent and sustainable. By the end of the 1970s, spending rates had risen above the 5 percent level at every one of these libraries; by the mid 1980s, spending rates in the 10 to 12 percent range were common (the Folger is the one exception to this generalization).

Not even the substantial infusions of operating income that resulted from these escalating spending rates eliminated deficits—but they certainly reduced their magnitude. In effect, because there was no reason to believe that such high spending rates could be sustained, the true extent of the current financial imbalances being experienced was disguised. It is useful to pose a hypothetical question: what would the average deficit have looked like over this period had all of the libraries adopted and enforced a spending rule that limited their annual take of investment income to 5 percent of the market value of the endowment? The answer to this question is given by the solid line in Figure 9.2. (For purposes of comparison, we also reproduce here, this time as a dotted line, the conventionally reported deficits shown in Figure 9.1.)

The general results of this exercise are striking.[3] Looking first at the 1960s, the full extent of the cushion enjoyed by the libraries at that time is now apparent. Actual spending rates were so low that if a full 5 percent of market value had been treated as current income, huge surpluses would have been recorded.[4] The central point is that whatever the mode of accounting and financial reporting, these libraries in fact had considerable untapped financial potential throughout most of the 1960s.

From about 1970 through 1978, the reported averages and the adjusted averages (the solid and the dotted lines in Figure 9.2) track each other fairly closely—which is only another way of saying that on average, spending rates were not very different from the hypothetical 5 percent level during those years. (As a careful inspection of Figures 8.4a and 8.4b will remind us, the Huntington and the AAS had spending rates quite a bit above the 5 percent level, but the Morgan and the Newberry were still spending roughly 4 percent of the market value of their endowments, which explains why the average was not far from 5 percent. We do

FIGURE 9.2. AVERAGE SURPLUS/DEFICIT AS A PERCENTAGE OF TOTAL EXPENDITURES, ADJUSTED FOR SPENDING RATE GREATER THAN 5 PERCENT, 1960–1993.

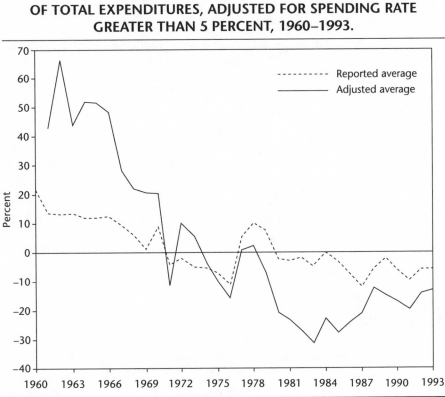

Source: Tabulations based on data in Appendix B.

not have data for the Folger for these years.) Much of the programmatic expansion under way in the 1970s was funded by new grants from the National Endowment for the Humanities (NEH) and foundations, so there was less pressure than in later years to look aggressively to investment income to pay the rising bills; also, the financial markets were hardly booming at that time and hence were not conducive to harvesting capital gains.

Starting in 1978, the picture changed dramatically, in essentially every respect. Spending rates now averaged well above 5 percent of the market value of the endowments, and the adjusted deficits begin to diverge substantially from the reported (conventionally defined) deficits. The year 1983 is the most extreme case in point: that was a year of very high spending rates, and the "adjusted" deficits—based on the imposition of a 5 percent spending rate—*averaged fully 30 percent of expenditures;* in contrast, the reported deficits, though hardly negligible, averaged only about 6 percent of expenditures. This was the period, it may be recalled, when these libraries were coping simultaneously with rising expenditures related to the programmatic initiatives of the late 1970s and with reductions in grant income. Encouraged, no doubt, by the buoyant financial markets of the early

1980s, large amounts of realized capital gains were taken into operating budgets in order to fill most (but not all) of the large budgetary gaps that resulted from these asymmetrical developments.

The last subperiod can be dated from the mid 1980s forward. For reasons discussed earlier, spending rates began to decline, and the adjusted and reported deficit lines began to converge. The adjusted line continues to show larger average deficits than those that were reported, even in 1992 and 1993, but the differential is much reduced. (This differential would disappear almost entirely if we used a 6 percent spending rate rather than 5 percent as the hypothetical standard. The choice of 5 percent is somewhat arbitrary, and a different yardstick would of course alter the magnitudes shown in Figure 9.2 but not the general picture.) Perhaps the main conclusion to be drawn from the data for these last ten years is that the libraries have made much more progress in addressing the fundamental imbalance in their operating budget than is evident from trends in the reported figures. That is the good news. The bad news is the reason: the extent of the underlying imbalance was, in truth, much greater in the mid 1980s than people acknowledged at the time.

Cycles and Dynamics

It would take a study all its own to analyze with requisite sophistication the various ways in which budgetary gaps emerge and are ultimately closed. An intensive analysis of this kind, which would have to parse out developments on a year-to-year basis, is outside the scope of the present study, which is focused more on long-term trends and patterns. Consistent with our general intent, we offer here only a suggestion of an approach that others may want to consider for a more detailed analysis and a few general comments.

Although the histories of deficits are inescapably institution-specific, it is useful to think about cycles and the dynamics of the process of adjustment a little more systematically. For this purpose, we have constructed a "balanced-budget diagram," which is designed to focus attention on the interrelated nature of year-to-year changes in expenditures, income, and deficits, as conventionally measured. This approach allows us to look simultaneously at the absolute amount of growth (or contraction) that is occurring, alongside operating deficits or surpluses, and to see how the events of one year feed into the next.

It is easiest to illustrate the type of analysis we wish to propose in the context of the data for a specific institution, and we have elected to begin with the Huntington (see Figure 9.3). Expenditures are plotted on the horizontal axis, income on the vertical axis. The straight line running from the origin to the northeast corner of the diagram is the balanced-budget line: expenditures equal income at any point on it. (It would be a 45-degree line if the figure were a square rather than a rectangle—that is, if the same units of measurement were used on the horizontal and vertical axes.) The levels of expenditures and of income for each year

FIGURE 9.3. SURPLUS/DEFICIT, INCOME, AND EXPENDITURES, HUNTINGTON LIBRARY, 1960–1993.

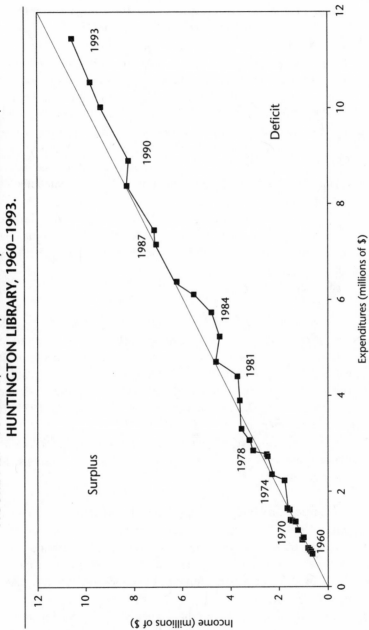

Source: Data from Tables B.1–1 and B.1–2 in Appendix B.

are shown by the location of a black square plotted for that year. The vertical distance between a square and the balanced-budget line measures the surplus for that year (if the square is above the 45-degree line) or the deficit (if the square is below the line). Squares for successive years are linked by straight lines so that we can see how the relationship between expenditures and income changes from one year to the next. Specific years (1960, 1970, 1974, and so on) are marked occasionally to permit the dating of events, but it should be understood that there is no special significance to the particular years identified on the graph. Since there has been quite steady growth in nominal expenditures and in income over the period covered by this study, there is a fairly regular progression of annual observations, with the square for 1960 near the bottom left-hand corner of the graph and the square for 1993 near the top right-hand corner. (It should be noted that this "upward" motion is by no means foreordained. As discussed earlier, growth is not always good. Also, the use of nominal rather than real data affects the appearance of the figure; see note 6.)

We have constructed similar graphs for the other four libraries, and we present them here too (as Figures 9.4, 9.5, 9.6, and 9.7) so that interested readers can examine the sequence of events in specific situations which they may know in detail.

Four general observations follow:

1. *In the figure for the Huntington, and in several of the other figures, one can detect the presence of minicycles, in the shape of curves.* Each of these cycle curves starts from a roughly balanced budget, moves "forward" into the deficit region (with increases in expenditures, not reductions in income, leading the way), and usually returns to balance only after additional growth in both expenditures and income. The cycle curves for the Huntington can be seen as early as the 1974–1976 period but are most prominent in 1979–1982, 1982–1986, and 1989–1991.

These recurring cycles can no doubt be interpreted in several ways. The interpretation that seems most plausible to us involves the following sequence of events and responses:

- The institution's budget is approximately in balance, as it was at the Huntington in 1970, 1979–1980, 1982, and 1989.
- Pressures of one kind or another for increased expenditures are felt—as a result of inflation, perceived new programmatic opportunities, or the need to do something about deferred maintenance or other "invisible payables" accumulated from earlier years
- Because the budget is currently in balance, the leadership and the trustees may well yield to these pressures and allow expenditures to increase more rapidly than in the preceding year or two—or they may even decide consciously that this is an opportune time to address some long-standing needs.
- Current income, however, does not increase as rapidly, if at all, and so deficits

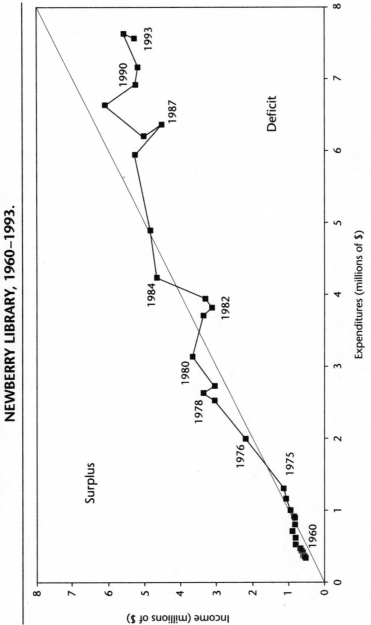

FIGURE 9.4. SURPLUS/DEFICIT, INCOME, AND EXPENDITURES, NEWBERRY LIBRARY, 1960–1993.

Income (millions of $)

Expenditures (millions of $)

Surplus

Deficit

Source: Data from Tables B.3–1 and B.3–2 in Appendix B.

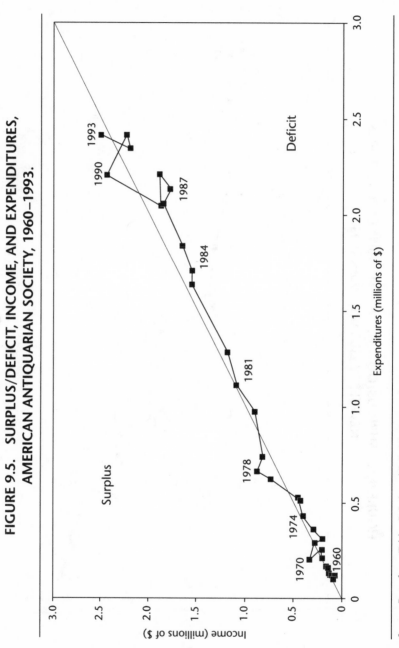

FIGURE 9.5. SURPLUS/DEFICIT, INCOME, AND EXPENDITURES, AMERICAN ANTIQUARIAN SOCIETY, 1960–1993.

Source: Data from Tables B.5–1 and B.5–2 in Appendix B.

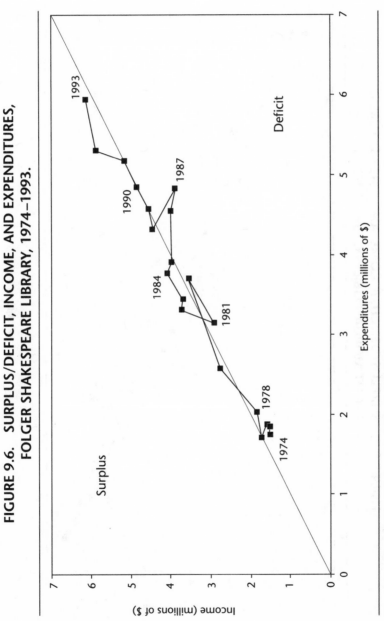

FIGURE 9.6. SURPLUS/DEFICIT, INCOME, AND EXPENDITURES,
FOLGER SHAKESPEARE LIBRARY, 1974–1993.

Source: Data from Tables B.4–1 and B.4–2 in Appendix B.

FIGURE 9.7. SURPLUS/DEFICIT, INCOME, AND EXPENDITURES, PIERPONT MORGAN LIBRARY, 1963–1993.

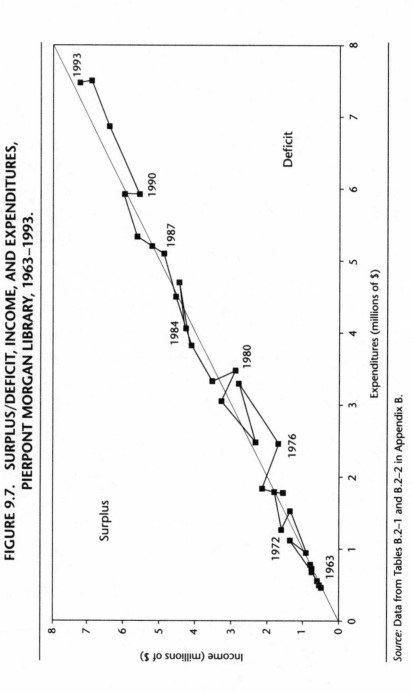

Source: Data from Tables B.2–1 and B.2–2 in Appendix B.

occur—and the next square will be below the balanced-budget line (as it was, for instance, at the Huntington in 1983 and 1990).

- Deficits continue for at least a year or two, as expenditures continue to rise without enough of a boost in income to make up for the initial shortfall.
- Facing recurring deficits, the leadership and trustees of the library both attempt to restrain expenditures and redouble their efforts to increase income—often through some combination of more aggressive fundraising and higher endowment spending rates.
- A balanced budget is again achieved (as in 1986 and 1991).
- The cycle may then repeat itself, as expenditures once again tend to rise ahead of current income.

In proposing a simple dynamic of this kind, we certainly do not mean to downplay continuing efforts to restrain expenditures. On the contrary, once history moved these organizations past the fully endowed years of the early 1960s, they were under more or less constant pressure to restrain expenditures. However, for institutions of this kind, with heavy fixed costs and predictable recurring costs (maintaining a physical plant, keeping a library open, and so on), substantial economies are not easy to achieve. The common pattern, we suspect, is to accumulate "invisible payables" while hoping for better financial conditions. Then, according to the logic of this scenario, when balanced budgets are achieved, the "dam breaks" (or at least cracks), and expenditures, including deferred expenditures, increase more rapidly than current income. Austerity is reimposed as rapidly as possible (though possibly only after one or two years because some projects must be carried through to completion), and renewed efforts are made to increase income.

There may also be situations in which it is necessary "to spend money to raise money." What we have in mind here is not so much the funding of more vigorous development efforts (though such efforts often do require the investment of "seed money") as it is expansions of activities designed to demonstrate the vitality of an institution and hence to attract new donors. The most recent cycle curve at the Huntington is, in this sense, a "growth curve," illustrating a strategy that the director, Robert Skotheim, has characterized as trying "to refinance the institution even as it is being programmatically revitalized."[5] There has been an increased focus on all elements of the revenue profile, even as the Huntington's programmatic sights were raised. Thus in 1990, expenditures grew significantly, while income did not. In 1991, the Huntington moved closer to a balanced budget, but as of this writing, balance has not yet been attained.

2. *External funding can create very volatile budgetary situations, and long-term financial problems can be caused by programmatic expansion fueled initially by new grant income.* The experiences of both the Newberry and the AAS illustrate this pattern. In the case of the Newberry (Figure 9.4), the difference between the period 1960–1975 and the period 1975–1994 is simply astounding. The fifteen years comprising the

earlier period—which occupies only a tiny area in the southwest corner of the graph—saw the Newberry's financial situation shift from one of substantial surpluses to modest deficits, but with relatively slow growth throughout (note the close bunching of the squares).[6] In the next three years—from 1975 to 1978— there was a veritable explosion of growth.

From the deficit/surplus perspective, the salient point is that reported income rose much more rapidly than expenditures at the Newberry, producing a very large reported surplus in 1978. Almost exactly the same pattern is evident at the AAS (Figure 9.7). The explanation is both straightforward and instructive. The Newberry and the AAS were, among these libraries, by far the largest beneficiaries of NEH grants during the mid 1970s (see Chapter Seven). At both institutions, the sudden—and very rapid—increases in income that drove the surpluses of the late 1970s were triggered in no small part by these appropriations, which either ran somewhat ahead of the programmatic expansions they were fueling or covered, at least for a time, expenditures that might otherwise have been a charge on regular sources of income. (We believe that the proceeds of capital campaigns at both institutions also contributed significantly to these apparent surpluses; it is impossible to know the magnitudes, however, because of the problems of distinguishing capital gifts from current gifts alluded to earlier.)

The turnaround in the fortunes of both of these libraries also occurred more or less simultaneously. The magnitude of the swing is most dramatic at the Newberry. By 1982, the large apparent surpluses of earlier years had become a very large deficit. The general pattern is again strikingly similar at the AAS. In the case of the Newberry, total income in 1982 was far below the 1980 level. One source of this abrupt reversal in circumstances is readily identified. Grant income was cut back greatly. At about the same time, or shortly thereafter, there was a dramatic spurt in expenditures at the Newberry (see the 1984–1986 interval in Figure 9.4); the proximate causes were increased operating costs associated with the major expansion and renovation of space and resumption of normal programs when the construction was completed.

It should also be noted that the reported deficits would have been even larger at both the Newberry and the AAS in these years had it not been for large increases in the endowment spending rate. At the Newberry, rapid increases in the endowment spending rate (which reached a peak of about 11 percent in 1985) played a significant role in achieving what proved to be a temporary balance between expenditures and income in 1984. At the AAS, spending rates peaked slightly earlier (at a rate above 12 percent in 1982 and 1983), which produced a near balanced budget in 1983. We see here clear evidence in specific settings of the more general point made earlier in the chapter about the role played by the spending of capital gains in funding what would otherwise have been much larger deficits. These extraordinarily high spending rates could not be maintained, and the consequences can be seen clearly. The return to deficits was more pronounced at the Newberry than at the AAS, though again the same pattern is evident at both libraries.

3. *Leadership transitions can have important effects—both short-term and long-term.*

4. *In recent years, these libraries appear to have become much more conscious of the need to manage their budgets carefully and to achieve a more sustainable balance between expenditures and income.*

These last two propositions, though different in character, are so interrelated in the recent histories of these libraries that they are most conveniently discussed together.

The arrival of a new director is often the occasion for the trustees and the director to take stock: to determine what the most pressing problems are and what should be done about them. This stock-taking process often leads to at least a brief pause in fundraising and sometimes in the growth of expenditures too; new staffing decisions have to be made, and (depending on circumstances) new plans must be drawn from both current giving and capital campaigns. These "plateaus" can be seen in the balanced-budget diagrams for several of these libraries. Gundersheimer arrived at the Folger in 1985, Cullen went to the Newberry in 1986, Skotheim arrived at the Huntington in 1987, and Ellen Dunlap has only recently taken over leadership of the AAS. (The impact of Charles Pierce's arrival at the Morgan in 1987 is obscured in the balanced-budget diagram by the effects of the expansion and the attendant campaign.)

Since settling in, each of the directors assuming office since the mid 1980s has adopted a program designed to lead the institution in question into a sustainable equilibrium. As shown in Figure 9.6, the Folger has been especially successful in balancing its operating budget—and without recourse to abnormally high spending rates for the endowment. Although the data are limited to the period 1974–1993, Figure 9.6 conveys a reassuring message: financial equilibrium can be achieved. It must be remembered that the apparent surpluses of the early 1980s at the Folger do not include the results for the theater (which was subsequently split off); including the theater, the Folger ran deficits in those years. It is during the period 1988–1991, under the direction of Werner Gundersheimer, that the Folger demonstrated its ability to grow while simultaneously maintaining balanced budgets.

At the Morgan (Figure 9.7), Charles Pierce has been very successful in simultaneously completing an ambitious program of physical expansion and moving the Morgan closer to long-term financial equilibrium. Deficits were historically less common at the Morgan than they were at some of the other libraries, but the most recent period (1989–1993) is particularly interesting. In 1989 and 1990, as the Morgan embarked on a capital campaign and expanded its building, the combination of borrowing from the endowment and capital fundraising cut into current income, which declined in absolute value. At the same time, closing the building meant that expenditures were lower as well, which prevented a large deficit. In 1991 and 1992, income and expenditures grew more or less in tandem; the operating deficit did not increase, but neither was the gap closed. Most of the money raised during this time was for the capital campaign. In 1993, expenditures were reduced, bringing the Morgan close to a balanced budget.

The recent history of the Huntington has already been summarized. As noted, Robert Skotheim has embarked on an ambitious program designed to restore financial equilibrium while simultaneously strengthening programs.

At the AAS, the budgetary gyrations of the late 1980s were tied in complex ways to the conclusion of a very successful capital campaign, and that part of Figure 9.5 is truly *sui generis*. Particularly encouraging are the good results achieved in the 1990–1993 period, when the highly respected director of the AAS, Marcus McCorison, transferred leadership to his successor, Ellen Dunlap. The results in 1993, the first full year of Dunlap's tenure, are also encouraging: income increased more rapidly than expenditures, and there was a surplus.

The situation at the Newberry continues to present the most daunting challenge. In recent years, under the leadership of Charles Cullen, the Newberry has succeeded in reducing very appreciably the rate of increase in expenditures. In fact, expenditures in 1988 were lower in absolute terms than in 1987. The current strategy, after the institution of cost-saving austerity measures, appears to be one of aggressive fundraising, and we have noted elsewhere that some encouraging progress has been made on this front. However, the events of the past have pushed the Newberry far into deficit territory, and, as can be seen from Figure 9.4, the path back is not yet clear.

To generalize, the directors and trustees of the independent research libraries have had to shift their focus from growth, new programs, and new users to cost-cutting, money-saving, and fundraising. Essays in the libraries' annual reports, not to mention persistent deficits (even as measured conventionally), testify to the nature of the current financial climate. The libraries' new leaders have focused on the need to manage operations more efficiently. Each took charge of an institution that, financially, needed to be made whole. Some libraries, such as the Folger and the Newberry, were experiencing substantial operating deficits. Others, such as the Morgan and the Huntington, had budgets that were balanced (albeit, in the case of the Huntington, by means of an unsustainable spending rate) or tolerably out of balance. All of the institutions were undercapitalized; all needed to rebuild their endowments. This process is now well under way.

Notes

1. The very concept of a deficit or a surplus requires a brief explanation. In principle, such bottom-line entries should sum up the operating results for an organization over the course of a year: if current expenditures exceed current income, a deficit should be reported; conversely, an excess of income over expenditures should result in a surplus. The figures for deficits and surpluses cited in this chapter reflect our effort to construct such summary measures by applying as consistently as possible the accounting template described in Appendix A. However, the nature of fund accounting and the various accounting conventions adopted by libraries have made this a more difficult exercise than it should be. Regrettably, neither the Financial Accounting Standards Board

(FASB) nor any other entity in the world of nonprofit accounting has found a way to require organizations to produce standardized operating statements (or, for that matter, operating statements of any kind). As a result, it is difficult to separate capital transactions from current accounts and to take account of interfund transfers.

2. To be more precise, deficits (or surpluses) as percentages of total expenditures were calculated separately for each library, and these percentage figures were then averaged to obtain the points plotted in Figure 9.1.

3. We use the expression "general results" to warn against attaching much weight to precise comparisons for any one year. If a 5 percent spending rule had been used, it almost certainly would have been applied in a less rigid, less simple-minded way than has been assumed for the purpose of this analysis. Specifically, some averaging scheme would surely have been used to prevent abrupt movements in financial markets from leading to sharp year-to-year fluctuations in investment income. Many mechanisms exist for this purpose.

4. We hasten to add, parenthetically, that it would probably have been unwise, as a tactical matter, for the libraries to show such large surpluses since reporting such results might have served both as an invitation to spend more and to discourage contributions from donors interested in helping institutions "in need." Many nonprofit organizations operate under what can be called a "balanced-budget constraint," which means that they are generally expected to spend the resources available to them in support of their missions, not to accumulate funds. From this perspective, large surpluses may be regarded with suspicion. This point of view can obviously be taken to foolish extremes and can interfere with orderly planning—especially when large capital outlays are anticipated.

5. R. A. Skotheim, letter to the board of trustees, April 13, 1993.

6. The visual appearance of bunching in the early years is magnified by the use of nominal values, but using real values would cause bunching in the late years; also, nominal data are easier to relate to published financial reports, which of course report nominal values.

CONCLUSION

ADDRESSING FUNDAMENTAL CHANGE

The five independent research libraries that are the subjects of this study have changed in such fundamental ways over the past thirty-five years that they can fairly be said to have been transformed: in scale, in "openness," in funding profiles, and in management and governance. In our view, these changes are irreversible. There is no going back to the institutional lifestyles of an earlier day. At the same time, these five libraries continue to serve essentially the same missions established for them at their founding, and they are at least as important to the scholarly world today as they were in the 1950s and 1960s.

Many of the changes that have occurred are for the better. But the path from "then" to "now" has not always been smooth, and the experiences along the way are instructive. At the minimum, they suggest propositions and raise questions that deserve thoughtful consideration. In this concluding chapter, we focus first on matters of program and mission, turn next to finances, and conclude with a brief discussion of organization, management, and board leadership.

Program and Mission

Although they were established in different times, with somewhat different goals in the minds of their founders, by the 1960s, the five libraries shared common elements: in essence, each was (and remains) a functioning research library, with collections, reference materials, and reading rooms and with distinguished scholars coming to use all three. Those basic attributes have only been enhanced.

- The collections at each of the libraries are stronger today than they were thirty-five years ago; new scholarly resources have been acquired, and conservation measures have been adopted.
- The collections are better housed. At each of the libraries, pressing needs for the addition and renovation of space have been met. In some instances (the Newberry may be the best example), a style of architecture that was thought suitable in another era has been supplemented with facilities and an organization of space and materials that are more conducive to the work of scholars in the modern day.
- Considerable progress has been made in taking advantage of new electronic technologies. Thanks to improved cataloging and new bibliographic tools, materials can be found more readily—and the knowledge of what is available at these libraries can be related to on-line information concerning other collections. At the same time, a new group of users—scholars working "off-site"—can now make use of at least some of the materials that have been collected by these libraries.
- Access has been broadened in other ways as well. Restrictions on "membership" have been eased or removed altogether. Whereas younger scholars and students were at one time made to feel less than welcome at these libraries (or were simply excluded), conscious efforts are now made to encourage them to take advantage of these collections.

In addition to enhancing their ability to serve established functions, the independent research libraries have taken on broader sets of educational responsibilities. They have launched new kinds of educational and research programs, including seminars and conferences—sometimes in conjunction with neighboring colleges and universities. The AAS's Program in the History of the Book, the Folger's Institute of Renaissance Studies, and the Newberry's undergraduate seminars are representative of these more activist tendencies.

Praiseworthy as they are, these efforts to "leverage" their distinguished collections raise an obvious concern: how broadly should these libraries define their missions? As the experiences of the Newberry, in particular, illustrate, there is a risk that in an effort to do good on many fronts, new obligations will be assumed that may stretch core resources too far. Is it realistic for an independent research library to seek to become, in some respects at least, a small university—and one without tuition-paying students? The decision by the AAS many decades ago to abandon incipient efforts to be a museum as well as a research library seems very wise in retrospect because it served to focus available energies and resources. In contrast, many of the extremely serious problems faced today by the New-York Historical Society—an institution whose origins are similar in certain respects to those of the AAS—can be traced to an overly all-embracing sense of what the society should be and should do.[1]

Finances

Over the past thirty-five years, the independent research libraries have evolved from income spenders to fund seekers. They remain, in any case, supplicants. An independent research library cannot survive without a committed cadre of supporters. It is an expensive enterprise to maintain and operate, and it cannot expect to depend on earned income. This is the first—and last—principle to be remembered in considering the future of these institutions. Some combination of private and public donors must be persuaded to provide enough support to subsidize core functions.

The founders were believers, and the endowments they provided obviated for many years the need to enlist other backers. Those days are over. For these libraries, one price of becoming larger and more active programmatically has been to become, simultaneously, less secure financially. The independent research libraries have outgrown their endowments and, in the process, entered the nonprofit marketplace. They have had to become far more active competitors for donations from individuals and foundations than they were in the 1960s, and as a consequence, they are now much more dependent on the goodwill of living constituencies, including governmental agencies. Maintaining genuine independence and freedom of action is inevitably more difficult for fund seekers than for income spenders.

Because many current donors have quite particularistic interests (as contrasted with the broad commitments of the founders to the overall health of the institution), one corollary is that all of these libraries must be more conscious of the balance between restricted and unrestricted sources of income than they were in previous eras. Overall measures of financial health can be misleading if the financial assets of the institution are more and more concentrated in restricted accounts. It is possible to have sizable assets and yet still be hard-pressed to meet current payrolls—or, to state the dilemma in less extreme form, to be unable to discharge core functions adequately.

Erosion of the relative size of the pool of unrestricted funds is a problem that is increasingly recognized by nonprofits in many fields, and the only real solution is to raise more unrestricted money—either through current gift programs or in the form of unrestricted endowment. Ultimately, there is no substitute for having an adequate amount of unrestricted endowment. It alone gives an organization sufficient confidence in its future to allow it to make long-term plans; it permits the leadership and trustees to exercise a reasonable degree of independence and not be too beholden to the large donor of today; and it permits a certain degree of entrepreneurial risk taking.

The combination of operating deficits and greater dependence on restricted funds has challenged all of these libraries. Fortunately, several of them appear to have reached a new equilibrium, in which the various sources of nonendowment income have become relatively predictable, the operating budget has been balanced, and the core endowment is again increasing in real value. This has entailed accepting a more disciplined approach to spending from the endowment as well as continuous fundraising. The Folger is the best example of a successful transition from the old, fully endowed regime to the new-style equilibrium, and the AAS and the Morgan have made noteworthy progress in achieving similar objectives. The Huntington started its own movement toward a new equilibrium more recently than some of the others, but it, too, gives evidence of having made substantial progress in restoring financial equilibrium while simultaneously reinvigorating its intellectual activities. The Newberry has had to face the most difficult process of adjustment—having, in retrospect, expanded programmatically beyond its long-term financial capacities in the late 1970s and early 1980s—and its financial future is the hardest to predict.

In reviewing these five financial histories, one is struck by certain truisms. Perhaps the most important is that in the world of the research library, assets are also liabilities. It was precisely the rapid growth in collections (assets) that played a major role in creating the needs (liabilities) that drained endowments. Acquisitions involve much more than just one-time outlays. Books and other scholarly materials must be cataloged, preserved, and made accessible—on a continuing basis.

A related truism has to do with what we have called invisible payables. It is possible to defer certain kinds of expenditures, sometimes for considerable periods of time; eventually, however, the payables come due. Buildings must be maintained and renovated, and new stack space always seems to be required; in addition, new programmatic developments stimulate the need for new types of space (conference rooms and lecture halls, for example). The larger and often more highly trained professional staff needed to provide key services must paid adequately. There are limits to the extent to which staff members can be expected to finance budgets by accepting low compensation—especially in a day when the workforce contains fewer volunteers and more women as well as men who expect adequate pay for professional work.

Over the course of the past three decades, all of these libraries have had to contend with invisible payables. It is to their credit that they have faced up to this problem, albeit sometimes belatedly. In looking ahead, one can hope that payables will be less invisible and that forward planning will take them into account. It is doubtful, however, if certain kinds of pressures on strained financial structures will ever be anticipated adequately. Inflation is the prime example. The inflation of the late 1970s (lasting into 1982) took a heavy toll on the finances of all five libraries; they simply could not increase income as rapidly as costs rose. Endowments lost purchasing power because of both inflation itself and the tendency to cope with the resulting financial distress by raising spending rates at the expense of reinvestments.

Fortunately, inflation has been kept under much better control over the course of the past dozen years or so. That single fact of economic life has probably made more of a contribution to the improved financial circumstances of these libraries than anything else. It is hard to imagine what would have happened to them (or, for that matter, to any number of other nonprofit organizations) had the inflation rate of the late 1970s persisted longer. Nor can one quite imagine how these libraries would respond today—or in the decades to come—if double-digit inflation were to reappear. It seems highly unlikely that reserves can be rebuilt to anything like earlier levels, and it seems just as unlikely that current gifts could be ratcheted up sufficiently to cover rising costs. Nor are these libraries able to increase fees or other forms of earned income to offset inflation in the way that many other entities can. For all of these reasons, the independent research libraries have more to fear from the possibility of renewed inflation than most other organizations in the for-profit and nonprofit worlds.

The other major threat to long-term financial stability in this sector is ongoing capital requirements driven principally by recurring needs to renovate, if not add space. There is no reason to believe that the most recent wave of renovations and new construction will prove to have been the last. Electronic technologies offer the best hope of offsetting the remorseless pressures for more storage space,[2] but it would be folly to assume that they will obviate altogether the large (if sporadic) requirements for capital that have put such great financial pressure on these institutions over the past twenty-five years.

The contrasting examples of the Morgan and the Newberry illustrate vividly the consequences of good and bad experiences with major construction and renovation projects. Each embarked on a major expansion that was to be paid for by a "largest-ever" capital campaign. The Newberry's $12.5 million campaign in the first years of the 1980s was equivalent to nearly half the value of its endowment at the time; the Morgan's $40 million campaign in the late 1980s was even more ambitious—equivalent to over 90 percent of the current value of its endowment. The sheer size of these projects meant that the consequences of poor planning or faulty execution would be dramatic.

The Morgan was successful in raising the large amount of money it needed and in retiring its debt as planned. The Newberry was much less successful in these respects, and it is fair to say that the financial stresses under which it labors today owe much to the debilitating consequences of having failed to meet capital obligations as planned. In analyzing the history of these divergent experiences, one is struck by the power of happenstance. The director of the Newberry at the time, Lawrence Towner, was known as an excellent fundraiser, and he accepted a great deal of personal responsibility for the campaign; tragically, he became ill, and his effectiveness was severely compromised. The Morgan was able to rely on an extraordinary fundraising effort by its entire board, which worked closely with the director, Charles Pierce. Of course, the Morgan launched its campaign later in the decade, and it was able to learn from the experiences of others, including the Newberry. By the end of the 1980s, the importance of collective commitments by boards of trustees was better understood.

A final point about capital requirements is both more general and more fundamental: it is difficult, if not impossible, for nonprofit organizations to raise capital funds in advance of the time when they will be needed. Donors asked for large gifts for capital purposes generally expect to see construction begin more or less immediately (and hence for planning to have gone on and commitments to have been made before they were solicited). Needs have to be visible and pressing in order to motivate large gifts.

Moreover, in sharp contrast to for-profit organizations, nonprofits have difficulty building up capital funds by generating substantial cash flows through the operating budget. Whereas for-profits are praised for running surpluses, which can then be reinvested if they are not distributed to shareholders, nonprofits would face many quizzical faces if they were to seek to finance expansion in a like way. Vigorous nonprofits always have more claims on available resources than they can meet from their operating budgets. It would also be hard for them to press donors for larger current contributions if they were seen to be running appreciable surpluses. The result is that the large sums needed for capital purposes almost always have to be raised "after the fact," which increases risk and can lead to serious long-term problems, even catastrophes.

Organization, Management, and Board Leadership

The combination of programmatic expansion and radical change in funding profiles has made much more daunting the tasks of organizing, managing, and leading these important institutions. As recently as the 1960s, the endowments provided by the founders sustained all activities of these libraries to such an extent that the directors were free to lead them with a light hand, to buy books, and to conduct research themselves. There were minimal professional staffs. The trustees managed the endowment, approved the budget for the year (if there was one), and enjoyed the privilege of being "bookmen."

All of this has changed. The organizational structures of these libraries have become both more professional and more bureaucratic (in other words, more orderly in the assignment of specific responsibilities within a defined hierarchy). Budgeting is today a more formal process, management of the endowment is often delegated to professional firms, and development staffs work closely with directors. Staff members are given specific responsibilities for maintaining good relationships with local groups, communities, governmental entities, and the public at large.

The directors, as the day-to-day leaders of the enterprise, have accepted more responsibility for financial as well as programmatic matters—and for managing the interrelationship between the two. The history of these libraries reveals clearly how important it is to have a highly competent director, and boards seem more and more inclined to look for individuals with a combination of talents, experiences, and skills. Familiarity with the scholarly activities of the institution remains of central importance, but trustees now seek individuals who are also able to discharge a wide range of duties beyond the provision of intellectual leadership. Directors must also be able to manage a complex institution, work closely with the trustees, be a skilled institutional advocate, and raise large sums of money effectively. This range of duties was no doubt always understood and accepted in some measure by directors; it is just that the balance among them appears to have shifted somewhat.

We suspect that the role of trustees has changed more radically than the role of the director. At one stage in the evolution of these institutions, trustees might have been expected to be friends of the founder or sympathetic to his vision for the library, but with little responsibility beyond that. Today, it is understood that effective boards are crucial to the success of the enterprise and that serving as a trustee is no sinecure. Board members must take seriously the ongoing responsibility to assess the leadership provided by the director, participate actively and knowledgeably in the making of strategic judgments, monitor the success of the organization in adhering to its short-term and long-term plans, be sure that the endowment is managed well, represent the institution before its increasingly varied publics, raise funds (in part by contributing generously, if they have the means to do so), and more generally, be seen as absolutely committed, by word and deed, to the success of the institution. The director and the board need to work together as partners. Boards, no less than directors, should be held accountable for their performance.[3]

For every kind of organization, prospects depend on the sum total of the resources that can be marshaled in support of the enterprise. In the case of the leading independent research libraries, these resources are by no means merely financial. In addition to endowments and other monetary assets, they consist primarily of the valuable cultural inheritances with which these institutions have been entrusted and which they continue to acquire. But these cultural resources cannot be seen as assets to be managed only passively. The success of these libraries has depended in the past, and will depend strongly in the future, on how effectively their collections are utilized, how skillfully priorities are set, and how well the libraries themselves are positioned both to address recurring problems and to anticipate new ones. One of the most encouraging signs for the future is that the directors of these libraries and their boards seem to appreciate more fully than in the past that the tasks they have to perform are demanding as well as important.

Notes

1. The forthcoming study of the New-York Historical Society by Kevin Guthrie will be instructive. The parallels and contrasts with the stories of the independent research libraries are highly informative, and these two studies serve as companion pieces of research.

2. The Mellon Foundation is now investing heavily in the pilot phase of a project designed to make back issues of journals available in electronic form. The objectives are to improve scholarly access and also to save space—and thus to reduce capital costs over the long run.
3. For a more extended discussion of the roles played by trustees, in the for-profit sector as well as in the nonprofit world, see Bowen (1994).

APPENDIXES

APPENDIX A

DATA SOURCES AND METHODOLOGICAL NOTES

The primary sources of data for the financial analysis in this book are annual audited financial statements from each library. Nonprofit financial statements are based on the principles of fund accounting, the weaknesses of which are well known and need not be recounted in great detail. It will suffice to mention four: the absence of an operating statement can lead to confusion as to which inflows and outflows are current and which are not, the use of separate funds can complicate efforts to understand the financial health of the institution as a whole, transfers between funds can make it hard to value particular flows or funds, and the wide variety of permissible accounting formats can make interorganizational comparisons all but impossible.

To help address these problems, the research staff of The Andrew W. Mellon Foundation developed an electronic spreadsheet that can be used to recast nonprofit financial statements and to make them more comprehensible and more consistent with one another. Current income and expenditures are tabulated, with capital flows excluded. The multiple-funds problem is countered by aggregating across funds. An entire section of the template tracks and nets interfund transfers. Interorganizational consistency is achieved by transferring each nonprofit's financial statements to the same spreadsheet. (Of course, another advantage of using an electronic spreadsheet is that the rapid, powerful, and extremely informative techniques of computer analysis can be brought to bear.)

Because the discussion of the five libraries included in this study is based in large part on the spreadsheet analysis and the financial statements they represent, key portions of the spreadsheet templates are reproduced in Appendix B. The remaining information (data for other years and additional items) is available on request. These notes provide an outline of the complete spreadsheet, with explanatory notes, when needed, about its structure and the translation process from the audited financial statements. The notes in this appendix are based on the spreadsheets used in the 1979/1981–1993 period. The analysis for earlier periods was less detailed but based on similar principles and definitions whenever possible.

Detailed Spreadsheet Templates (1981–1993)

I. *Revenue and support.* Revenue and support is divided into two sections: current income and capital gifts. The distinction is an important one. Current income refers to the year-in, year-out inflows that support current operations. Capital gifts include other inflows, especially gifts to endowment and to building funds, which do not affect the operating budget.

A. *Current income.* Current income is divided into four categories, reflecting the income structure of the independent research libraries. (These categories could be altered for analysis of other types of nonprofits.)

1. *Gifts, grants, and contributions.* This category includes all forms of contributed current income. The libraries' own accounting standards were usually followed in this breakdown. "Contributions upon admission," for instance, were included in this category even though they could also be construed as earned income.

The subcategories used depend on the institution and on the presentation used in its audited financial statements. In most cases, the line items used by the libraries could be transferred directly to the spreadsheet. The Newberry, for instance, has one line-item for contributed income and divides it by fund. The subcategories in Figure 3.5 (unrestricted and restricted) reflect that breakdown. The American Antiquarian Society reports separately contributed income from private sources and from governmental sources, and as a result the contributed income subcategories for the AAS are "governmental" and "private."

2. *Investment income.* Investment income as reported on the spreadsheet is "investment income spent." In other words, it represents the earnings on the endowment or other invested funds that were spent in the course of a year. No distinction is made among interest, dividends, and realized gains. Again, the subcategories vary by institution.

3. *Earned income.* Earned-income figures are reported gross, without adjusting for related costs.

4. *Miscellaneous and other.* A catchall category used to aggregate all other income sources.

5. *Total current income.*

a. *Nominal dollars.* This figure is the sum of income categories 1 through 4. It represents the total dollar value, unadjusted for inflation, of the current income received by the organization in question during a single year.

    b. *Real (year 1) dollars.* This entry adjusts the nominal dollars figure for inflation, indexed to the first year of the spreadsheet. (For the recent period, for which our analysis is more detailed, the Huntington's, the Morgan's, and the Newberry's spreadsheets begin in 1981; 1981 is therefore used as year 1 for all five libraries, even though the corresponding spreadsheets for Folger and AAS start in 1979.)

        The deflators used in this study are the implicit price deflators for the gross domestic product. (See *Economic Report of the President,* February 1994, p. 272.)

  B. *Capital gifts.* This measures all inflows not included in current income. For the most part, these flows are contributions to the endowment or to the plant fund. Capital gifts are usually reported either in the endowment fund or "below the line" on the statement of revenues and expenses.

    1. *Gifts to endowment.* These figures are usually taken directly from the financial statements. Gifts to quasi-endowment funds are included here as well, even though those gifts are not restricted by law to the endowment (the analysis is based on operational principles, not legal ones).

    2. *Gifts to plant.* Gifts to the plant fund are usually for a specific expansion or renovation. Since most institutions have a separate plant fund, gifts to that fund are commonly listed separately on the financial statements.

II. *Expenditures and surplus / deficit.*

  A. *Functional distribution.* The share of expenditures devoted to a given function, and the fluctuations in that share over time, are useful indicators of changes in programmatic focus. Four out of the five libraries (all except the Newberry) divide their expenses along functional lines. Functional expenditures are subdivided into two categories: program services and support services. Although the balance between the two is partly a function of accounting conventions and allocation decisions, the split can be seen as one measure of efficiency: all other things being equal, the greater the share of expenditures devoted to program services, the more efficient the organization.

    1. *Program services.* The specific subcategories within program services vary by institution and usually match those used on the audited statements. In some cases, the categories were changed from one year to another. Wherever possible (at the Folger, for instance), supplementary audited statements were used to construct identical categories;

otherwise (as in the Morgan's case for 1992 and 1993), only totals were presented.

Because they can be construed either as a functional outlay or as a line-item cost, acquisitions are treated in widely different ways by the five libraries. The Huntington subsumes acquisitions into the programmatic division of expenditures, with library acquisitions included as part of library expenditures and art gallery acquisitions included as part of art gallery expenditures. The Morgan, which has substantial restricted acquisitions funds, reports acquisitions separately from operating expenditures. The Newberry uses an object breakdown but treats acquisitions as a capital expense. The Folger also reports acquisitions as a capital expense. The AAS treats acquisitions as a normal program expenditure.

The spreadsheet template treats all acquisitions as a current expenditure. We adopted this practice for two reasons. The first was consistency. The second, in some ways the more important of the two, is that even though acquisitions add to a library's capital stock, they do not add monetary assets. The funds, once spent, are gone. Thus acquisitions should not be viewed as a transfer from one type of asset to another. Also, because acquisitions are a regular part of a library's activities, we included them as current, as opposed to capital, expenditures.

2. *Support services.* Two common subcategories of support services are management and fundraising.

3. *Total expenditures.* Total expenditures is the sum of program services and support services. (In the Newberry's case, it represents the total of the object breakdown plus acquisitions.) This figure represents the amount spent for current purposes in the course of a single year. It is presented in both nominal and real dollars.

B. *Object distribution.* Although object distributions were not used frequently, this section tracks any data that the libraries provided. Usually this included salaries and benefits, or total "compensation" and depreciation. Due to insufficient data, the sum of object categories does not necessarily equal total expenditures.

C. *Surplus/deficit.* The surplus or deficit is the difference between total current income and total expenditures.

1. *Including depreciation.* This series computes the surplus or deficit with depreciation counted as an expense, as is done in most audited financial statements. Although depreciation is technically the amortization of plant assets over the life of the asset, it also provides a proxy for some measure of the wear and tear on the physical plant.

2. *Excluding depreciation.* Depreciation is the single largest noncash expenditure line item for the independent research libraries in this set.

Excluding it produces a surplus/deficit figure that reflects more closely the difference between cash received and cash spent.

3. *Other measures of the surplus/deficit.* In some cases, there are other revenue and expenditure streams that can be compared instructively. The Huntington's spreadsheet, for instance, computes a surplus/ deficit figure for the operating fund, which is often a better indicator of performance than the global figures. Since the Morgan is also a museum, its acquisitions expenditures are both large and highly variable; as a result, its spreadsheet computes a surplus or deficit for the operating fund as well as for the organization as a whole. The spreadsheet for the Newberry computes separate figures for the unrestricted and restricted funds. The Folger's spreadsheet tracks the surplus/deficit for the "with theater" income and expenditure streams.

III. *Transfers.* The use of interfund transfers is one of the most confusing aspects of nonprofit accounting. The transfers section of the spreadsheet tracks all interfund transfers on a double-entry basis. In other words, each transfer is noted in two places: in the originating fund (as a "transfer out," or negative number) and in the receiving fund (as a "transfer in," or positive number). Thus the subtotal for each fund represents the total inflows or outflows (as transfers) for that fund in a given year. By definition, the entries for each year should net to zero for the organization as a whole.

IV. *Endowment.*

A. *Market value of endowment.* The market value of the endowment is often different from the book value shown on the balance sheet which, due to accounting conventions, usually reflects historical costs. Market values can usually be obtained from the notes to the audited statements. Both nominal and real values are included on the spreadsheet.

B. *Total return.* The total return is the return achieved on a given principal, or corpus of funds, regardless of the form the return takes. Dividends, interest, realized gains, and unrealized gains are the components of the total return, which is usually expressed as a percentage of the corpus's market value at the beginning of the year.

Estimating the total return from audited statements is a complicated task; all of the flows of funds into and out of an organization's endowment corpus, except those related directly to investment performance, must be isolated and held constant in order to produce a total return figure that is unpolluted by other effects. Authoritative figures that originate with investment managers are usually preferable, if they are available and accurate. The method used here is particularly valuable in cases where no other data are available. Its strength is that it allows one to compute total returns based solely on audited statements.

The formula used in computing total return is as follows:

$$\frac{(MV_{EOr} - MV_{BOr}) + CF_{OUT} - CF_{IN} + (\Delta \text{ NC Assets}) - (\Delta \text{ NC Liabilities})}{MV_{BOr} + [\frac{1}{2} * (-CF_{OUT} + CF_{IN} - (\Delta \text{ NC Assets}) + (\Delta \text{ NC Liabilities}))]}$$

The variables are defined as follows:

MV_{BOr}, MV_{EOr}: Market value of the corpus at the beginning and end of the year, respectively. The corpus includes the endowment fund as well as any other invested funds.

CF_{OUT}: Cash outflows. The principal cash outflow is usually investment income spent during the course of the year (whether interest and dividends or realized capital gains), since all investment income and gains form the total return numerator. Another outflow is the depreciation-excluded deficit or surplus (a surplus being nothing more than a "negative deficit"), which is used to hold constant changes in the endowment based on operations. Deficits are paid out of invested funds, but because such expenditures are not related to investment performance, they must be excluded from the total return calculations. Other cash outflows include transfers to other funds, and any other spending from the corpus not included in the surplus/deficit.

CF_{IN}: Any cash inflows that are not included in the surplus/deficit. Gifts to endowment are a common example; like the surplus/deficit, they are not part of investment performance and must therefore be excluded.

Δ NC Assets and Δ NC Liabilities: If any noncash asset rises in the course of a year, the amount of the increase should be added back because it was created by a cash outflow. For example, if there were $100,000 worth of accounts receivable last year and this year there are $200,000, a noncash asset has increased. Because this increase represents cash that has been spent, it must be added back. By the same logic, an increase in a noncash liability should be subtracted.

The denominator of the equation includes the same flows as the numerator, with the signs reversed. Since the precise timing of the inflows and outflows is unknown, we make the simplifying assumption that they occur evenly over the course of the year and multiply by 0.5.

This method, convoluted as it may seem, provides a reasonably accurate estimate of the total return. In the Folger's case, for instance, where there were authoritative numbers with which our calculations could be compared, the average difference between our calculations and the "correct" figures was one-half of one percentage point.

C. *Spending rate.* The spending rate is defined as the total level of spending from the endowment as a percentage of the endowment's market value. For purposes of this analysis, spending was usually taken directly from the investment income line on the financial statements.

The numerator of the spending rate is total spending, including spending from the endowment and any other invested funds. The

denominator, which in the simplest case would be just the market value
at the beginning of the year, is adjusted for the various inflows and outflows over the course of the year.

V. *Balance sheet.* The spreadsheet collapses the typical nonprofit balance sheet,
    in which each fund is a self-balancing entity, into a single statement. The
    asset side is arranged in terms of decreasing liquidity.

  A. *Assets*

   1. *Cash and investments.* This category includes the endowment, quasi-
       endowment, money in the plant fund, and any other pools of cash
       or marketable securities.

   2. *Noncash assets.* This category includes all other current assets.

   3. *Net fixed and noncurrent assets.* The single largest asset in this category
       is usually the physical plant.

   4. *Other assets* (interfund loans, and so forth). Interfund loans can be
       accounted for in one of two ways. The loan can be listed as an asset
       in one fund and the obligation to repay as a "negative asset" in
       another fund; or the loan can be listed as an asset and the obligation
       to repay as a liability. The latter overstates the value both of assets
       and of liabilities for the organization as a whole. The spreadsheet
       includes all interfund loans in this section, which net to zero.

   5. *Total assets.* The sum of items 1 through 4.

  B. *Liabilities.* These are divided into current and noncurrent liabilities. The
      latter category includes long-term debt such as mortgages or bonds.

  C. *Fund balances.* The fund balance is the difference between assets and lia-
      bilities. Fund balances are roughly analogous to "retained earnings" or
      "owners' equity" in for-profit accounting. The balance is listed sepa-
      rately for each fund or group of funds.

  D. *Total liabilities and fund balances.* The sum of liabilities and fund balances.
      By definition, total liabilities and fund balances are equal to total assets.

APPENDIX B

DATA TABLES

TABLE B.1-1. SUMMARY FINANCIAL DATA, HUNTINGTON LIBRARY, 1956–1980 (THOUSANDS OF $).

	1956	1957	1958	1959	1960	1961	1962	1963	1964	1965	1966	1967	1968
Income													
Investment income	791	854	865	908	948	1,035	1,058	1,110	1,150	1,212	1,266	1,353	1,409
Total income	802	860	879	920	952	1,040	1,067	1,118	1,156	1,217	1,277	1,368	1,417
Operating fund income	802	860	879	920	952	1,040	1,067	1,118	1,156	1,217	1,277	1,368	1,417
Expenditures													
Total expenditures	692	749	900	1,002	991	1,034	1,028	1,072	1,148	1,311	1,278	1,393	1,507
Operating fund expenditures	692	749	900	1,002	991	1,034	1,028	1,072	1,148	1,311	1,278	1,393	1,507
Surplus/deficit													
All funds	110	111	(21)	(83)	(39)	6	39	46	8	(94)	(2)	(26)	(90)
Operating fund	110	111	(21)	(83)	(39)	6	39	46	8	(94)	(2)	(26)	(90)
Endowment													
Market value	21,230	20,781	21,776	23,924	24,786	28,052	25,701	30,761	32,490	32,310	30,023	30,192	31,399
Spending rate (%)	N.A.	4.0	4.2	4.2	4.0	4.2	3.8	4.3	3.7	3.7	3.9	4.5	4.7

Table B.1-1, cont.

	1969	1970	1971	1972	1973ᵃ	1974	1975	1976	1977	1978	1979	1980
Income												
Investment income	1,484	1,554	1,693	1,731	1,900	2,156	2,113	2,156	2,228	2,235	2,682	3,135
Total income	1,490	1,559	1,699	1,737	2,679	3,779	3,209	3,046	4,025	3,902	8,026	5,677
Operating fund income	1,490	1,559	1,699	1,737	2,015	2,265	2,522	2,582	3,019	3,171	3,529	3,499
Expenditures												
Total expenditures	1,491	1,509	1,755	1,771	2,263	2,279	2,843	2,996	2,949	3,183	3,421	4,215
Operating fund expenditures	1,491	1,509	1,755	1,771	2,208	2,314	2,716	2,771	2,824	3,048	3,232	3,687
Surplus/deficit												
All funds	(1)	50	(56)	(34)	415	1,500	366	50	1,076	719	4,605	1,462
Operating fund	(1)	50	(56)	(34)	(193)	(49)	(194)	(190)	195	123	296	(188)
Endowment												
Market value	30,773	27,174	31,512	32,334	30,821	29,308	32,110	32,329	32,778	33,889	31,961	33,522
Spending rate (%)	5.0	5.0	6.2	5.5	5.9	7.0	7.2	6.7	6.9	6.8	7.9	9.8

Source: Audited financial statements of the Huntington Library, Art Collections, and Botanical Gardens, 1956–1980.

Notes: Data are for years ending June 30. N.A. means not available.

ᵃIn 1973, a new reporting format was adopted, allowing a distinction to be made between the "operating fund" and all other funds.

TABLE B.1-2. SUMMARY FINANCIAL DATA, HUNTINGTON LIBRARY, 1981–1993 (THOUSANDS OF $).

	1981	1982	1983	1984	1985	1986	1987	1988	1989	1990	1991	1992	1993
Current income													
Gifts and grants	1,271	941	1,223	1,891	1,613	2,068	2,657	2,466	2,897	2,812	3,894	4,616	6,635
Investment income	3,606	3,949	3,524	3,484	3,854	4,080	4,372	4,362	4,443	4,831	4,350	4,289	4,423
Earned income	529	650	800	823	1,465	862	1,375	1,213	1,299	1,694	2,200	2,165	2,541
Total current income	5,406	5,540	5,547	6,198	6,932	7,010	8,404	8,040	8,639	9,337	10,444	11,070	13,598
Operating fund income	3,776	4,452	4,473	4,853	5,714	6,391	7,098	7,317	8,153	8,126	9,664	10,265	11,038
Capital gifts													
Total capital gifts	2,209	2,394	1,891	6,325	1,509	2,682	3,812	2,378	1,170	536	6,349	5,665	2,764
Gifts to endowment[a]	2,209	2,394	1,891	3,784	553	2,682	3,812	2,278	777	536	3,863	5,660	2,764
Expenditures by function													
Program services	3,413	5,224	6,142	4,194	4,960	5,231	5,815	7,178	6,246	7,322	7,760	8,595	12,022
Support services	668	1,202	1,440	1,680	1,849	2,014	2,305	2,599	2,908	3,142	3,992	4,301	4,905
Total expenditures	4,082	6,426	7,582	5,875	6,809	7,244	8,120	9,776	9,154	10,464	11,752	12,896	16,927
Operating fund expenditures	4,177	4,476	5,015	5,447	6,066	6,387	7,052	7,409	8,087	9,046	9,932	10,558	11,509

Expenditures by object[b]													
Compensation and benefits	2,675	2,856	3,166	3,428	3,743	3,880	4,088	4,312	4,742	5,417	6,237	6,647	7,430
Depreciation	0	0	0	0	0	0	0	0	0	0	0	315	966
Acquisitions	598	2,144	2,677	482	728	664	795	1,761	645	1,371	780	858	3,627
Library acquisitions	369	460	352	435	454	449	562	616	468	430	467	346	288
Surplus/deficit													
Including depreciation	1,324	(886)	(2,035)	323	122	(234)	284	(1,736)	(515)	(1,127)	(1,309)	(1,826)	(3,329)
Excluding depreciation	1,324	(886)	(2,035)	323	122	(234)	284	(1,736)	(515)	(1,127)	(1,309)	(1,511)	(2,363)
Operating fund	(401)	(24)	(543)	(593)	(352)	4	45	(92)	66	(919)	(268)	(294)	(471)
Endowment													
Market value	28,881	25,008	36,360	37,057	46,981	59,682	66,829	62,628	67,786	66,305	66,543	77,077	82,916
Total spending	3,606	3,949	3,524	3,484	3,854	4,080	4,372	4,362	4,443	4,831	4,350	4,289	4,423
Total return (%)	N.A.	-1.1	57.8	-0.8	34.0	31.3	13.4	-0.8	15.2	5.5	3.0	15.6	12.2
Spending rate (%)	10.8	13.8	14.3	9.0	10.6	8.6	7.3	6.5	7.2	6.4	6.3	5.7

Source: Audited financial statements of the Huntington Library, Art Collections, and Botanical Gardens, 1981–1993, except where noted.

Notes: Data are for years ending June 30. N.A. means not available.

[a]Based on unpublished data provided to The Andrew W. Mellon Foundation.

[b]The sum of the object categories does not equal total expenditures because not all object categories are presented.

TABLE B.2–1. SUMMARY FINANCIAL DATA, PIERPONT MORGAN LIBRARY, 1963–1980 (THOUSANDS OF $).

	1963	1964	1965	1966	1967	1968	1969	1970	1971	1972	1973	1974	1975
Income													
Investment income	366	380	427	481	519	551	556	568	592	595	608	631	620
Other income[a]	166	84	186	240	200	211	770	305	744	911	1,159	953	1,449
Total income	532	464	613	721	719	762	1,327	873	1,335	1,507	1,766	1,585	2,068
Operating income	366	380	516	607	603	639	637	654	877	1,086	974	1,009	1,189
Expenditures by object[b]													
Compensation and benefits	249	262	281	304	328	366	376	429	471	518	562	622	652
Acquisitions	37	31	112	177	138	156	579	248	806	363	738	508	475
Capital expenditures	0	0	0	0	0	0	0	0	0	50	95	1	293
Total expenditures	516	491	577	678	692	736	1,168	967	1,504	1,253	1,760	1,744	1,826
Operating expenditures[c]	479	459	465	502	554	580	589	719	698	841	928	1,235	1,058
Surplus/deficit													
All funds	16	(27)	36	43	27	26	158	(94)	(169)	253	6	(159)	242
Operating surplus/deficit	(113)	(79)	51	106	49	59	47	(66)	179	245	46	(226)	130
Endowment													
Market value	13,283	11,798	14,057	14,323	14,189	14,304	14,822	12,763	15,045	16,363	16,875	14,302	12,783
Spending rate (%)	N.A.	2.9	3.6	3.4	3.6	3.9	3.9	3.8	4.6	4.0	3.7	3.7	4.3

Table B.2–1, cont.

	1976	1977	1978	1979	1980
Income					
Investment income	609	723	870	893	893
Other income[a]	1,106	2,055	1,575	2,264	1,955
Total income	1,715	2,778	2,446	3,156	2,849
Operating income	1,178	1,673	2,269	2,941	2,758
Expenditures by object[b]					
Compensation and benefits	774	796	881	1,000	1,128
Acquisitions	291	606	779	904	511
Capital expenditures	917	1,303	317	256	254
Total expenditures	2,534	3,267	2,543	3,051	3,473
Operating expenditures[c]	1,326	1,359	1,447	1,891	2,708
Surplus/deficit					
All funds	(819)	(489)	(97)	106	(624)
Operating surplus/deficit	(148)	315	821	1,050	50
Endowment					
Market value	13,848	13,533	12,780	12,327	10,299
Spending rate (%)	4.8	5.2	6.4	7.0	7.2

Source: Audited financial statements of the Pierpont Morgan Library, 1963–1980.

Notes: Data are for fiscal years ending March 31. N.A. means not available.

[a]Other income includes gifts, grants, and earned income.

[b]The sum of the object categories does not equal total expenditures because not all object categories are presented.

[c]Operating expenditures is total expenditures less acquisitions and capital expenditures.

TABLE B.2–2. SUMMARY FINANCIAL DATA, PIERPONT MORGAN LIBRARY, 1981–1993 (THOUSANDS OF $).

	1981	1982	1983	1984	1985	1986	1987	1988	1989	1990	1991	1992	1993
Current income													
Gifts and grants	1,837	2,051	2,422	1,804	1,875	2,199	2,474	2,672	2,570	2,665	3,507	3,837	4,220
Investment income	1,044	1,193	1,550	1,720	2,057	2,158	2,143	2,320	2,481	2,530	2,437	2,066	2,243
Earned income	449	914	424	459	457	447	480	469	878	379	437	702	759
Other income	105	87	70	85	88	64	67	77	117	121	117	203	337
Total current income	3,434	4,246	4,466	4,069	4,477	4,869	5,164	5,538	6,046	5,695	6,497	6,809	7,558
Operations fund income	2,438	2,680	3,105	3,331	3,665	3,973	4,255	4,967	5,537	4,570	5,054	6,004	6,706
Acquisitions fund income	995	1,566	1,361	737	812	895	909	570	508	1,125	1,443	805	633
Capital gifts													
Gifts to endowment	1,873	2,888	708	2,260	1,585	2,816	1,932	2,735	5,726	462	817	7,587	1,403
Gifts to fixed-asset fund	1,873	2,888	708	2,260	1,585	2,816	1,932	2,735	3,710	1,781	5,000	665	1,813
Total capital gifts	3,745	5,776	1,415	4,520	3,170	5,632	3,865	5,470	9,436	2,243	5,817	8,252	3,216
Expenditures by function													
Program services	N.A.	N.A.	N.A.	N.A.	3,232	3,653	3,635	3,833	4,480	4,753	5,742	5,476	4,999
Support services	N.A.	N.A.	N.A.	N.A.	1,236	1,439	1,573	1,529	1,514	1,237	1,207	2,098	1,867
Total expenditures	3,307	4,091	4,667	3,882	4,468	5,092	5,208	5,362	5,993	5,990	6,949	7,575	6,865
Operations fund expenditures	2,373	2,619	3,087	3,219	3,690	4,009	4,442	4,955	5,382	5,171	5,778	6,770	6,865

Expenditures by object[a]	1981	1982	1983	1984	1985	1986	1987	1988	1989	1990	1991	1992	1993
Compensation and benefits	1,314	1,434	1,684	1,886	2,104	N.A.	N.A.	N.A.	N.A.	N.A.	N.A.	N.A.	N.A.
Depreciation	0	0	0	0	0	0	0	0	0	0	227	693	768
Acquisitions fund expenditures	934	1,472	1,580	663	778	1,083	766	407	611	818	1,171	805	646
Surplus/deficit													
Including depreciation	127	155	(201)	186	8	(224)	(44)	176	52	(295)	(452)	(766)	693
Excluding depreciation	127	155	(201)	186	8	(224)	(44)	176	52	(295)	(225)	(73)	1,461
Operations fund (including depreciation)	66	60	18	112	(25)	(36)	(187)	12	155	(602)	(951)	(1,459)	(927)
Endowment													
Market value	15,142	16,542	21,283	23,458	28,357	38,498	45,217	43,086	40,000	39,988	36,122	40,008	47,268
Total spending	1,044	1,193	1,550	1,720	2,057	2,158	2,143	2,320	2,481	2,530	2,437	2,066	2,243
Total return (%)	N.A.	2.5	32.5	5.1	17.8	35.9	15.3	-2.2	11.3	13.4	15.1	13.2	13.5
Spending rate (%)	10.1	7.9	9.4	8.1	8.8	7.6	5.6	5.1	5.8	6.3	6.1	5.7	5.6

Source: Audited financial statements of the Pierpont Morgan Library, 1981–1993.

Notes: Data are for fiscal years ending March 31. N.A. means not available.

[a]The sum of the object categories does not equal total expenditures because not all object categories are presented.

TABLE B.3–1. SUMMARY FINANCIAL DATA, NEWBERRY LIBRARY, 1960–1980 (THOUSANDS OF $).

	1960	1961	1962	1963	1964	1965	1966	1967	1968	1969	1970	1971	1972
Income													
Gifts and grants	0	0	0	0	0	0	0	0	0	0	0	35	24
Investment income	546	570	583	597	622	606	710	757	799	695	709	759	763
Other income	99	75	68	91	100	108	104	53	89	132	129	72	110
Total income	645	645	650	688	721	714	814	810	889	827	838	866	897
Income—"Trustees' Table"[a]	N.A.	N.A.	N.A.	N.A.	N.A.	N.A.	N.A.	N.A.	N.A.	N.A.	N.A.	N.A.	N.A.
Expenditures													
Total expenditures	397	417	469	491	530	557	589	664	729	794	882	956	962
Expenditures—"Trustees' Table"[a]	N.A.	N.A.	N.A.	N.A.	N.A.	N.A.	N.A.	N.A.	N.A.	N.A.	N.A.	N.A.	N.A.
Surplus/deficit													
Including depreciation	248	228	182	197	191	157	225	146	160	33	(44)	(90)	(65)
Surplus/deficit—"Trustees' Table"[a]	N.A.	N.A.	N.A.	N.A.	N.A.	N.A.	N.A.	N.A.	N.A.	N.A.	N.A.	N.A.	N.A.
Endowment													
Market value	15,294	19,266	15,794	18,653	18,117	18,983	18,550	18,550	21,491	19,666	17,083	21,249	24,561
Spending rate (%)	N.A.	3.7	3.0	3.8	3.3	3.3	3.7	4.1	4.3	3.2	3.6	4.4	3.6

Table B.3–1, cont.

	1973	1974[b]	1975	1976	1977	1978	1979	1980
Income								
Gifts and grants	25	N.A.	N.A.	1,052	1,847	2,247	1,642	2,037
Investment income	819	892	860	870	935	950	1,182	1,374
Other income	131	197	271	229	258	207	190	191
Total income	976	1,089	1,131	2,150	3,039	3,405	3,013	3,603
Income—"Trustees' Table"[a]	1,454	1,820	2,045	1,784	2,402	2,927	2,941	3,328
Expenditures								
Total expenditures	1,030	1,196	1,349	2,048	2,495	2,608	2,741	3,152
Expenditures—"Trustees' Table"[a]	1,519	1,821	2,315	2,048	2,495	2,608	2,741	3,152
Surplus/deficit								
Including depreciation	(55)	(107)	(217)	102	544	797	273	451
Surplus/deficit—"Trustees' Table"[a]	(65)	(2)	(270)	(264)	(93)	319	200	176
Endowment								
Market value	23,682	19,353	20,086	20,626	19,436	18,623	19,436	18,932
Spending rate (%)	3.3	3.8	4.4	4.3	4.5	4.9	6.3	7.1

Source: Audited financial statements of the Newberry Library, 1960–1980, except where noted.

Notes: Through 1973, data are for fiscal years ending October 31; starting in 1974, data are for fiscal years ending June 30. N.A. means not available.

[a]"Trustees' Table" data are taken from the minutes of a meeting of the finance committee held September 8, 1982; these data begin in 1973.

[b]Data for 1974 are based on the eight-month period between November 1, 1973, and June 30, 1974, extrapolated to twelve months.

TABLE B.3–2. SUMMARY FINANCIAL DATA, NEWBERRY LIBRARY, 1981–1993 (THOUSANDS OF $).

	1981	1982	1983	1984	1985	1986	1987	1988	1989	1990	1991	1992	1993
Current income													
Gifts and grants—unrestricted	444	345	399	494	433	611	367	748	795	822	835	1,322	1,269
Gifts and grants—restricted	1,240	744	548	1,412	1,697	1,819	1,632	1,567	1,494	1,232	1,118	1,125	819
Investment income—unrestricted	1,135	1,352	1,354	1,727	1,648	1,455	1,280	1,236	1,432	1,338	1,226	1,115	933
Investment income—restricted	275	481	458	757	877	1,042	1,026	1,031	1,267	1,342	1,436	1,462	1,471
Earned income—unrestricted[a]	215	168	180	162	199	266	290	354	374	444	507	546	543
Earned income—restricted[a]	2	4	3	3	12	24	9	35	46	53	42	30	99
Other income	31	23	338	4	(5)	11	(15)	11	611	0	0	0	146
Total current income	3,343	3,117	3,280	4,560	4,860	5,228	4,589	4,982	6,019	5,231	5,164	5,600	5,280
Total unrestricted income	1,794	1,864	1,933	2,383	2,280	2,332	1,937	2,338	2,601	2,604	2,568	2,983	2,745
Total restricted income	1,518	1,229	1,009	2,173	2,585	2,885	2,667	2,633	2,807	2,627	2,596	2,617	2,389
Capital gifts													
Endowment—unrestricted	N.A.	N.A.	N.A.	N.A.	500	813	410	394	1,292	508	320	110	81
Endowment—restricted	N.A.	N.A.	N.A.	N.A.	677	1,250	148	1,441	594	806	467	1,496	1,264
Endowment—other[b]	N.A.	303	339	375	N.A.	N.A.	N.A.	N.A.	N.A.	757	14	N.A.	N.A.
Centennial fund gifts	2,286	1,929	1,595	1,034	1,644	938	0	0	0	0	0	0	0
Total capital gifts	2,286	2,232	1,934	1,409	2,821	3,001	559	1,836	1,886	2,071	801	1,606	1,345
Expenditures by object[c]													
Compensation and benefits	2,236	2,292	2,081	2,353	2,533	2,701	2,866	2,890	2,867	3,037	3,424	3,637	3,739
Depreciation	39	161	335	420	534	630	641	653	681	659	632	655	641

Acquisitions—unrestricted												
206	196	151	134	161	263	238	92	220	209	203	190	275
Acquisitions—restricted												
108	43	73	114	132	465	460	319	251	338	346	321	334
Other												
1,100	1,130	1,315	1,274	1,572	1,932	2,247	2,300	2,607	2,723	2,612	2,883	2,632
Total expenditures												
3,689	3,821	3,955	4,296	4,932	5,992	6,453	6,255	6,626	6,966	7,217	7,686	7,621
Total unrestricted expenditures[d]												
2,114	2,286	2,302	2,750	2,832	3,165	3,364	3,210	3,273	3,509	3,705	4,078	4,456
Total restricted expenditures[d]												
1,295	1,188	1,050	964	1,273	1,468	1,749	1,982	2,207	2,257	2,337	2,448	2,530
Centennial fund expenditures												
2,837	5,820	3,465	3,326	2,770	855	0	0	0	0	0	0	0
Surplus/deficit												
Including depreciation												
(346)	(704)	(675)	264	(71)	(764)	(1,864)	(1,272)	(607)	(1,735)	(2,053)	(2,086)	(2,341)
Excluding depreciation												
(307)	(544)	(340)	684	463	(134)	(1,223)	(619)	74	(1,076)	(1,421)	(1,431)	(1,700)
Unrestricted surplus/deficit[d]												
(526)	(618)	(520)	(501)	(713)	(1,097)	(1,665)	(964)	(892)	(1,114)	(1,340)	(1,285)	(1,986)
Restricted surplus/deficit[d]												
115	(2)	(114)	1,095	1,181	952	457	332	349	32	(87)	(152)	(475)
Endowment												
Market value												
26,267	21,393	26,791	22,538	26,209	28,217	29,174	28,155	30,172	30,953	31,470	32,473	32,733
Total spending												
1,411	1,833	1,812	2,484	2,525	2,498	2,306	2,267	2,699	2,680	2,662	2,577	2,404
Total return (%)												
N.A.	1.4	42.1	0.9	26.7	16.9	10.3	1.4	10.1	8.8	9.9	11.6	9.7
Spending rate (%)												
7.5	7.0	8.5	9.3	11.2	9.5	8.2	7.8	9.6	8.9	8.6	8.2	7.4

Source: Audited financial statements of the Newberry Library, 1981–1993.

Notes: Data are for fiscal years ending June 30. N.A. means not available.

[a] From the category called "Operations" in the library's financial statements.

[b] Includes gifts to endowment that could not be divided between unrestricted and restricted gifts. Figures for 1982–1984 are from unpublished data provided to The Andrew W. Mellon Foundation.

[c] A breakdown of expenditures by function was not available.

[d] Includes expenditures for acquisitions.

TABLE B.4–1. SUMMARY FINANCIAL DATA, FOLGER SHAKESPEARE LIBRARY, 1969–1978 (THOUSANDS OF $).

	1969	1970	1971	1972	1973	1974	1975	1976	1977	1978
Income										
Investment income	887	833	N.A.	898	929	994	1,006	1,037	1,065	1,166
Other income (including theater)	63	67	N.A.	186	303	581	645	764	1,071	1,180
Total income (with theater)	950	900	N.A.	1,084	1,232	1,575	1,651	1,801	2,136	2,346
Total income (without theater)[a]	N.A.	N.A.	N.A.	N.A.	N.A.	1,506	1,506	1,544	1,649	1,916
Theater income[b]	N.A.	N.A.	N.A.	N.A.	N.A.	N.A.	N.A.	N.A.	487	534
Expenditures										
Theater expenditures[b]	N.A.	N.A.	N.A.	N.A.	N.A.	108	223	347	498	667
Acquisitions expenditures	N.A.	N.A.	N.A.	N.A.	100	110	115	120	110	130
Total expenditures (with theater)	605	796	N.A.	1,131	1,334	1,828	2,038	2,186	2,198	2,685
Total expenditures (without theater)[a]	605	796	N.A.	1,131	1,334	1,720	1,815	1,838	1,699	2,018
Surplus/deficit										
With theater	345	104	N.A.	(47)	(101)	(253)	(387)	(385)	(62)	(339)
Without theater[a]	N.A.	N.A.	N.A.	N.A.	N.A.	(214)	(309)	(294)	(51)	(101)

233

Endowment									
Market value	24,533	19,886	25,151	26,941	26,611	20,904	22,799	24,412	22,797	21,656
Total return (%)	N.A.	-16.2	N.A.	11.9	1.1	-15.9	10.2	7.3	4.9	-5.1
Spending rate (%)	N.A.	3.4	N.A.	3.6	3.4	3.7	4.8	4.5	4.4	5.1

Source: Audited financial statements of the Folger Shakespeare Library, 1969–1978.

Notes: Data are for fiscal years ending June 30. N.A. means not available.

[a]The "without theater" series exclude the theater's income and expenditures and include quasi-endowment gifts and expenditures for acquisitions. See note 15 in Chapter Four for further details.

[b]Theater operations began in 1970, but expenditures and income were not reported separately until 1974 and 1977, respectively.

TABLE B.4–2. SUMMARY FINANCIAL DATA, FOLGER SHAKESPEARE LIBRARY, 1979–1993 (THOUSANDS OF $).

	1979	1980	1981	1982	1983	1984	1985	1986	1987	1988	1989	1990	1991	1992	1993
Current income															
Gifts and grants	959	1,437	1,057	1,220	1,039	1,215	1,547	1,680	1,631	1,519	1,419	1,473	1,611	2,095	2,052
Investment income	1,368	1,451	1,252	1,688	1,742	2,006	1,967	1,627	1,627	2,063	2,160	2,281	2,547	2,767	3,039
Earned income	464	726	686	810	913	864	489	705	656	852	1,029	1,135	1,000	1,119	1,143
Total income (without theater)[a]	2,791	3,613	2,996	3,718	3,695	4,084	4,002	4,011	3,914	4,435	4,608	4,890	5,158	5,981	6,233
Total income (with theater)[a]	3,337	4,646	4,373	4,542	4,492	5,058	5,476	4,352	4,260	4,435	4,715	5,086	5,185	5,955	5,963
Theater income[b]	624	1,176	1,352	1,208	1,138	1,222	1,461	N.A.	N.A.	N.A.	N.A.	N.A.	N.A.	N.A.	N.A.
Capital gifts															
Gifts to endowment	5	5	26	219	206	577	203	259	541	398	516	483	75	639	530
Gifts to quasi-endowment	N.A.	N.A.	N.A.	N.A.	N.A.	N.A.	N.A.	N.A.	N.A.	348	411	210	141	280	1,390
Gifts to plant	872	1,549	544	626	966	502	43	376	538	463	129	766	193	440	304
Total capital gifts	877	1,554	569	845	1,172	1,080	247	635	1,079	1,208	1,056	1,459	409	1,359	2,225
Expenditures by function															
Program services	1,986	2,876	2,158	2,107	2,120	2,461	2,840	3,463	3,496	3,095	3,201	3,515	3,817	3,869	4,400
Support services	606	797	923	1,231	1,327	1,295	1,109	1,093	1,323	1,276	1,396	1,370	1,372	1,481	1,537
Total expenditures (without theater)[a]	2,592	3,673	3,081	3,338	3,447	3,756	3,949	4,556	4,819	4,371	4,596	4,886	5,189	5,350	5,937
Total expenditures (with theater)[a]	3,311	4,989	4,812	4,589	4,475	5,122	5,669	4,397	4,659	4,196	4,416	4,702	5,010	5,167	5,662

Expenditures by object[c]															
Compensation and benefits	N.A.	N.A.	N.A.	N.A.	N.A.	N.A.	1,694	1,950	2,021	2,059	2,298	2,342	2,595	2,611	2,802
Depreciation	0	0	0	0	0	0	0	0	0	0	0	0	327	338	348
Acquisitions expenditures	110	110	110	120	110	115	125	159	160	175	180	184	179	183	275
Theater expenditures	719	1,316	1,731	1,370	1,138	1,481	1,845	N.A.	N.A.	N.A.	N.A.	N.A.	N.A.	N.A.	N.A.
Surplus/deficit															
Including depreciation (without theater)[a]	200	(60)	(85)	379	247	328	53	(545)	(905)	64	11	5	(32)	631	296
Excluding depreciation (without theater)[a]	200	(60)	(85)	379	247	328	53	(545)	(905)	64	11	5	295	969	645
Including depreciation (with theater)	26	(343)	(439)	(47)	16	(64)	(193)	(45)	(399)	239	299	384	175	789	301
Excluding depreciation (with theater)	26	(343)	(439)	(47)	16	(64)	(193)	(45)	(399)	239	299	384	502	1,127	650
Endowment															
Market value	18,364	19,028	21,500	19,838	26,653	25,617	32,074	41,811	46,579	45,051	48,925	50,353	49,308	53,631	59,582
Total spending	1,368	1,451	1,252	1,688	1,742	2,006	1,967	1,627	1,627	2,063	2,160	2,281	2,547	2,767	3,039
Total return (%)	10.6	10.3	20.3	-1.5	42.8	1.4	32.3	36.2	15.4	0.3	12.6	6.8	2.9	13.1	15.2
Spending rate (%)	7.3	9.1	7.8	8.9	9.8	8.1	8.4	5.7	4.4	4.9	4.7	4.6	5.0	5.6	5.6

Source: Audited financial statements of the Folger Shakespeare Library, 1979–1993.

Notes: Data are for fiscal years ending June 30. N.A. means not available.

[a]The "without theater" series exclude the theater's income and expenditures and include expenditures for acquisitions; they include quasi-endowment gifts until 1990 and exclude them thereafter. See note 15 in Chapter Four for further details.

[b]The theater began operating as a separate entity in 1986.

[c]The sum of the object categories does not equal total expenditures because not all object categories are presented.

TABLE B.5–1. SUMMARY FINANCIAL DATA, AMERICAN ANTIQUARIAN SOCIETY, 1960–1978 (THOUSANDS OF $).

	1960	1961	1962	1963	1964	1965	1966	1967	1968	1969	1970	1971	1972
Income													
Gifts and grants	26	12	19	14	12	16	18	22	32	29	69	18	35
Investment income	87	90	87	102	112	118	124	137	143	157	185	215	161
Other income	10	17	13	18	20	17	20	25	38	39	57	46	38
Total income	122	119	119	134	144	151	163	184	213	225	312	279	234
Expenditures	106	118	121	124	123	122	147	159	198	256	216	273	298
Surplus/deficit	16	1	(2)	10	20	28	16	25	15	(30)	96	6	(64)
Endowment													
Market value	2,206	2,817	2,625	3,230	3,394	3,465	3,040	3,594	3,741	3,733	3,314	4,173	4,402
Spending rate (%)	N.A.	4.1	3.1	3.9	3.5	3.5	3.6	4.5	4.0	4.2	5.0	6.5	3.9

Table B.5–1, cont.	1973	1974	1975	1976	1977	1978
Income						
Gifts and grants	81	142	161	151	326	391
Investment income	207	220	242	217	271	319
Other income	31	67	105	106	122	166
Total income	319	430	509	474	720	875
Expenditures	423	554	535	525	654	699
Surplus/deficit	(104)	(124)	(26)	(51)	65	177
Endowment						
Market value	4,050	3,348	3,673	4,009	4,164	5,352
Spending rate (%)	4.7	5.4	7.2	5.9	6.8	7.6

Source: Audited financial statements of the American Antiquarian Society, 1960–1978.

Notes: Data are for fiscal years ending August 31. Financial statements were prepared on a cash basis. N.A. means not available.

TABLE B.5–2. SUMMARY FINANCIAL DATA, AMERICAN ANTIQUARIAN SOCIETY, 1979–1993 (THOUSANDS OF $).

	1979	1980	1981	1982	1983	1984	1985	1986	1987	1988	1989	1990	1991	1992	1993
Current income															
Gifts and grants	429	433	512	461	625	583	639	657	636	665	559	722	720	695	807
Investment income	349	400	491	690	878	929	1,016	1,111	1,113	1,207	1,264	1,359	1,347	1,332	1,438
Other income	61	89	91	72	80	60	61	140	94	60	99	132	218	238	239
Total current income	839	922	1,094	1,223	1,583	1,572	1,716	1,908	1,843	1,932	1,922	2,213	2,285	2,265	2,483
Capital gifts															
Gifts to															
endowment	101	25	453	1,611	556	483	452	563	1,752	625	189	756	158	483	268
Gifts to plant	0	75	29	321	158	27	0	0	0	40	10	0	28	181	211
Total capital gifts	101	100	482	1,932	714	510	452	563	1,752	665	199	756	186	664	478
Expenditures by function															
Program services	624	760	844	982	1,269	1,285	1,445	1,603	1,663	1,674	1,537	1,682	1,819	1,739	1,692
Support services	164	216	262	325	354	432	402	444	463	525	491	510	559	576	677
Total expenditures	788	976	1,106	1,307	1,623	1,717	1,847	2,047	2,126	2,199	2,028	2,192	2,378	2,314	2,368

Expenditures by object[a]															
Compensation and benefits	N.A.	N.A.	N.A.	N.A.	N.A.	N.A.	N.A.	N.A.	1,027	1,064	1,124	1,168	1,279	1,092	1,184
Depreciation	37	38	46	63	78	82	83	82	81	78	48	58	57	65	79
Surplus/deficit															
Including depreciation	51	(54)	(12)	(84)	(40)	(145)	(131)	(139)	(283)	(267)	(106)	21	(93)	(49)	115
Excluding depreciation	88	(16)	34	(21)	38	(63)	(48)	(57)	(202)	(189)	(58)	79	(36)	16	194
Endowment															
Market value	5,506	5,686	5,427	6,816	9,684	9,782	12,334	14,335	16,684	15,726	19,144	17,270	20,242	21,824	25,871
Total spending	349	400	491	690	878	929	1,016	1,111	1,113	1,207	1,264	1,359	1,347	1,332	1,438
Total return (%)	7.7	9.0	-4.4	2.4	45.0	5.5	32.8	21.1	11.7	-2.5	29.5	-6.7	24.8	11.3	22.0
Spending rate (%)	6.5	7.3	8.6	12.7	12.9	9.6	10.4	9.0	7.8	7.2	8.0	7.1	7.8	6.6	6.6

Source: Audited financial statements of the American Antiquarian Society, 1979–1993.

Notes: Data are for fiscal years ending August 31. N.A. means not available.

[a]The sum of the object categories does not equal total expenditures because not all object categories are presented.

REFERENCES

Achilles, R. (ed.). *Humanities' Mirror: Reading at the Newberry, 1887–1987*. Chicago: Donnelly, 1987.

Adams, F. B., Jr. *An Introduction to the Pierpont Morgan Library*. New York: Pierpont Morgan Library, 1964.

Andrews, W. *The Pierpont Morgan Library: Mr. Morgan and His Architect*. New York: Spiral Press, 1957.

Baumol, W. J., Blackman, S.A.B., and Wolff, E. N. *Productivity and American Leadership: The Long View*. Cambridge: Massachusetts Institute of Technology, 1989.

Baumol, W. J., and Bowen, W. G. *Performing Arts: The Economic Dilemma*. New York: Twentieth Century Fund, 1966.

Baumol, W. J., and Marcus, M. *Economics of Academic Libraries*. Princeton, N.J.: Mathematica, Inc., 1973.

Berman, R. *Culture and Politics*. Lanham, Md.: University Press of America, 1984.

Billington, R. A. "The Genesis of the Research Institution." In *The Founding of the Henry Huntington Library and Art Gallery*. Los Angeles: Anderson, Ritchie & Simon, 1969.

Bowen, W. G. *The Economics of the Major Private Universities*. Berkeley, Calif.: Carnegie Commission on the Future of Higher Education, 1968.

Bowen, W. G. *Inside the Boardroom: Governance by Directors and Trustees*. New York: Wiley, 1994.

Bowen, W. G., Nygren, T. I., Turner, S. E., and Duffy, E. A. *The Charitable Nonprofits: An Analysis of Institutional Dynamics and Characteristics*. San Francisco: Jossey-Bass, 1994.

Bowen, W. G., and Rudenstine, N. L. *In Pursuit of the Ph.D.* Princeton, N.J.: Princeton University Press, 1992.

Bright, C. B., and Cary, W. L. *The Law and the Lore of Endowment Funds: A Report to the Ford Foundation*. New York: Ford Foundation, 1969.

Bright, C. B., and Cary, W. L. *The Developing Law of Endowment Funds: "The Law and the Lore" Revisited*. New York: Ford Foundation, 1974.

Buddington, W. S. "To Enlarge the Sphere of Human Knowledge: The Role of the Independent Research Library." *College and Research Libraries*, July 1976, p. 299.

Burkett, N. H., and Hench, J. B. (eds.). *Under Its Generous Dome: The Collections and Programs of the American Antiquarian Society.* Worcester, Mass.: American Antiquarian Society, 1992.

Cummings, A. M., and others. *University Libraries and Scholarly Communication: A Study Prepared for The Andrew W. Mellon Foundation.* Washington, D.C.: Association of Research Libraries, 1992.

Ennis, R. M., and Williamson, J. P. *Spending Policy for Educational Endowments.* New York: Common Fund, 1976.

Fleming, J. F., and Wolf, E., III. *Rosenbach: A Biography.* Cleveland: World, 1960.

Folger Committee of the Trustees of Amherst College. *Folger Shakespeare Library Long-Term Plan (The Thalheimer Report).* Washington, D. C.: Folger Shakespeare Library, 1992.

Ford Foundation, Advisory Committee on Endowment Management. *Managing Educational Endowments: A Report to the Ford Foundation.* New York: Ford Foundation, 1969.

Greene, E., Millar, B., and Moore, J. "The Midwest's Charitable Advantage." *Chronicle of Philanthropy,* Feb. 22, 1994, p. 1.

Griffin, D. "The Collector: How Bill Towner Turned Chicago's Newberry Library into a Mecca for the World's Scholars." *Chicago Tribune,* Jan. 13, 1985, Magazine section, p. 17.

Gundersheimer, W. "Two Noble Kinsmen: Libraries and Museums." *Rare Books and Manuscript Librarianship,* 1988, *3*(2), 91–101.

Hansmann, H. "Economic Theories of Nonprofit Organizations." In W. W. Powell (ed.), *The Nonprofit Sector: A Research Handbook.* New Haven, Conn.: Yale University Press, 1987.

Hansmann, H. "Why Do Universities Have Endowments?" *Journal of Legal Studies,* 1990, *19*(1), 3–42.

Hardison, O. B. "The Ivory Tower in the Arena: Research Libraries and Public Outreach." *Wilson Library Bulletin,* Jan. 1979, pp. 384–391.

Herzlinger, R. "Why Data Systems in Nonprofit Organizations Fail." *Harvard Business Review,* Jan.-Feb. 1977, pp. 81–86.

Huntington, H. E., and others. *Policies: The Future Development of the Huntington Library and Art Gallery.* San Marino, Calif.: Huntington Library, 1925.

Kane, B. A. *The Widening Circle: The Story of the Folger Shakespeare Library and Its Collections.* Washington, D.C.: Folger Shakespeare Library, 1976.

King, S. *Recollections of the Folger Shakespeare Library.* Ithaca, N.Y.: Cornell University Press, 1959.

Longstreth, B. *Modern Investment Management and the Prudent Man Rule.* New York: Oxford University Press, 1986.

Metcalf, K., with Leighton, P. D., and Weber, D. C. *Planning Academic and Research Library Buildings* (2d ed.). Chicago: American Library Association, 1986.

Pierce, C. E., Jr. *Advancing the Great Legacy: The Pierpont Morgan Library, 1988–1992.* New York: Stinehour Press, 1993.

Pierpont Morgan Library. *Space Problems and Proposed Solutions.* New York: Pierpont Morgan Library, 1987.

Salamon, L. M. "Partners in Public Service: The Scope and Theory of Government Nonprofit Relations." In W. W. Powell (ed.), *The Nonprofit Sector: A Research Handbook.* New Haven, Conn.: Yale University Press, 1987.

Salamon, L. M. "Foundations as Investment Managers. Part 1: The Process." *Nonprofit Management and Leadership,* 1992, *3*(2), 117–137.

Salamon, L. M. "Foundations as Investment Managers. Part 2: The Performance." *Nonprofit Management and Leadership,* 1993, *3*(3), 239–253.

Skotheim, R. A. *Financing the Humanities and Fine Arts.* Unpublished essay, 1993.

Taylor, F. H. *Pierpont Morgan as Collector and Patron.* New York: Pierpont Morgan Library, 1957.

Thorpe, J. "The Creation of the Gardens." In *The Founding of the Henry Huntington Library and Art Gallery.* Los Angeles: Anderson, Ritchie & Simon, 1969a.

Thorpe, J. "The Founder and His Library." In *The Founding of the Henry Huntington Library and Art Gallery.* Los Angeles: Anderson, Ritchie & Simon, 1969b.

Thorpe, J. *At the Huntington Library: A Time for Changes.* Unpublished essay, 1994a.

Thorpe, J. *The Huntington Library: The First Years.* Unpublished essay, 1994b.

Towner, L. W. *Past Imperfect: Essays on History, Libraries, and the Humanities.* Chicago: University of Chicago Press, 1993.

Turner, S. E., and Bowen, W. G. "The Flight from the Arts and Sciences: Trends in Degrees Conferred." *Science,* 1990, *250,* 517–520.

Wheatcroft, G. Review of *Churchill: The End of Glory* by John Charmley. *Atlantic,* 1994, 273(2), 116.

Williamson, W. L. *William Frederick Poole and the Modern Library Movement.* New York: Columbia University Press, 1963.

Wolpert, J. *The Structure of Generosity in America.* New York: Twentieth Century Foundation Press/Priority Press Publications, 1993.

Wright, L. B. *Of Books and Men.* Columbia: University of South Carolina Press, 1976.

INDEX